GAYLORD			PRINTED IN U.S.A.

Complications

Columbia Studies in Political Thought / Political History

COLUMBIA STUDIES IN POLITICAL THOUGHT / POLITICAL HISTORY

Dick Howard, General Editor

Columbia Studies in Political Thought / Political History is a series dedicated to exploring the possibilities for democratic initiative and the revitalization of politics in the wake of the exhaustion of twentieth-century ideological "isms." By taking a historical approach to the politics of ideas about power, governance, and the just society, this series seeks to foster and illuminate new political spaces for human action and choice.

Pierre Rosanvallon. *Democracy Past and Future*, edited by Samuel Moyn   2006

Complications

Communism and the Dilemmas
of Democracy

Claude Lefort

Translated, with an Introduction, by Julian Bourg

Columbia University Press   New York

Columbia University Press
Publishers Since 1893
New York   Chichester, West Sussex

Library of Congress Cataloging-in-Publication Data
Lefort, Claude.
[Complication. English]
Complications : communism and the dilemmas of democracy /
Claude Lefort ; translated, with an introduction, by Julian Bourg.
p. cm. — (Columbia studies in political thought/political history)
Includes bibliographical references and index.
ISBN 978-0-231-13300-5 (cloth : alk. paper)
1. Communism. I. Title. II. Series.

HX21.L43913   2007
335.43—dc22   2006036788

Columbia University Press books are printed on
permanent and durable acid-free paper.
Printed in the United States of America
c 10 9 8 7 6 5 4 3 2 1

CONTENTS

FOREWORD

No Political Thought Without History—No History Without Political Thought: Communism, Modernity, and Democracy in Claude Lefort

Dick Howard

W HY RETURN TO COMMUNISM more than a decade after its actual demise, and long after its intellectual attraction had disappeared? Why would a philosopher who has been a major force in the renewal of French political theory—beginning with his massive study of Machiavelli (1972); sharpening his insights through encounters with Michelet, Quinet, and Tocqueville; and returning to earlier historical figures like Dante and La Boétie—be convinced of the need for a renewed analysis of the desiccated corpse of a failed utopia? True, Claude Lefort has always also written on contemporary political problems, publishing a devastating critique of Trotsky in *Les Temps modernes* in 1948 before beginning a vigorous polemical exchange with Jean-Paul Sartre, the journal's editor, in 1953 and 1954. While traditional leftists denounced the anarchism of the May 1968 youth revolts, he underlined the radical political implications of this "rupture" in a book published already on June 21 of that year. In the 1970s and 1980s, Lefort's work (even when read superficially by the so-called New Philosophers) was a fundamental source for the French antitotalitarian revival that made human rights central to foreign policy, while renewing reflection on the nature of democratic politics. Why, then, at the height of his power and influence, would Claude Lefort return to Communism? Why beat a dead horse?

Lefort's interpretation of the end of Communism is important because it helps the reader understand its origin and therefore its trajectory, which Lefort sees as a reaction to the indeterminacy of democracy. He calls into question the idea that Communism's demise consecrates democracy's triumph, as if politics were a zero-sum game. Democracy is more complicated; it has to be understood as a framework of social relations within which everyday politics finds its place. As such, it poses problems rather than offers solutions; indeed, democracies may harm themselves, as we have known since the Athenians condemned Socrates. Communism emerged as an attempt to overcome the complications of democratic society. The merely formal institutional framework that is said to ensure and legitimate capitalist domination was denounced as creating an illusory equality. But things are not so simple, once again. These same formal institutions also protect the rights that permit a challenge to social domination; they guarantee that political power is regularly subjected to popular electoral approbation; they ensure that laws can be changed by organized popular mobilization. But all of this can still be criticized as merely incremental change. Reformism is challenged by the revolutionary will to overcome, once and for all, the traces of exploitation, alienation, and oppression: social inequality in all its ethnic, gendered, nationalist, and other forms must be eliminated. Under Communism, division will be overcome, unity must prevail, and, as Friedrich Engels famously put it, "the government of men must be replaced by the administration of things." The *real* democracy that will replace its merely formal precursor is then realized by means of the Communist unification of party and state, which then sets out to crush every velleity of individual or social independence.

Haunted by division, indeterminacy, and the resulting inability that anchors itself to a shared vision of the Good Life, democracy constantly seeks a fixed point. But such a point, Lefort cautions us, if it were ever in fact achieved, would destroy the roots of democracy's own creativity. In the guise of the quest for a final, really real democracy, the Communist vision and temptation to permanently institutionalize social order through unchecked power inheres in the very nature of modern democracies. As Lefort analyzes the avatars of Communist history (in the Soviet Union, in France, and among theorists from Arendt to Aron), this pattern of the systematic movement toward oppressive closure repeats itself.

But those contemporary historians who seek to conduct the autopsy on the now mute corpse of a regime that seemed to threaten the world— Martin Malia, François Furet, and their followers—make the opposite mistake. They reduce the history of Communism to the pursuit of an idea, an illusion. They don't recognize that the unitary logic that seeks to overcome the indeterminacy of democracy is, on its side, even more

complicated than it appears. On this point, Marx was being more faith-
ful to reality than his ideological followers when he insisted, in a famous
passage, that men "make their own history," but that they do not "make
it as they please." Historical action is no more determined by material
conditions than it is the result of ideological deception. In other words,
political thought cannot be understood apart from the history in which
it is embedded, any more than that history makes sense without considering the intentions of the actors.

This complication affects contemporary political choices. The traditional alternatives of reform or revolution remain. The reformers recognize the weight of history; their radical critics insist on the power of the will
to overcome all remaining traces of social division. Lefort's reconstruction
of the paradoxical history of Communism shows that neither side is, in
fact, ultimately right—but neither is wrong in any absolute way. Indeed,
both are part and parcel of the same history of modernity. They need each
other, and will continue to do so in our own present and future.

I summarize here these somewhat abstract elements of Lefort's argument because the demise of Communism has still not been fully understood. That failure of understanding continues to stunt contemporary
democratic political thought. Talk of a new world order while the first
Bush was president was nothing more than idle chatter; the eight years
of the Clinton administration were mostly spent treading water (save
for the Kosovo intervention). Since September 11, 2001, the appearance of a new enemy (called, vaguely and anachronistically, Islamo-fas-
cism) has largely spared the remaining global superpower the trouble
of thinking deeply about democracy. As a label, *totalitarian* has gained
new currency, but its indiscriminate use is incoherent, if not biased.
The bad money of political sloganeering drives the good money of political thought from circulation. Contemporary Western democracy is
dominated by a politics of fear and false memory that re-creates, in its
own way after the downfall of the Soviet Union, a society that villanizes
division. Joining philosophical reflection with historical reconstruction,
Lefort's arguments make it clear that we should not make the leap that
equates the new threat with the old enemy until we understand just how
much that old totalitarianism was a response to the profound and long-
standing historical and philosophical problem of democracy—how
much, in other words, totalitarianism was embedded in the flesh of our
own modernity.

Lefort's analysis of Communism insists not only on its denial of difference but also on its inability to recognize novelty. That weakness is not unique to the Communist deformation of democracy. The politics of fear that surrounds us today is another instance of the same paralysis of judgment in the face of the new and the possibilities for real democracy—as well as for its decline.

ACKNOWLEDGMENTS

F OR THEIR SUPPORT AND ADVICE I would like to thank Véronique André, Jonathan Bourg, Julie Chansel, Peter Dimock, Elizabeth Durden, Tim Harte, Dick Howard, Anthony Kammas, Tom Lacey, Stéphanie Lebassard, Kiril Levinson, Samuel Moyn, Irene Pavitt, Jan Plamper, Roberta Ricci, Anne Routon, Thibaut Schilt, and Ann Tlusty.

Claude Lefort showed me in conversation that ceaseless thought can be humane.

Complications

Translator's Introduction

Julian Bourg

The past is never dead. It's not even past.
—William Faulkner

C OMMUNISM DIED in the twentieth century.
    The evidence for such a resounding claim is overwhelming. To many people's minds, the collapse of the Soviet Union and its Eastern European dependent states brought to a close an era in which Marxism-Leninism had served as a viable ideology, movement, philosophy of history, and system on a world scale. For some, the story line of the flagship Soviet regime, from 1917 to 1991, has come to define the bookends of the short twentieth century.[1] In the West, philo-Communism did not survive the upheavals of the 1960s and 1970s in any widespread way, and Western liberal capitalism, reconfigured as globalization, has marched forward from the end of the cold war unchallenged, it seems, by any coherent world-historical alternative. Where remnants of the Marxist-Leninist inheritance persisted in the early twenty-first century, they were largely unrecognizable when compared with the sometimes conflicting, sometimes coordinated world Communist movements of the twentieth century. Those remnants bespoke local dynamics (disgruntled pensioners in Moscow, guerrillas in Nepal and Peru), aging figures (Cuba), isolated states (North Korea), or market–party hybrids (Vietnam, China). Protozoan signs of Marxisant life—a not-uninteresting academic neo-Marxism; renascent, if stymied, social movements—have disavowed the darker sides of the Communist past. The preponderance of evidence simply suggests that Communism is unlikely to achieve the kind of

influence and impact it had circa 1917 to 1991. Surely, there is nothing like a new historical period to help leave behind a previous one, and terrorism has replaced Communism, in the United States at least, as an enemy in a variety of ways for a variety of reasons.

Saying that Communism has died is tantamount to saying that it was mortal. While there is little doubt that the period from 1917 to 1991 was distinctive, the claim for the death of Communism as a historical phenomenon also encounters the fact that history itself keeps moving and is indeterminate. Who knows what will happen next and what the future will bring. It was Mikhail Gorbachev himself, standing amid the rubble of the edifice he had helped demolish, who wrote in 1992, "I am entirely certain that [the Stalinist model's] death does not affect socialism itself. The idea of socialism lives on, and it is my feeling that the quest—the desire to experiment and to find a new form for putting the socialist idea into practice—is ongoing."[2] That general trends to date have not exactly confirmed his forecast in no way detracts from the contrast between a closed past and a future that remains open. And it is precisely this prosaic point that raises a serious interpretive problem for Communism and its histories.

Since the fall of the Berlin wall, a range of analysts have approached Communism with its death certificate in hand, conducting autopsies on its corpse in order to show that it had always been terminally ill, that its very birth had in some sense made it mortal. Its life over, its story concluded, certain kinds of antihagiographical biographies have been written of late. However, the metaphor of Communism's life and death is complicated by the fact that history does not obey either organic cycles or the stages of human life. Nor is it so simple to stand outside history and sum it up. Ironically, Communists themselves excelled at doing exactly that: trying to determine once and for all the meaning and ends of history. At stake is not the resuscitation, resurrection, or rebirth of Communism, or even a séance that would summon the haunting "specter" that Karl Marx and Friedrich Engels famously described in the opening lines of *The Communist Manifesto* (1848). Rather, questioning what Communism was when it was alive is indeed profitable because history is not over—it continues to twist and undulate, to exceed and surprise.

Patients, it is often said, develop complications. Communism, though, when laid out on an examination table, seems moribund. For Claude Lefort, it is not the patient but the diagnosis that must develop complications. After all, one did not, according to him, have to wait for Communism to pass away to know and to judge that all was not well.

Complications: Communism and the Dilemmas of Democracy was first published in France in 1999 as *La Complication: Retour sur le communisme*. In it, Lefort argues that recent explanations of the Communist phenomenon in the Soviet Union and the West, notably those that describe the disastrous misadventures of the Communist *idea*, tend to be too simplistic. We need to complicate our understanding of Communism because the phenomenon, and history itself, are complicated. By implication, the popular view that the breakdown of Communism certifies the health of Western liberalism, as if the fact of being alive confirmed one's moral superiority over those who have departed—this view stands in need of correction. Lefort resituates the Communist phenomenon in the context of modernity after the democratic revolutions of the eighteenth century and in the field of an emergent and common "world-space" he sees as one of the most important developments of the twentieth century, even prior to widespread discussion of globalization. Communism, liberalism, and democracy all took root in the modern terrain, and they shared this same world. That is why Lefort asserts that "the question of Communism remains central to our time." Exploring its intricacies has something to teach us about our own historical condition and, what amounts to the same thing for Lefort, our own political condition. The original French *retour sur le communisme* does not mean a return to Communism as a program; rather, it suggests a turning or a looking back, a revisiting. One is reminded of André Gide's reflections published in 1936 in his *Return from the USSR* but also of the return of the repressed in the psychoanalytic and even political senses, as suggested in the title of an early article by Lefort, "The Return of Poland," on the suppression of the 1956 Poznań workers' movement.[3] Now, in returning to the Communist phenomenon and investigating its political, historical, and philosophical meanings, Lefort asks us to consider the difficulty of coming to grips with it as well as with the catches and dilemmas—the complications—of political life.

This book, it is not an exaggeration to say, is the result of his more than fifty years of sustained critical engagement with and reflection on Marxism, Communism, bureaucracy, democracy, human rights, and the political. One of the most significant political theorists in France today, Lefort has yet to achieve extensive, well-deserved recognition, and therefore still requires an introduction.[4] Born in 1924, a student of Maurice Merleau-Ponty and an early critic of Stalinism, in the late 1940s Lefort rejected the Trotskyism to which he had been briefly attracted and cofounded the noteworthy journal *Socialisme ou Barbarie* (1949–1965) with the Greek émigré Cornelius Castoriadis. At the height of the early cold war, this group and journal, while often in the quiet margins of French intellectual life, pioneered a critique of Soviet bureaucratism and an anti-Stalinist vision of autonomist revolutionary politics. In the early 1950s, Lefort and Jean-Paul Sartre engaged in a heated debate in the pages of *Les Temps modernes* over the Soviet Union and the role of the working class. In 1958 he broke with the *Socialisme ou Barbarie* group on the grounds that its members were unwittingly replicating the vanguardism and bureaucracy for which they had criticized Communists and that they were failing to squarely confront the quandary of the relation of knowledge to power. Also in the late 1950s, he began work on a doctoral dissertation on Niccolò Machiavelli under the supervision of Raymond Aron. It was Merleau-Ponty, though, who remained Lefort's mentor. After Merleau-Ponty's tragic death in 1961, Lefort became the editor of his posthumously published works.[5] In a moving and rigorous reflection called "Politics and the Thought of Politics," he declared that "nothing . . . can make us forget the resolution, recognizable in each of [Merleau-Ponty's] writings, to tie reflection on the political philosophy of the day to the experience of events."[6] This axiom can be found forty years later in *Complications: Communism and the Dilemmas of Democracy*.

The 1960s marked Lefort's explicit, post-Marxist turn toward properly political questions and philosophy. It took the watershed events of May 1968, however, to propel him into prominence as a theorist *avant la lettre* of the kind of spontaneous, associational, and communicative—in a word, *democratic*—spirit those events embodied.[7] In the decade following the completion of his thesis in 1971, Lefort turned out a flurry of articles and essay collections, as well as timely interventions, for instance, in debates on the fate of Marxism then galvanizing French intellectual politics. He emerged as an inspiration for a new generation of thinkers who sought to reinvigorate political thinking—figures such as Pierre Rosanvallon, Marcel Gauchet, Bernard Manin, Pierre Manent, and others eventually associated with the Institut Raymond Aron (later the Centre de Recherches Politiques Raymond Aron) at the École des Hautes Études en Sciences Sociales in Paris, where Lefort was *directeur d'études* from 1976 until 1989. During the 1980s and 1990s, he was a crucial voice in far-reaching debates in France on democracy, liberalism, human rights, literature, and the political.

Complications: Communism and the Dilemmas of Democracy introduces Lefort's career as a whole, condensing and distilling his rich thought. It is a concise, navigable synthesis. Those familiar with him will find that the book gathers, focuses, and expands lines of reflection he has long pursued; for those unfamiliar, it is an indispensable primer. Students of modern politics, revolution, totalitarianism, Communism, the Soviet Union, Europe, the cold war, and the twentieth century will be provoked to reconsider fundamental questions and to reflect on foundational categories. One need not be put off by the fact that Lefort is a philosopher, for his philosophical reflections here derive precisely from considering how what happened came to pass, the advent of historical events in their details and relationships. Yet, for such a short work, *Complications* is indeed complex. Occasionally, Lefort's style is difficult, but he cannot be counted among those theorists who confuse opacity with insight. The book often turns on and refers to itself, on more than one occasion arriving at a conclusion, pausing briefly, and then yielding an interpretation or approaching it from another angle. Thus there is a layering, interweaving, and even returning within the structure of *Complications* that conveys his larger claims about the indeterminacy of history and politics.

Furthermore, Lefort presents his own arguments in a thoroughgoing dialogue with other thinkers. His thought emerges from exchanges that are sometimes critical, sometimes accommodating. Here, too, are performative lessons about historicity and the political. As he says at one point in concluding a discussion of Hannah Arendt's views on totalitarianism, "To tell the truth, the entire argument I am trying to summarize hides slippages or twists of thought that reveal a desire to rush to produce an ultimate explanation." Lefort himself is in no such hurry, since ongoing and open-ended interchange with others is the democratic standard he champions. *Complications* condenses Lefort's development, and this point is worth emphasizing. He is summarizing, elaborating on, and tying together decades of analyses and judgments.

It is a curious kind of summa, synthetic and accumulative in a way, but decidedly compact. One can recognize previously disparate elements gathered together and "intertwined."[8] This is the case with the notion of *complication* itself. For example, discussing *The Prince* in his dissertation on Machiavelli, Lefort remarks that rulers' "extraordinary" acts exceed their private concerns and "leave their mark in time, fully responding to the *complication* that rules the history of societies." If the prince is to "discover in the patient exploration of possibilities the signs of historical creation and leave the mark of his own action in time," then even he "must be open to indetermination."[9]

If there is a single point of departure, at once biographical and intellectual, for Lefort's analysis of the Communist phenomenon, it is his independent, non-Communist Left perspective. Leftists had been among the earliest, consistent, and most vociferous critics of Communism, whether by accusing leftist parties and regimes of not living up to their own emancipatory ideals and standards or, more potently, by using the methods of the Left to go beyond the limitations and distortions of actually existing thought and practice. This perspective was often articulated in the name of social, not utopian, critique. (Lefort reminds us that Marx himself had lambasted utopian thinking, which anyway more readily characterizes today's prevailing neoliberal and market-security orthodoxies.) As he concedes, however, the non-Communist Left had difficulty carving out territory for itself amid the polarizations of the cold war. Moreover, since the fall of the Berlin wall, that perspective seems to have been similarly disregarded; the view that Communism was once alive and is now dead has given afterlife to the cold war's black-and-white logic. Recently, as before, the position of those in the West who denounced Stalinist terror as well as capitalist callousness and imperialist bellicosity has fit uncomfortably with reigning logics of the day (in the same way that Soviet and Eastern European dissidents who spoke in favor of socialism confounded, say, the U.S. State Department). As noted, the non-Communist Left did not require the so-called death of Communism to criticize the rottenness of the Soviet system or the perfidy of many of its defenders outside the USSR. Lefort's virtue is to have maintained relatively consistent positions from the late 1940s to the turn of the twenty-first century, even as the foci of his attentions have shifted and as the sophistication and depth of his insights have increased over the course of those decades. Ronald Aronson has appealed for a "post–Cold War approach to Communism" that would at last escape that event's reductive either-or logic.[10] Lefort's contribution to this enterprise is notable.

Lefort wrote *Complications* after having been provoked by two books on Communism published after its fall: François Furet's *The Passing of an Illusion: The Idea of Communism in the Twentieth Century* (1995) and Martin Malia's *The Soviet Tragedy: A History of Socialism in Russia, 1917–1991* (1994).[11] In them he found the signs of a new historiographical sensibility which suggested that the collapse of the Soviet and Eastern European Communist regimes proved that their historical and sociological incoherence had resulted from the folly of trying to realize the Communist "idea." For Furet, this idea was the illusion of radical equality established by revolution; for Malia, it was the dream of a socialist utopia. In *Complications*, Lefort does not disparage these historians; instead, his assessment of their works occasions a return to his own intellectual and, at times, biographical itinerary, leading him to argue, in so many words, that yes, ideas are important, but matters are much more complicated. Unlike things, ideas cannot stand alone. Because ideas interact and circulate and because they can be tested, put into practice, and embodied, the history of ideas is inadequate to grasp the complex dimensions of the historical experience of Communism. Since it was this post-1991 historiography of the Soviet Union that provoked Lefort, and to which his intervention contributes inter alia, it is worthwhile to pause on Furet, Malia, and the search for a post–cold war history of Communism. Writing as a political philosopher drawing theoretical lessons from historical experience, Lefort shines a light on a tangled and twisted field, and a complicated set of shadows, contours, and depths is reflected back.

The fall of the Soviet Union and its related regimes surprised almost everyone in the West, Lefort included. But this surprise was accompanied by the impulse to find signs and causes of its eventual demise. As Lefort cautions, it has recently become easy to forget that while the Soviet regime existed, many people seriously weighed the possibility that it could be reformed. Even its harshest cold warrior critics assumed that it would be around for some time. But as Lefort notes, the fact that there are "degrees in the unforeseeable" sometimes relates to people's desires not to see. In the West, the events of the fall instigated a crisis in the otherwise solidly established field of Sovietology.

Building on early accounts by eyewitnesses to the revolution of 1917, and then by those of sympathetic fellow travelers and suspicious skeptics during the interwar period, Soviet studies had its first major phase in the West during the early cold war, fueled by the ready parallels between the Nazi and Soviet totalitarian systems, geopolitical pressures, the policy establishment, and insistent émigrés. After Nikita Khrushchev broke with Stalinism in 1956 (Lefort does not think a meaningful rupture occurred) and the period of détente began in the 1960s, the chapter in Soviet studies known as revisionism opened. A climate of peaceful coexistence, modernization theory, and the turn toward the social associated with the social sciences and the popular movements of the 1960s cast revisionism as postideological in its rejection of a totalitarian model. Revisionists tried to parse the differences between the putatively healthy and the disastrous aspects of the Russian Revolution and Soviet society. But neither they nor their cold warrior interlocutors anticipated the events of 1986 to 1991. Thus the 1990s saw the emergence of what might roughly be called third-wave histories of twentieth-century Russia. The availability of new archives, the halting steps of the new Russian democracy, the creativity of the methods of cultural history, and, of course, the need to come to terms with the unexpected breakup of a superpower regime, among other factors, have all contributed to a robust scholarship on twentieth-century Russia and Eastern Europe, notably in journals such as *Kritika*. Since 1991. we also have been invited to attend what Aronson has called "Communism's posthumous trial."[12]

As the Soviet and East European regimes were coming apart, Malia, a specialist in nineteenth-century Russian socialism and longtime professor of history at the University of California, Berkeley, criticized those who at first believed that Communism was capable of refashioning itself.[13] In early 1990, he achieved notoriety from a well-known *Daedalus* article, "To the Stalin Mausoleum," which he signed only "Z" and in which he expressed deep skepticism about Gorbachev's reforms, then being widely lauded. The Soviet system, he said, could not be redeemed: "This circle cannot be squared."[14] *The Soviet Tragedy* extended this analysis, targeting revisionist historiography directly. Against the mixed assessment of putatively healthy and disastrous elements in postrevolutionary Russia, Malia insisted that the regime was intractably perverse. Countering the emphasis on the social, he asserted the primacy of the political, by which he meant the ideological: socialism's utopian idea. Modern democratic equality had led inexorably to the demand for economic equality, or socialism. Marx had designed the utopian vision from which Vladimir Lenin and Joseph Stalin drew practical consequences. "Ideocracy" led to "partyocracy," and socialism was fulfilled in totalitarianism. Malia's thesis that the Soviet tragedy was the result of political ideology took some time to be digested by scholars in the field.[15] However, the book was the opening salvo in what proved to be an unrelenting public engagement. The virulence with which Malia went on the offensive in the 1990s and early 2000s revealed a long-simmering impatience with scholarship considered soft on Soviet Communism. This offensive culminated in a controversial 2002 article in the *National Interest* in which he compared revisionist Sovietologists with Holocaust deniers. While associating the two showed that the postwar comparison of Communism and Nazism was not a dead letter, the incendiary equation of two kinds of revisionisms demonstrated the intense emotional and moral stakes of historicizing Communism. Not surprisingly, the article elicited debate and rebuttals.[16]

Malia's prominent role in the prosecutorial historiography of Communism had been evidenced further in his writing the foreword for the 1999 English translation of *The Black Book of Communism: Crimes, Terror, Repression* by Stéphane Courtois and others.[17] No other book embodied the nail-in-the-coffin view of Communism better. Although admonished, even eventually by some of his coauthors, for his obsession with adding up victims of Communism to reach the magic number of 100 million, Courtois successfully popularized the posthumous trial approach; the only lesson to be drawn from the collapse of Communism was that it had been nothing more than a relentless machinery of death on a global scale. Moving beyond the Soviet Union and Eastern Europe, *The Black Book* addressed the global impact of Communism. (Lefort does not contend with this book in *Complications: Communism and the Dilemmas of Democracy.* Like Malia and Furet, he focuses on Communism in Russia, Europe, and, briefly, the United States.) The work of Courtois and his collaborators is important to mention because it introduces the specifically French features of the case, which play a crucial role in the prosecution's indictment.[18] From the Russian Revolution until the 1970s, French intellectuals were renowned for their flirtations, flings, marriages, and affairs with Marxism, Communism, and the Soviet Union. That *The Black Book* appeared in France was presumably significant.

The testimony of Furet, who was slated to introduce *The Black Book* before his untimely death, is important in this regard. Best known for his pioneering work on the historiography of the French Revolution, Furet, from the 1970s until his sudden death in 1997, contributed mightily, in some ways single-handedly, to prying the grip of Marxist historians from the events of 1789.[19] His provocation that "the French Revolution is over" shifted debate from questions of economic class to those of cultural and political representation, indirectly instigating a revival of liberal political thinking about modern France's foundational event. When Furet turned to twentieth-century history with *The Passing of an Illusion*, it was to some extent the foray of a nonexpert, though the book marked the full-circle completion of his own intellectual-biographical trajectory. Furet had joined the French Communist Party in the late 1940s. Part of a generation attracted to and indulgent with the party, due to its legitimating role in the resistance of World War II and to general philo-Soviet opposition to American cold war clout (according to the principle that the enemy of one's enemy is a friend), Furet was not alone in his renunciation of Communism after the Soviet invasion of Hungary in 1956, though he was, broadly speaking, early. Only during the "antitotalitarian moment" of the 1970s did the French intellectual-political Left generally come to grips with Communism.[20] Furet's de-Marxification of the French Revolution, occurring when French intellectuals finally refused to renew their infatuation with revolutionary politics, was an integral part of this turnaround.

In *Interpreting the French Revolution*, written between 1971 and 1978, Furet attacked the truism of Marxist historiography that the French Revolution was a prelude to the Russian Revolution. In *The Passing of an Illusion*—the title confirmed the autopsy model—he told the story from the other end, writing in the 1990s of the French Revolution's abuse at the hands of twentieth-century Communists inspired by 1789 and the idea of revolution. Communism in the Soviet Union and the West (that is, France) was a surrogate religion based on an idea, an illusion—hence the implicit reference to Freud's *The Future of an Illusion* (1927). Furet criticized the post-Enlightenment confidence that linked the meaning and direction of history with the institutional form of the party, according to him an updated version of French revolutionary Jacobinism. The illusion of radical equality established by revolution was the functional equivalent of Malia's utopia. Following Communism's career from 1917 to 1956, Furet combined established historiographical positions (World

War I's destabilizing effect opened the door for the Bolsheviks; Nazism and Communism paralleled each other) with his own emphases (revolutionary passion as the consequence of bourgeois self-hatred; antifascism as the coagulant of Communist legitimacy in the West). It is not surprising that North American readers have approached *The Passing of an Illusion* in tandem with *The Black Book*, since such impassioned exorcisms of Communism from the French soul were historically significant.[21] The verdict: Communism was defunct; a circle had closed.

Again, Furet's and Malia's books merely provided the occasion for *Complications*, and Lefort was not overly severe with them. However, insofar as they, together with Courtois, represent a formidable strain of post-1991 historiography, they are indispensable for understanding Lefort's compelling book. To be sure, Malia and Furet softened their claims in the end, the former admitting that the struggle between socialism and liberalism was a hallmark of modernity and thus unavoidable, and the latter evoking the return some day of a solidaristic politics impossible for the time being.[22] But in them one finds something of the urgency, passion, and single-mindedness of the cold warrior and the former Communist; in other words, something of the love–hate relationship with Communism maintained by Sovietologists and by believers who lost their faith. Lefort has a completely different approach to the Communist phenomenon. He had never been a warrior-ideologue and had never belonged to the church.

Complications: Communism and the Dilemmas of Democracy can be described as a phenomenological history of Communism or, more generally, as a phenomenology of the political. True to the philosophical legacy of Merleau-Ponty and Edmund Husserl, and explicitly evoking Marcel Mauss's corresponding notion of "*total* social facts," Lefort argues that Communism must be grasped in its "concrete" circumstances and its "political, social, economic, juridical, moral, and psychic" depth. Against the monocausal approach of ideas (or the socioeconomic one that discounts them), Lefort advocates complication or, to use a term he avoids, multicausality. Against the simplified psychological analysis of leaders' intentions, he examines the "intentionality" of a system and a complex. Twentieth-century Communism emerged at the "conjuncture" of a range of factors and forces that cannot be reduced to simple choices between necessity or contingency, top or bottom, ideas or practices, totalitarianism or democracy, and so forth. To grasp the phenomenon, one's analysis must be conjunctive, not disjunctive. Lefort pursues the significance of social forms, organizations, and institutions (especially the Communist Party); the way Communism answered people's needs, gave them identities, and thereby "captured" them; the mistake of blaming Marx for the gulag; democratic, Communist, and fascist senses of revolution; differences between the French and Russian revolutions and the February and October revolutions of 1917; Soviet leaders for whom expediency overrode ideological coherence; a Soviet legal system that was peculiar and perverse, but not unintelligible; the appeal of Communism in the West according to local circumstances; Marx's old theory of "semi-Asiatic" autocracy or "Oriental despotism" applied to Russia; the nature of the political; and the significance of a world-space for both the advent of totalitarianism and contemporary history. His assessment of Furet and Malia returns to the analyses of Aron and Arendt, both of whom had led the way during the 1950s in theorizing the Communist phenomenon as political and especially as new, and he makes thorough use of other early, now largely forgotten investigations by Ante Ciliga and Boris Souvarine, among others. Throughout *Complications*, one finds the firm insistence that many critical intellectuals did not need to wait for Communism's demise to judge and criticize it. Lefort and others had never been deluded about its promises. Returning now to vantage points articulated earlier is crucial. In this complicated analysis of the Communist phenomenon, illusion and utopia come across as rather weak explanatory engines.

I would like briefly to introduce two threads in *Complications* regarding the party and the political as examples of the kind of "interweaving" (*intrication*) Lefort advances. In his eyes, the twentieth-century Communist Party was an unprecedented social and organizational form. One looks in vain to the French Revolution and Jacobinism, or for that matter to Marx, for any concrete precedent or design. It did emerge prior to 1917, but in Russia. It did not spring fully formed from the mind of Lenin, even if he did much to shape and influence it, capitalizing on and condensing previously existing organizational forms. Bolshevism and the party were thus interwoven. Bolshevism became monolithic under the force of organizational requirements and the unitary principle of Communism. The party became tied to the state, its bureaucracy, and the cadres who came to occupy elite positions while repeating the ideological mantra of a classless society. Marx's views on ideology remain useful in understanding this situation, as do Lefort's.[23] The party became the great qualifier of Soviet law. Soviet constitutional provisions, whose rhetoric was surprisingly democratic (especially the constitution of 1936), were subsumed under the party's so-called democratic centralism. Citizens' rights were compressed by their duties. Although not lawless, Soviet society represented a "perversion" of law to the extent that it removed the perspective of the arbitrating "third," forcing accusers and accused to face one another directly, the accused sometimes facing themselves, within the horizons set by the party in whose immanence all could and should partake. Law thus surrendered its universality to the false claim made to it by the party—the ultimate adjudicator and manipulator of Soviet jurisprudence.

Lefort strongly insists that people did not join and serve the Communist Party of the Soviet Union and those of Western countries—his example is obviously France—out of illusions. They knew very well what they were doing. He stresses that beneath party members' idealized rhetoric was the material reality of their "love of the discipline of action and thought; their love of authority, culminating in the cult of the supreme leader; their love of order, for which the system provided them the criteria; and their love of uniformity, which they fulfilled already in the spectacle of their unanimity." The party was the conduit for and pillar of a new social form, providing an answer for everything, a reference point for all inside its ranks, and a cutting blade against all those on the outside (the step from inside to outside being sometimes very short). This new social form represented a "society without divisions" to which individuals surrendered and abnegated themselves. In Lefort's powerful conception, it involved the composition of "a new kind of person: a man endowed with the capacity to not let himself *be affected* and therefore surprised by *what happens*." Social relations were therefore recast via a party that provided the fixed conditions for both uniformity and separation, for the "being-together" of those who belonged and the ever-present potentiality of enemies to be eliminated (again, those who belonged sometimes eliminated themselves). Lefort returns to Étienne de La Boétie's sixteenth-century notion of voluntary servitude and "the One" to help explain the population's complicit oblation to the Communist *we*. "In short," he concludes, "one must always return to the interweaving [*intrication*] of power, law, and knowledge in the party. Yet, I must insist, the party is only the concretion of the social, the motor element of the exclusion of plurality and division."

For Lefort, the Communist Party was a concrete social organization operating as a hub for the spokes of other formations such as the state, law, judiciary, and bureaucracy. Irreducible to the ideas that served it, the party profited from petty machinations and sweeping revolutionary ambitions; it captured individuals and served their interests; it reconditioned the social as it embodied and expressed the social—"a kind of closing [*bouclage*] of the social around itself"—in such a way as to break strongly with the fundamental features of a democratic society ("plurality and division") while simultaneously remaining thoroughly modern. It is this modernity that distinguishes totalitarianism from traditional tyranny or despotism. When one focuses, for instance, on the Soviet constitutions or on the show trials of the 1930s, one can view the party itself as a subsidiary, a spoke on another hub. However, taking these forms together, we see a complex network of ideas, practices, motives, and forms, irreducible to one primary cause but altogether intelligible and criticizable. Although Malia and Furet marshal much empirical evidence in their books, the motor driving Communism in their view is ideational. Lefort, despite his more theoretical language and argumentation, sets his sights on the intricate convergence of concrete forces, as the example of the party demonstrates. His efforts might be described as a kind of revisionism, except that he has been developing his own unique perspective since the late 1940s and that he rejects the classic revisionist positions that see October 1917 as a proletarian revolution and Stalinism as a distortion of Leninism. (Still, with the historian Marc Ferro, and contrary to Malia, he insists on the democratic significance of the February revolution).

The passing reference earlier to the plurality and division constitutive of a democratic society leads to the second thread that needs to be briefly introduced: the political. This theme rests at the heart of Lefort's mature project. As those familiar with his work are aware, he distinguishes the political (*le politique*) from politics (*la politique*), the former being the constitutive condition of the latter. The political comes first. It involves a forging and shaping of meaning. It is a form or space defined in part by its opposite, the nonpolitical, and it provides the elementary bed in which the social, the economy, culture, and politics inhere. In contrast, for instance, to the contractualist view, which gives modern politics the goal of healing preexisting social disparities, Lefort thematizes such divisions as always already political. Dialogue and work on the common thus transpire in and through that form. Lefort defines democracy as a genre of the political, while elsewhere he seems to amalgamate the terms *democracy* and *the political* (merging content and form). By definition, the political, like democracy, is open, irreducible, indefinite, plural, and composed of differentiated spheres of activity. He gives his political theory a French cast by rooting the emergence of modern democracy in the shift from Old Regime monarchical power to the post-1776 and, especially, post-1789 regimes. As opposed to the sovereign's embodiment of power during the era of divinely sanctioned kingship (notwithstanding the fact that that power was also limited), democracy leaves the site of power "empty." For any one person or group to fully occupy it is not merely illegitimate, but antimodern, antipolitical, and therefore antidemocratic. That is why democratic regimes emphasize the primacy of the separation of powers and the peaceful, regular transfer of authority. In a democracy the throne is empty, and Humpty Dumpty, having fallen, cannot be put back together again. To do so would be to contrive a new unity and identity subsumed in the One. Therein lies the appeal of pluralism. The virtue of a democratic society is exactly the irreducible diversity of spheres of activity that coexist, interact, and are transformed within the empty constitutive space of modern political society. There is a parallel and a correspondence between, on the one hand, the spatial dynamic of democratic plurality pitted against the monocratic One and, on the other, the temporal dynamic of historicity set against the restriction of past forms and the form of the past. Lefort has made this empty/full point on a number of occasions, and he makes it again here most directly in chapter 15, "Disincorporation and Reincorporation of Power."

Totalitarianism tries to fill, occupy, and totalize the space of the political. Under Communism, though mutatis mutandis the picture applies to Nazism as well, the party takes upon itself the audacious presumption to reduce an irreducibly divided society as well as to decide in advance and once and for all the meaning of historical community. Totalitarianism, paradoxically, forecloses the political. On the face of it, it seems to politicize everything by drawing all activity under the tutelage of the party-state and thereby paving over democracy's requisite differentiations. But in Lefort's sense, totalitarianism is antipolitical, since it tries to refill the constitutive emptiness that is the sine qua non of the political. If everything is political, nothing is. The attempt to totalize representation leads to the destruction of representation. The symbolic negation of otherness and difference is related to the literal negation of others identified as different and abnormal outsiders. Obviously, attempts by all the king's horses and all the king's men to put Humpty Dumpty back together again have exacted catastrophic damage on the human community.

Complications makes the case that the February revolution and the soviets, before the Bolsheviks rose to power, expressed the uncontrolled, populist sensibilities of "untamed democracy."[24] On this point, Lefort is consistent with an earlier leftist councilist tradition that underscored the virtues, among earlier examples, of the East Berlin worker strikes of 1953, the Hungarian and Polish insurrections of 1956, and the French student/worker revolts of 1968. By the same token, Lefort has adamantly resisted the trap of trying to divide the allegedly good and bad sides of or moments in revolutions. Appropriately, the thrust of this book instead is on the antidemocratic and antipolitical topography of Communism. Lefort does not dispute that Soviet Communism was totalitarian, but he wants to bring rigorous and intricate reflection to the question of how this was the case. It will not do to presume that Communism stemmed from the application of a ready-made ideological formula engineered by a few notorious characters; or that, as Malia says, its tragedy resulted from the unintended consequences of that ideology; or even, as Arendt argues, that it expressed a "law of movement" conceived in a modern world that believed it could know and control everything. The originality of Communism was its ability to exclude the political in practice under cover of a revolutionary rhetoric and ideology that, on the surface, seemed to try to fulfill an egalitarian politics. Soviet institutions, however, were never egalitarian: not the party or the state and its laws. The "majoritarian principle" of democracy succumbed to the "unitary principle" of Communism, as Aron had noted. The tragedy of Communism came not from trying to fulfill egalitarianism but from trying to fill the space of the political. Such attempts at capture and occupation are as modern as the resistances and critiques they occasion.

The relationship between Communism and democracy is complex. Furet and Malia see Communism as an illiberal consequence of heightened and unrealistic expectations in the democratic era. Before them, Alexis de Tocqueville and others had identified the problems and dangers of democracy's promise of equality. Lefort wants to restore the specificity of Soviet Communism—hence his emphasis on the distinctive circumstances of the Bolshevik Party and Russian semi-Asiatic authority. At the same time, when considering the political domain, he does underscore the significance of the fact that Communism emerged subsequent to the events of 1776 and 1789. He writes, "Communism is intelligible only in the framework of a world transformed by democratic revolution, but I will not go so far as to say that they were part of the same matrix." In both Communism and democracy, power is "unlocalizable." In a democracy, this is the case due to the emptiness discussed earlier. Unlike in a democracy, however, power in a Communist society (or within the party itself) is everywhere. The party can point to the law, the law can point to the proletariat, the proletariat can point to the leaders, the leaders can point to the cadres, the cadres can point to the party, and so forth. This round-robin circulation bears similarities to the view of totalitarianism as politicizing everything while effectively stripping the political of any sense; since power is everywhere, it cannot be localized in any one place. Stalin, for instance, did not embody power in the way Louis XVI had. Thus, despite their otherwise considerable differences, Communism and democracy share the modern feature of the unlocalizability of power.

For Lefort, the formation of the Communist phenomenon took place on pre-empirical levels to which he refers in the explicitly psychoanalytic language of the symbolic and the imaginary.[25] The attempt to create, in reality, a new society without divisions required a shift and reorientation in the collective social and political imaginary. In the same way that plurality and division as well as the people and rights are part of the democratic imaginary, the Communist imaginary envisioned homogeneity, uniformity, discipline, and order. These were ultimately antihistorical, since even though they were articulated and instituted in the name of the historical vocation of proletarian revolution, they rejected the openness, variability, and transformations of our historical condition, our historicity. Lefort is aware that this picture of Communist immobility contrasts with Arendt's argument in *The Origins of Totalitarianism* that Communism and Nazism legitimized themselves by appealing to laws of movement, history, and nature, respectively. So, too, he engages Arendt's subsequent argument that ideology provided the required glue to patch up the holes in those systems when the founding laws of movements proved insufficient. Again, he discourages us from appealing in the final instance to ideas and ideologies. Prior to symbolic representation and empirical instantiation, one finds constitutive "phantasmagoria" and "a frantic denial of social division." The Communist imaginary that installed a "new mode of domination" was characterized by two main qualities. First, there was a confusion between top and bottom, as Communist leaders supposedly embodied the party, which in turn supposedly embodied the proletariat, allegedly freeing Soviet society from class hierarchies altogether. Second, the boundaries of the separate spheres of activity one finds in democratic society were erased, diversity and differentiation being paved over by uniformity and unanimity, movement by hardened totality. The Communist imaginary reflects a "petrification of the social in its depths or . . . a kind of closing [*bouclage*] of the social around itself." The psychoanalytic facet of the analysis thus rejoins the phenomenological. Lefort is after the conditions of possibility for and constitutive elements of the Communist phenomenon. He skirts talk of necessity and contingency and is even less interested in conclusive explanations and singular causes, meanwhile affirming that Communism is nevertheless intelligible. If the causative refers to actors and drama on the historical stage, then the constitutive is the scene and background, the imaginary. All of this helps us understand Lefort's insistent description of the formation or shaping (*mise en forme*) of Communism and its forging of meaning (*mise en sens*).

Finally, from his argument about Communism's voluntary servitude and individuals' submission to the One, Lefort reaches a surprising conclusion. While it is true that World War I, especially its legitimation of violence, contributed significantly to the unexpected advent of the Communist event, the war was a crucial step in a process already under way: globalization. What is one to make of Communism, he asks, if we situate its desire for a *single social state* in the context of a historically emergent *single world-space*? Perhaps the Communist imaginary of a unified and uniform society was itself symptomatic of a larger field of historical meaning and direction characterized by an experientially genuine contraction of the world. This fact would make the international character of Communism into much more than a malevolent conspiracy and would raise the question of the continuity of the pre- and post-1991 eras. It would mean that globalization is less the harried release of liberal market energies, previously pent up and hemmed in by the Iron Curtain and other proxy barriers, and more a longer historical process haunted at all times, the early twentieth century like the early twenty-first century, by dangers. Not least of these dangers is the modern temptation to try to fill the empty space of the political with final answers to the question—ongoing and constitutively unanswerable in any definitive way (at the risk of social, political, and historical destruction)—of what it means to live in common within history.[26]

Also making Lefort's book timely are the interrelated contemporary circumstances whose capture on the world has intensified since *Complications: Communism and the Dilemmas of Democracy* appeared in 1999. Whether or not it is appropriate to describe Baathism and Islamic fundamentalism as species of totalitarianism,[27] the parallels between the West's cold war with Communism and its broadly conceived war on terrorism warrant reflection. The analogy may not prove to be a sound one, the war on terror may not last as long as the cold war, and terrorism may not become the protracted excuse the West uses to ignore its own systematic difficulties. Nevertheless, there is no doubt that the totalitarian linkage quickly became a part of Western responses to political realities and exigencies after September 11, 2001. That neoconservatives have drawn this linkage is less interesting than the emergence of liberal hawks who, rightly or not, place themselves directly in the non-Communist, antitotalitarian, independent leftist tradition.[28] This phenomenon predated the September 11 event. Already in the 1990s, talk of humanitarian intervention had occasioned crises of conscience for some on the European and American Lefts insofar as the values of peaceableness and military action were seen to collide. Lefort himself supported the 1999 bombing of Belgrade. To take another example: the inability of the Left to articulate a forceful and effective response to the Iraq war, in defense of the democratic principles at stake but in coherently critical opposition to the nature of the war's prosecution, has been a further sign that the dynamics of the cold war era continue to play themselves out. The point is that totalitarianism and antitotalitarianism have been given post–cold war afterlives.[29] The return to a simple formula obviously risks constricting thought; yet, thinking through and with the present also involves considering how the twentieth century weighs on all our living brains. Not such a distant memory after all, the question of Communism remains, as Lefort says, central to our time.

A related aspect of our early-twenty-first-century conjuncture also needs to be broached, and it bears more directly on the West's systematic difficulties. Although the giddiness of neoliberalism, palpable in the immediate post–cold war moment, has seemingly passed to sobriety, the sense strongly persists that markets and rights are ultimately the only games in town (qualified in the United States by religion and militarism). Incessant appeals to "freedom-loving people" are the signature of this sensibility, illustrating the strengthening of what Lefort in the 1970s called the West's "invisible ideology." Inflated rhetoric about the virtues of freedom finds a compelling counterpoint in *Complications: Communism and the Dilemmas of Democracy*. As Lefort observes in the concluding chapter, if there is a totalizing, utopian force in the world today, it is liberalized globalization.[30] In the monism of this best-of-all-possible worlds, the West exports its systematic difficulties for multiplication, rather than confronting them. In opposition to the antipolitical, utopian view that markets and rights solve all problems, Lefort rejuvenates the notion that freedoms are social. Again, the social involves more the expression and incorporation of fundamentally political divisions than disparities to be healed by politics. Freedom requires "the recognition of a civil life"; freedom of belief and opinion are "irreducible to the property of the individual; [they become] open to all, public, and recognized in a common space." Tied to this notion of sociality is that of social equality. While some might be tempted to see Lefort's emphasis on the constitutive division and emptiness of the political as a retreat to liberal rights, he has always insisted that socially interactive freedoms condition the advancement of social solidarity. Against a liberal-market utopianism that sees freedom as the endgame, Lefort suggests that democracy is a project that moves forward from the diversity and intercourse of the common. Endorsing Harold Rosenberg's 1950s critique of liberal anti-Communism, he writes, "I would emphasize the word 'equality,' which clearly means that the liberalism Rosenberg embraced implied absolutely no concession to the conservatism for which inequality in our societies is simply a given fact." Without the notion of equality, law, human rights, fairness, public education, and even market contracts are inconceivable. Equality is not uniformity, homogeneity, or the stifling of uniqueness. It is not a utopian or an illusory idea. In the face of sustained attacks on this Enlightenment value, Lefort reminds us that if the Soviet Union and Communism gave equality a bad name, it is because they never experienced it. They were never democratic.

Author's Introduction

C OMMUNISM BELONGS TO THE PAST, but the question of Communism remains central to our time. In what follows, I attempt to bring this question to light and to show that it remains repressed in recent interpretations presenting the development of totalitarian regimes as merely a deviation in the course of the twentieth century. This essay makes use of scholarly studies of the Russian Revolution and the Soviet system that have nourished my reflection for a long time, and I rely on accounts of authors who, to different degrees, have played a political role in Russia. Furthermore, from time to time, I rely on my personal experience. Nevertheless, my intentions are not those of a historian. I would like to contribute to our understanding of the political societies of the world in which we live. I would not, though, have conceived of this "return to Communism" had I not been provoked by reading two remarkable works that, by different approaches, tried to evaluate the Communist enterprise in light of its failure.

The first book is François Furet's *The Passing of an Illusion*, which I read as soon as it was published in 1995.[1] Having maintained a long personal and intellectual friendship with Furet, I knew from him something of his investigation's scope. I was confident that his book would make an original contribution, disturbing those nostalgic for the Bolshevik Revolution in the same way his earlier, audacious analysis of the mythology grafted onto the French Revolution had disturbed guardians of the Jacobin tradition.[2] Furet and I shared the same interest in the Communist phenomenon and the same conviction that the Soviet Union embodied a previously unknown and unimaginable mode of domination, to some extent more enigmatic than fascist domination had been. Committed to a professional craft that demanded historical knowledge be linked to a rigorous handling of the facts, Furet rejected all forms of positivism, including structuralism, and instead embraced conceptual history. Only the formulation of a problem, he used to say, enables the historian to connect a series of seemingly independent facts and open the way toward comprehending events that affect the ensemble of society. His approach in this sense seemed inspired by Max Weber. As many of his readers know, however, his true guide for many years had been Alexis de Tocqueville. I thus had been expecting a great deal from Furet's study of the Communist phenomenon. My disappointment, though, was great when I discovered that he had made illusion (the title of his book had already forewarned me) the first and constant mainspring of the Soviet system and of the politics of parties in the West that had taken that system as a model. He had directed all his knowledge and talent toward solving a precise problem: Why was the illusion able to resist failure and disappointment for so long—longer in the West than in the Soviet Union—once confronted with knowledge of the facts? Although his investigation focused on Western Europe, Furet, it is true, gave an overview of the vicissitudes of a drama that unfolded in all corners of the globe over a long period of time. He restored meaning to events that had been either falsified, credited to the heroic defense of revolutionary Russia against imperialism, or passed over in silence by sectarian historians. He spared his reader nothing of the violence and lies of Communist politics inside the Soviet Union and outside its borders, and he did not hesitate in many places to call by the name *totalitarian* the regime in place, if not since the time of Vladimir Lenin, at least since the 1930s.

Still, despite such a rich and brilliantly driven story, the conceptual history on this occasion was spoiled by recounting the misadventures of tens of millions of people obstinately attached to an idea. I shared with Furet my reaction, which surprised him, and said that I intended to write a critical review of his book—a project he enthusiastically welcomed, as I had anticipated. But it soon occurred to me that I could not ignore an entire set of considerations that propped up, and not merely accompanied, his interpretation of Communism—considerations that touched on Marxism, the relation of the Russian Revolution to the French Revolution, the destiny of liberalism, the dynamic of egalitarianism, the appearance of voluntarism in politics, and the notion of history itself.

Furthermore, Furet's use of Tocqueville's and Raymond Aron's thought merited discussion. In short, I discerned the scattered signs of a conception of politics and modernity that I had to explicate and connect in order to fully explain my criticisms. To do this in a review of twenty to thirty pages was not possible. Moreover, I will not deny that I was displeased at the idea that others would see a polemical purpose in my analyzing a book by François Furet.[3]

I had given up on my project when reading Martin Malia's *The Soviet Tragedy* convinced me that I had to take it up again in an entirely different form.[4] I learned of Malia's book late; it had appeared in the United States in 1994 and was published in France several months after Furet's. The author limited his inquiry (if I dare use that word since the topic was immense) to the history of the Soviet Union from its beginning to its end. He saw that history as a whole ruled by a utopia—socialism—in the only version, namely, Marxism, that according to him allowed one to accurately grasp its meaning. I was struck by the affinity of intention in both historians. They seemed all the closer in the way that Malia put Communism back into the field of modernity, discovering the sources of the utopia that brought about the Soviet tragedy in eighteenth-century rationalism and liberalism, in nineteenth-century Hegelian and Marxist philosophies of history, and no less in the errors of democratic egalitarianism and voluntarism.

In Malia's book the idea reigns absolutely. That the idea was expressed in the practice and organization of a party-state and in social institutions did not change this fact. Communists, beginning with their leaders—Joseph Stalin, like Lenin; Nikita Khrushchev, Leonid Brezhnev, or Mikhail Gorbachev, like Stalin—showed themselves guided alike by the idea. They all believed in socialism. Malia frequently affirmed that the Soviet system was intelligible only on condition of recognizing the "primacy of the political." He called the regime a "partyocracy." But he did so in order to add that, when all was said and done, it was an "ideocracy." Recognized as a creation of Lenin, the party appeared entirely instrumental. It provided an efficient means for multiplying the agents of a doctrine and submitting them to a rigorous discipline of action. Thus the study of Soviet social and economic relations taught us nothing about the regime. In a concise formula, Malia declared that "in the world created by October, we were never dealing in the first instance with a *society*; rather, we were always dealing with an ideocratic *regime*."[5]

The convergence of these two eminent historians' analyses made me think that a new interpretive schema for totalitarianism had emerged in recent years. Indeed, their arguments were not easily assimilated into the framework of debates that had long structured explanations of the nature and evolution of the Soviet regime and, more generally, of the Communist enterprise. From the observation that this regime suddenly collapsed or, more exactly, that it fell apart not because of the military defeat of Russia but through disintegration, pure and simple, one drew the conclusion that it never had either consistency or a historical or sociological standpoint. Resituated in the course of twentieth-century events, it seemed a parenthesis (Furet's term) or a deviation. Considered in its workings, the Communist idea appeared the product of raving minds, never taking root in reality. To the image of the new regime's inconsistency, however, was joined that of a coherent political system. It would be exaggerating to say that the mechanism of illusion or utopia in these interpretations was equivalent to the mechanism of paranoia described by psychologists. Yet, to examine the obstacles encountered by the builders of socialism is certainly inadequate to grasp the rationale for their politics. Their political reasoning does not give the impression of improvised responses to unforeseeable events. Even if there were improvisations, they gave rise to decisions that depended on a logic and an ideology. Thus Furet and Malia could, while denying the formation of a new kind of society, admit the validity of the concept of totalitarianism as Hannah Arendt had defined it.[6]

In discovering this new schema, I understood that it would have been useless for me to restrict myself to a critique of Furet's book and that it would be necessary to return to the analyses I had previously made of totalitarianism and modern democracy in order to clarify and "complicate" them. Such is the motive for this essay.

To my mind, the concept of totalitarianism has pertinence only with respect to Communism, even more than to Nazism or fascism, if it designates a regime in which the source of power becomes unlocalizable. That source supposedly resides neither in someone (a monarch, despot, or tyrant) or a group of people (aristocrats or oligarchs) nor, properly speaking, in the people altogether, if one understands by "the people" the ensemble of individuals recognized as citizens by law and not merely by those who govern. When the distinction between the political and the nonpolitical finds itself challenged, one might as well conclude that in a regime all becomes political or that nothing no longer is. The assertion that everything is political seems justified when, indeed, neither individual and collective activity nor relations among persons and groups are independent in economics, society, and culture. But the second assertion (the collapse of the political) is also well founded, since what has always been defined as political decisions and actions bears the mark of a source of authority, no matter the range of its domain of competence. In fact, no one who considered the Communist regime totalitarian doubted that the party, its directing core, or its supreme leader alone had at their disposal the means of decision, constraint, information, and propaganda. Nevertheless, the party presented itself as the expression of a social power. Nothing was foreign to it. Law and knowledge were written into it, producing in reality the obligation to *incorporate oneself* into the Soviet community and the need to *organize oneself* according to the rationality of the division of labor. *Totalitarian* is thus the right word to explain the advent of a mode of domination in which many kinds of signs were effaced at one and the same time: the signs of a division between the dominating and the dominated; of distinctions among power, law, and knowledge; and of a differentiation among the spheres of human activity. This effacement of boundaries took place in such a way as to bring the institution of the social back into the framework of the supposed real. In other words, it effected a kind of closing [*bouclage*] of the social around itself. Consequently, once one evaluates the enterprise and acknowledges that it is impossible to reduce the new regime to a despotism, tyranny, or dictatorship analogous to those that emerged in twentieth-century Latin America or Southeast Asia, or even to reduce it to a democracy misguided by egalitarianism, one must recognize the historical innovation and ask about its origin.

The destruction of the Soviet regime, and the model it represented to tens of millions of people around the world, does not spare one from observing that an attack had been launched against the foundations of every society, that humanity did not escape unscathed from this adventure, and that a threshold of the possible had been crossed. To say that a totalitarian society could have been born only in the twentieth century is not adequate; one must furthermore make clear that this was the century during which a world-space was rapidly constituted, with relationships increasing among countries whose levels of development, traditions, and political structures had been previously incomparable. Communism appears in a new light when one views it as an unforeseeable product of this process. As soon as one wants to explain its formation, one risks trapping oneself in an alternative—necessity or contingency—instead of investigating the phenomenon as it presents and delivers itself to thought. Out of fear of giving in to the fiction of necessity and thus falling back into the orbit of grand theories of history, one is tempted to retreat to the argument of contingency: fortuitous events, World War I above all, explain what seemed to be a new society. However, the phenomenon itself, as long as one looks for meaning in it, bears traces of the past from which it emerged, traces of heterogeneous institutions, practices, and beliefs. As the reader will see, the idea of Communist society's origin implies absolutely no concession to determinism. We are led back once again to sources in history: the despotism of the tsarist Old Regime; conspiratorial or terroristic revolutionary movements acting on the Russian stage during the second half of the nineteenth century; and democracy, industrial capitalism, and the rise of social democracy in Western Europe. It is true that the historians considered here, whose first concern was to reject belief in necessity, were no more satisfied invoking contingency. For them, the new regime seemed from the beginning born from illusion or the utopia of socialism. But this judgment does violence to the phenomenon in a new way, reducing it to either the manifestation of an idea or the political will of individuals struggling relentlessly to construct a system conforming to this idea. Totalitarianism becomes, in this manner, an abstraction.

The first task is to return to the *concrete*. I use this word—without overlooking the abuses done to it, notably in Marxist language—in order to restore the rigorous meaning given it by Marcel Mauss, one of the founders of social anthropology, in a programmatic text that concluded his famous "Essay on the Gift" (1923–1924). After having introduced the notion of "*total* social facts," Mauss expressed the wish that "one succeed in seeing social 'things' themselves, in concrete form and as they are."[7] Immediately clarifying this remark, he added, "In societies one grasps more than ideas or rules; one takes in humans, groups, and their different forms of behavior."[8] Mauss's approach, I would note in passing, was not foreign to Edmund Husserl's phenomenology in its call for a return to "things themselves." It implied a break with intellectualism as much as with empiricism, the latter being the dominant point of view in the modern sciences. Mauss's method led to uncovering the experience hidden beneath constructions that defined and delimited "objects" corresponding to the well-ordered exercise of knowledge. Mauss criticized the reduction of social phenomena to the status of objects together with the strict separation of disciplines within the human sciences.

Following this inspiration, I maintain that we can achieve some understanding of the Communist phenomenon only if we grasp the interweaving [*intrication*] of political, social, economic, juridical, moral, and psychic facts (as anthropology asks us to do). Furthermore, we should not prejudge the definition of these facts but grasp them as they are presented in the society under consideration. In this case, the political facts will become clear by examining not only leaders' policies and their justifications for them but also the nature of a new institution, the Bolshevik Party, which resembled no other parties that had appeared until then. We must consider how the party's rules (democratic centralism, for example) did not immediately reveal the meaning of its actual workings. We must assess the representations—for which ideology does not provide the key—commanding or driving party members' behavior (their inclusion in a collective body and the plain efficacy of "organization"). Social facts will become clearer by examining not only the destruction of old class relations but also the formation of new discriminations and hierarchies in society. Juridical facts must be inspected not only in constitutions promulgated by the party-state but also in the instauration of a "Soviet legality," which destroyed all prior distinctions between legal and illegal. Moral facts should be examined not only from the perspective of explicitly declared ethics but also from the point of view of practices that eliminated, in good conscience, entire groups or masses of individuals without particular affiliations who were assigned the role of enemies of the people. Psychic facts ought to be analyzed not only as a language governed by the certainty of a historical logic but also as a system of thought that implied the abolition of the subject and the swallowing up of the individual in the Communist *we*.

Without denying the role of illusion, in this essay I ask a question that no doubt will seem scandalous even today: Did the totalitarian model and the chances it afforded the formation of a party-state and a new elite exercise a more tremendous attraction on all the continents of the planet than the image of a society delivered from class exploitation in which all citizens enjoy the same rights?

It is true that understanding a regime and a model of political society (this last term no longer referring to a particular domain of actions but designating that which constitutes society as an ensemble) leads us out of the anthropological framework. A regime confronts us with a formation, a shaping [*mise en forme*], which is also a forging of meaning [*mise en sens*] of social relations in a community ordered under a pole of authority, in such a way that those social relations are supposed to conform to good ends (even despotism is not an exception in this respect). From this point of view, every regime defines itself only by virtue of principles that oppose it to others at a given time. No political thinker, whether or not he sees himself as a philosopher, ignores either this agonistic relation or the fact that it puts in play a conception of the world that escapes the perspective of the historian's or sociologist's knowledge. Less than all others, the totalitarian Communist regime, in its opposition to democratic regimes as well as its attempt to attack the foundations of political society, leaves no place for neutrality. It poses more than just a new problem. It constitutes a challenge for thought whose significance we have not yet fully grasped. It puts to the test history's *complications*.

I have not erased the traces of the two interpretations to which I owe my reflections. Furet and Malia provided me with a guiding thread. In following them, I was led to reconsider the older interpretations of Raymond Aron and Hannah Arendt. The wisdom of Aron, author of *Democracy and Totalitarianism* (1958), struck me more than it had on other occasions.[9] He expressed all too clearly the worthwhile distinction between the two meanings of the political. The attention he paid to properly social facts is remarkable, especially to the formation of a new dominant stratum—bureaucracy—that refused reduction to the model of bureaucracies characteristic of industrial societies. I continue to wrestle both with his idea of the vestiges of the democratic spirit in Communist ideology and, more generally, with his conception of ideology. Arendt, to whom I have always felt the closest as a thinker, has led me to ask, from a point of view different from her own, what law becomes "in the concrete" at the heart of the totalitarian universe.

1

Wisdom of the Historian

D ID THE END OF COMMUNISM reveal the meaning of its beginning? It is a tempting image: a ruined edifice whose foundations and frame are suddenly revealed. Martin Malia suggested as much in *The Soviet Tragedy*, starting in the preface, where he warned, "Soviet history is now for the first time really history, and this closure permits us to see the pattern or 'logic' of its life course."[1] Even more explicit was his assertion in the introduction, eloquently subtitled "A Time for Judgment":

> For the first time it is possible to see Soviet Communism as a closed historical episode, with a clear beginning, a middle, and an end. Until 1989–91, in assessing the erstwhile Soviet enigma, we were always somewhere in medias res, and our analyses of Soviet development were thus accordingly governed by a range of expectations as to how the experiment might turn out. Now that we know the real denouement of the drama the guessing game is over, and what we believed we understood about the story's beginning and middle appears far from the mark indeed. Hence, the real process of assessing the Soviet adventure can at last begin; to draw on the historical wisdom of Hegel: "the owl of Minerva takes flight only as the shades of night are falling."[2]

It is worth pausing on these lines, since they show signs of the confident discovery of a truth. Such a discovery is unusual for a historian; I believe the phenomenon of Communism alone can inspire it. Malia eschewed a debate that, one should recall, had constantly engaged often unforgiving participants—whether the argument concerned the origins and nature of the Soviet system or, during its final years, the meaning of its evolution. Consigning this debate to the obscure time of riddles, he expressed the same ardor, if not the same passion, as his predecessors in stating the diagnosis. He simply added the claim of the right to knowingly conclude, since the history of Communism was itself at an end. In spite of what he said, however, his tone gave the feeling that he was still in medias res. That expression—in the middle of things—grabs one's attention. How does one cease to move and think in the middle of things? How can one attain a position that achieves a clear view of the past on the question of Communism? Neither Alexis de Tocqueville nor Max Weber, to whom Malia liked to refer, claimed this power. No less eloquent, it seems to me, was this other formula: "to see Soviet Communism as a closed historical episode." Where is the book from which one could extract this chapter? It is curious to find an author who placed the myth of historical Reason at the origin of Communism, himself referring to Hegelian wisdom. For Hegel would not have dreamed of defining Communism without situating it as a particular moment in the becoming of the World Spirit.

No, we have not finished reflecting on Communism. It is one thing to say that its breakup revealed flaws in its construction present from the beginning or brought to an end Sovietologists' speculations on its future. But it is another thing to affirm that the final event produced the "solution" to problems posed by the rise of that unprecedented Russian regime and by its extraordinary influence outside its borders. *The Soviet Tragedy* offered us exactly that: a solution. What was it? The reader was spared having to look for it, since Malia phrased it clearly: Soviet Communism was the product of a utopia called socialism.

Before examining this thesis and its implications, let me return to the passage I cited. Availing himself of his position at the end of the history of Communism, Malia spoke of a "time for judgment," as if one had been incapable of judging beforehand and had instead been condemned to express opinions impenetrable to reason. In short, everyone was wrong. This amounts to saying that even if not all interpretations are equivalent, at least one cannot decide among them. And yet, had not Communism mobilized the faculty of judgment? The fact is that Communists always presented themselves as people who judged everything, while those who supported them tried to find the most convenient arguments for justifying Communist politics. Furthermore, a conspicuous characteristic among Communists was judging non-Communists and reducing the behaviors and beliefs of their adversaries, indeed their allies, to objective causes known only to them.

Malia lived through the era he later considered as having not yet been the time for judgment, a time during which one certainly took sides, but not knowing the future, he seemed to say, without being able to judge. He overlooked the fact that during that era the question of judgment was asked in terms that have in no way been effaced by the destruction of the Soviet regime. Judging did not depend on merely a precise knowledge of the regime, its character, and evolution, of Communist parties and their character and evolution, of the relationship between Marxism and Leninism or between Leninism and Stalinism, or of detailed facts. Judging required in the first place the freedom or the right to judge. It was as a matter of fact this right and freedom that Communists refused to those who were not Communists. To gauge the significance of this refusal, one must still distinguish between, on one hand, the fabricated image of the bourgeois adversary who, embedded in the capitalist system, occupied the role assigned to him in the scientific scenario of history and, on the other hand, the image of the leftist non-Communist. Against the latter, Communists exercised constant intimidation, not without success. They suspected or accused leftist non-Communists of betraying the cause of the exploited and playing, as was said at the time, the "game of imperialism." Within the party framework, no one was supposed to evade discipline of action or thought. Outside the party, no one could criticize Communist politics without finding himself placed in the category of the proletariat's enemies. For a long time, questioning the role of Lenin or Stalin was taken as blasphemy.

Malia wrote *The Soviet Tragedy* at a time of large consensus. Where Communists or Communist parties continue to exist, we see them condemning "errors" committed in the past and declaring themselves the best defenders of democracy. As for ex-Communists, many of them like to emphasize the fact that they left the party "at the right moment," intentionally forgetting the assistance they had brought to Stalinist practices. On the whole, for both Communists and ex-Communists it is not disagreeable to see themselves now called victims of a *utopia* and thus to offer the double image of innocence and repentance. However, the memory of an epoch when it was urgent to judge and denounce not utopia, but the lie—this memory must remain.

2

Critique of "Couch Liberalism"

COMMUNISM HAS FALLEN APART, and passions have cooled. The time for judgment has arrived. This line of thinking reminds me of that held by apparently liberal American intellectuals forty years ago when Communist engagement was discredited in the United States because of the Senate investigations led by Joseph McCarthy, the fanatical politician. In a 1955 article of rare lucidity and ferocity, "Couch Liberalism and the Guilty Past," Harold Rosenberg commented on those intellectuals. The essay was published in French in 1962.[1] I believe it worthwhile to mention because it seems to me to have illuminated for the first time the political stakes of a debate often readily dressed up as a metaphysical drama. It will help introduce some reflections I would like to develop.

A highly talented writer, art and literary critic, and poet, Rosenberg was the author of some dazzling articles on modern politics, Marx, and Leninism published in American Left-liberal journals, notably *Dissent*, *Encounter*, and *Partisan Review*. In France he published in *Les Temps modernes*. The article I mentioned contained certain considerations that are no longer pertinent, since they were tied to accusations made against two Communists, Whittaker Chambers and Alger Hiss, the former avowing, the latter denying his collaboration with the Soviet secret services. And yet Rosenberg's claims have kept their sharpness when he described the attitude of "couch liberals" and took apart the arguments of intellectuals obsessed with presenting Communists and their former allies as victims of a Marxist-Leninist utopia. Rosenberg was interested in the confessions of repentant Communists, and he underscored their haste in denouncing a collective guilt surrounding duly identified spies, the leaders of the Communist machinery, simple militants, fellow travelers, and, with them, liberals (in the American sense of the term that associates liberalism with a libertarian spirit). "Everyone is familiar, or should be," he wrote, "with the Communist method of transforming the past. . . . Through a series of public confessions a new collective Character is created, and made retrospectively responsible for the way things happened."[2] These confessions were compared with dark humor to those by the accused in the earlier Moscow trials, notably Karl Radek, who revealed that there were "semi-Trotskyites, quarter-Trotskyites, one-eighth Trotskyites . . . and people who from liberalism . . . gave us help."[3] The American penitents were certainly not exposed to the same fate as the victims of Andrei Vyshinsky, but their confessions similarly lent themselves to verdicts handed down through a kind of person, "a collection of individuals who constitute a single 'we.'" In other words, Rosenberg concluded, "the guilty Enemy is *one*."[4] If this representation, transposed onto the scene of the American universe, offered only another sign of the Communist mentality, it would not have been terribly astonishing. But the fact is that it had the advantage of the cooperation of intellectuals who defined themselves as liberals and were delighted to be able to slip into the community of those who were guilty and had repented:

> In America the part of the repentant history-maker has been played by the ex-radical intellectuals, some former Communists, others liberals and rebels who suddenly discovered that all roads of dissent cleared the way for Communism. . . . All threw themselves into the same melting pot, were changed into the same character, and assumed the identical guilt. Looking backwards, paying dues to the party, following its line, were only deeper shadings of any criticism of capitalism, any questioning of the motives of American foreign policy, any making of distinctions between Red and White totalitarianism.[5]

Rosenberg attacked in particular the work of Leslie Fiedler, an intellectual who presented himself as a liberal and provided the most remarkable specimen of couch liberalism. Fiedler opened his book *An End to Innocence* (1955) by paraphrasing a famous citation from Chambers "to the effect that History will get you if you don't get it first."[6] In focusing on this essay, Rosenberg gives us a suggestion that is not yet out of date. The widespread confusion today among historians of Communism between the idea of history, which cannot possibly be abandoned, and the theory of Reason, which controls the development of human societies and leads toward its fulfillment, cautions us as to the impression one might have of the Communist adventure. Having believed the fiction of Necessity, the Communist adventure apparently demonstrated by its failure that it was henceforth necessary to mourn a meaning and direction of history expressed in social institutions and then be interested only in actors (Lenin, the foremost leader) whose voluntarism had collided with the resistance of the real and produced unintended consequences. Rosenberg's critique of Fiedler's book was too long and touched on many events that are outside my interests here—notably the trial of Julius and Ethel Rosenberg—so I will not go through the trouble of reconstructing it. However, it seems worthwhile to freely extract several arguments that merit consideration by those today who ponder the history of Communist movements. The first touched on the notion of innocence, the second on the defense of liberalism and radicalism, the third on Communists' mentalities and how they adapted to American society, and the fourth on conflicts between Communists and left-wing anti-Communists.

Rosenberg summed up Fiedler's thought in this way: we were guilty of being innocent. Fiedler had bemoaned Hiss's refusal to confess once accused of spying because he "failed all liberals, all who had, in some sense and at some time, shared his illusions (and who that calls himself a liberal is exempt?), all those who demanded of him he speak aloud a common recognition of complicity. And yet . . . at the bottom of their hearts, they did not finally want him to admit anything, but preferred the chance he gave them to say, 'He is, we are, innocent.'"[7] Rosenberg vehemently contested the expression "all liberals," which presented a made-up character equipped with an arbitrary past. To the parenthetical remark—"who that calls himself a liberal is exempt?"—Rosenberg objected: "I raise my right hand and reply that I never shared anything with Mr. Hiss, including automobiles or typewriters; certainly not illusions."[8]

In fact, we quickly realize, Rosenberg attributed to Hiss neither illusions nor errors of judgment. He saw him acting in step with party orders. Furthermore, Rosenberg did not believe that the non-Communist intellectual Left lived under the sway of illusion: "Fiedler's 'common recognition of complicity' is simply slander, ex-Communist style."[9] The way he dismantled Fiedler's argument remains instructive. The idea of a shared illusion points back to a time of innocence, by which I mean a time when intellectuals had not learned how to distinguish the real and the imaginary, since they had only "a caste vocabulary made of universals and idealistic abstractions" (I will add that they distinguished no better the good and the bad, the true and the false).[10] Suddenly, according to Fiedler, they discovered to their great displeasure that the man in the street does not make mistakes, that "buffoons and bullies, those who *knew* really nothing about the Soviet Union at all, were right— stupidly right, if you will, accidentally right, right for the wrong reasons, but damnably right." The task of intellectuals, after having "erred out of generosity and open-mindedness," was thus to recognize this fact without joining the McCarthyites.[11] In short, Rosenberg noted, once the time of innocence was over, then came apprenticeship and self-criticism, the time of evenhanded assessment and the return to the good American community as a substitution for the community of which they had dreamed: "The Left intellectual is given the chance of gaining self-knowledge and rehabilitating himself via confession; all the Communist fakers, fools, and position-seekers of yesterday became not only 'innocent' but 'generous and open-minded.'"[12]

The second point is this: Rosenberg protested against falsifying the history of Communism in America, defending those few liberals who, even if they did not fully understand what Communism was, had never been collaborators. "It is false to say," he wrote, "that a belief in freedom, equality, individuality, induced adherence to the Red band, with its underband of party bosses, spies, and masterminds. The liberal sentiment for radical equality and freedom was, in fact, the single intellectual mooring that held against the powerful drag of the totalitarian 'we,' supported by the offer of a heroic part and material reward through social scheming. Moreover, the sentiment of freedom alone presented Marxism itself in its living intellectual form, that is, as a problem."[13] I would emphasize the word *equality*, which clearly means that the liberalism Rosenberg embraced implied absolutely no concession to the conservatism for which inequality in our societies is simply a given fact. As for the characterization of Marxism as a problem, it seems to me fortunately to make short work of the new commonplace that converts Marx into an inspirer of totalitarianism.

The third point concerns Communist engagement. If Rosenberg made the mistake of passing over the extent to which belief was involved, he had the merit of illuminating one of its dimensions too often left in the shadows. It is true that he did not discuss the generation contemporary with the Soviet regime's rise, but rather those that followed. More precisely, he treated engagement in the Communist Party or on its margins within a democratic society—the United States—and, even more exactly, intellectuals' engagement. Instead of citing the most significant passages at length, I will mention a few parts of the picture he drew: Communists and Communist sympathizers were not at all troubled by the execution of the Old Bolsheviks,[14] the liquidation of revolutionaries in Spain, the Hitler–Stalin pact, the division of the Resistance under the Nazis, the partition of Poland, or other widely observed events (there were many examples). Commenting ironically on the supposed innocence of intellectuals who witnessed these events and remained imperturbably loyal, Rosenberg asserted in a language that could still seem irreverent in our day: "These scoundrels were, as a type, middle-class careerists, closed both to argument and evidence, impatient with thought—psychopaths of 'radical' conformity."[15] Speaking of an idealism that masked cynicism, he detailed their portrait in this way: "Delirious at finding themselves on the Stage of History, they eagerly carried out the intellectual atrocities assigned to them, while keeping one eye on a post in the future International Power, the other on the present good spot in the government, the university, Hollywood, or publishing."[16] I do not disagree that this judgment is one-sided. Taking and transposing an expression of the author, I would say that I love thought too much to remain satisfied with the idea that Communist intellectuals were all, or for the most part, scoundrels. On the other hand, to restrict myself to the period that I know, since I lived through it, it seems to me fair to denounce the cynicism of many of these intellectuals and to emphasize the symbolic and material benefits they received from their engagement. Many benefited from belonging to a milieu that secured for each person the feeling of social recognition via participation in a knowledge elite that fed on contempt for the non-Communist Left and on the hope of winning posts in government administration, the university, publishing houses, and cultural organizations (not to mention writers whose books, distributed in the Communist world, achieved a readership whose scale exceeded their dreams). Rosenberg made a simple remark: "Their social respectability did not conflict with their support of Communist treachery and violence committed against non-party leftists or radical democrats throughout the world."[17] More generally, I should point out that, contrary to the image to which they devoted themselves, Communist intellectuals did not remain on the margins of the official world. They mapped out their own special territory.

Here is the fourth and final point: Communists did not speak, or hardly spoke, about their persecution of nonconformist intellectuals and about the resistance some of the latter offered: "Like their master in Moscow, the Communist intellectuals in America detested above all, not capitalism nor even fascism, to both of which the switching party line taught them to accommodate themselves—their one hatred which knew no amelioration was toward the independent radical. . . . Soft to the point of servility to its foes on the Right, the Stalinist Front never varied in its violence against those who struck in any form against its radical pretensions."[18] This observation seems to me once again very pertinent when considering those who are tempted to include in the same category Communists and those who opposed Stalinism. The latter in Marxist or anarchist movements were the most precocious and constant critics of the Soviet regime and the Comintern's politics. As Rosenberg furthermore noted, the ex-Communist often exploited information furnished by the radical Left. Recalling the vigor with which independent intellectuals were opposed to Communists, he cited in particular the "Statement of the League for Cultural Freedom and Socialism" published in *Partisan Review* in 1939 and signed by thirty-four writers. This document denounced the so-called cultural organizations controlled by the Communist Party for being "among intellectual circles in the United States the most active forces of reaction today. . . . Pretending to represent progressive opinion, these bodies are in effect but apologists for the Kremlin dictatorship. They outlaw all dissenting opinion from the Left. They poison the intellectual atmosphere with slander."[19]

I should not leave Rosenberg behind without mentioning the portrait he painted in his essay "Death in the Wilderness" of the representatives of the new generation freed from "the problems of their elders." Significantly, this rich essay followed "Couch Liberalism and the Guilty Past" in the same collection. Here, one notably finds that Fiedler's swindle in *An End to Innocence* was followed by Daniel Bell's in *The End of Ideology* (1960).[20] As few can now forget, Bell's book briefly aroused broad interest, especially among distinguished sociologists in Anglo-Saxon countries and in France. Its arrival marked a change of scenery. Rosenberg saw Bell playing the role of the prophet of the impossible. In the last small part of his essay, entitled "The Open Road of Im-possibility," he deciphered a message that might be summed up in several propositions: the intellectual-ideologue was at an impasse; he scorned the ordinary person for his indifference to grandeur, believed that he dedicated himself to an authentic passion, and waited on the salvation of humanity in the Revolution. All illusion had vanished, and all that remained was "daily routine without heroism." Let me limit myself to three useful observations on this point. The first is that the praise of pragmatism and the slogan of adapting to reality hid traces of the posture of the ideologue. Second, the so-called illusion of Communism and its liberal allies went hand in hand with the "routine" of the lie as well as the falsification of history and the facts they witnessed. Third, the delimitation of the possible and the impossible presupposed that we could depend on the reality of American society—an absurdity. In fact, as Rosenberg wrote, "American Life is a billboard; individual life in the U.S. includes something nameless that takes place in the weeds behind it. In America everything is possibility—or it is sham. You cannot *fit* into American life except as a 'camp.'"[21] It is true that he was speaking only about America. But what he said concerns all democratic countries unsettled and upset by transformations of technology, economy, social relations, and mores. The ideology of realism conceals the fact that the possible is something entirely different from illusion.

3

Autopsy of an Illusion

I T IS WORTHWHILE TO ASK about the role attributed to illusion in the constitution and development of Communism. I am struck by this fact: two books appeared at more or less the same time (one ought not think they borrowed from each other). Both invited the reader to discover a utopia, an illusion, or an idea as the principle at the heart of Communism. The first, already considered, was by Martin Malia. The second was François Furet's *The Passing of an Illusion*. Their intentions, it is true, were different. Whereas one proposed to write the history of the Soviet regime, the other had for his object "not a history of Communism, even less a history of the Soviet Union . . . [but] a history of the illusion of Communism during the time in which the USSR lent it consistency and vitality."[1] Still, Malia's and Furet's routes intersected on several occasions. According to Malia, the history of the Soviet regime allegedly demonstrated that utopia—by way of "unintended consequences"—governed its course from beginning to end, whereas for Furet the history of the illusion or the idea (the two terms were interchangeable) led the investigator to state, relate, and interpret changes occurring both in Russia between the October revolution and perestroika and in Western Communist politics. I would immediately add that the two works were equally stimulating. They neither disguised nor toned down any traits of a system of domination justly called totalitarian, they fortunately refused to explain that system's formation and evolution as a mere matter of circumstances, and they demonstrated the continuity of the Communist enterprise in spite of the upheavals provoked by Stalin's death and his successors' reforms.

One of Furet's arguments immediately seizes one's attention, not only because it bears witness to the affinities between the two interpretations but because it bears on the reconstitution of a history controlled by illusion. While Malia, as I indicated, asserted that the end of the Soviet regime inaugurated the time for judgment, Furet declared in his preface:

> What historians of the Communist idea in the twentieth century will find is an entirely closed circuit of the modern political imagination, beginning with the October revolution and ending with the dissolution of the Soviet Union. Beyond what it actually was, the Communist world always glorified what it wanted and what it would therefore become. With its disappearance, the question of what it would have become has been answered: today, Communism is completely contained within its past.[2]

The first proposition—the closed circuit of the Communist idea—goes without saying, though we cannot forget the case of China. But I would dispute the interpretation that the question of the regime's nature and orientation could not have been broached previously. Likewise, I deny that the illusion was such that it blinded even those who did not belong to the Communist world. Indeed, Furet specifically argued that if it had been possible to "diagnose the debilitating disease that afflicted the Soviet Union . . . international public opinion could hardly imagine the possibility of a radical crisis in the social system established by Lenin and Stalin."[3]

No one seems exempt from this opinion. Like Harold Rosenberg, I protest. Already in 1956, learning of the astonishing state of affairs brought about by Khrushchev's secret speech to the Twentieth Party Congress, I wrote in an article entitled "Totalitarianism Without Stalin" that the regime designed to be the most solid and well-locked-down among systems of domination showed itself wrought by insurmountable contradictions and eminently vulnerable.[4] I have reformulated this diagnosis on many occasions. Without wanting to belabor this point, I will briefly mention the judgment I made in the 1970 postscript to my *Éléments d'une critique de la bureaucratie* (1971) that "one may well expect that in the USSR—at some unpredictable day of reckoning—there will be a crisis of the regime, whose consequences would have unprecedented significance in Eastern Europe as well as in the Western world."[5] Then again, as I wrote in my 1977 essay "Another Revolution": "Totalitarianism constitutes the most efficient system of domination, but also the most vulnerable. After such an event (the 1956 Hungarian insurrection whose memory I had been evoking), it is permitted to think that if a crisis emerges at the heart of the totalitarian edifice, the Soviet Union, a generalized, unmasterable revolt will break out, leaving power naked as nowhere else."[6] Others shared the same analysis and the same expectation. Did the fact that they belonged to a non-Communist, nonofficial Left make their opinions negligible?

I assure the reader that I was thoroughly astonished at the spectacle of Communism's downfall.[7] I had imagined a popular revolt and absolutely did not foresee that the crisis would spring from a top-down initiative (which should not lead anyone to underestimate the extraordinary effervescence released in that society, preventing Gorbachev from realizing his program of reforms). That is to say, I agree that there are degrees in the unforeseeable. The script of the regime's decomposition had not been conceivable ahead of time, especially for the actors who were to play leading roles. The event that we have difficulty calling a revolution—although it is tempting to use that term to qualify the destruction of a regime so powerful that it had subjugated an empire and part of Europe and challenged a coalition of Western states—this event has lessons for us and sheds a new light on the past. What was singular in that event's unfolding cannot be deduced from accidental causes or structural defects. Nevertheless, that does not mean that, during the time we will henceforth call the Old Regime, we were unable to foresee its collapse.

In *The Gulag Archipelago* (1973–1975) Aleksandr Solzhenitsyn described how, once liberated and rehabilitated, he had appeared before a group of judges indistinguishable from those who had condemned him. He wrote of his stupefaction at seeing them so pleasant and informal, even rushing to compliment him now that they themselves had been released from the organs in which previously the law had been applied in conformity to Stalin's will. "If the first tiny droplet of truth has exploded like a psychological bomb," Solzhenitsyn wondered, "what then will happen in our country when whole waterfalls of Truth burst forth? And they will burst forth. It has to happen."[8] No doubt he had too much confidence in the effects of truth, but he was not mistaken about the

magnitude of the explosion. All the same, his commentary on this episode is worthwhile in another way. The judges, Solzhenitsyn reported,
"were explaining that their intentions were of the best." But, he asked
himself, "if things turn full circle and it is once again up to them to try
me? . . . Well, so they will convict me."[9] How does one record this phenomenon in terms of illusions? Solzhenitsyn did not suggest that his
interlocutors had been prey to illusions in the past and that, after having been liberated from them, they could again fall under their spell.
He makes us understand something else entirely. These men, who were
supposed to have sought the good, only saw good and bad with the eyes
of the law—that is, with the eyes of the party. I do not doubt the efficacy
of Communist belief. But can one analyze it without connecting it to the
political formation in which it found its element, prospered, and would
long endure even as it decayed?

In one sense, Furet's project was more ambitious and audacious than
Malia's. Their objects of research largely coincided in the factual details,
since they both analyzed the existence of the Soviet regime from its birth
to its disappearance. The interpretation of the regime was grounded in
historical reconstruction. Confidently setting events and actors into a
specific relief and discerning continuities and ruptures, Malia followed
a well-known course already explored by other historians, though the
latter had been yet unaware of how that course was to end. For his part,
Furet had to construct an object—"the idea of Communism in the twentieth century"—that he made consistent by gathering and selecting data
from different epochs and spaces. Of course, his investigation remained
limited. It excluded China, Korea, Cambodia, and Vietnam, not because
there was nothing to learn from them, but because confronting the destiny of the Communist idea in the Soviet Union and Europe (along the
way, an incursion was made into the American milieu) was particularly
instructive, since the project of a proletarian revolution had been born
in nineteenth-century Europe before it subdued Russia and then made
its return to its first setting.

Furet posed the following questions: In what did the Communist illusion consist? How was it distinguished from the reality of Communism?
How was it formed, preserved, and then renounced in Russia, while during the same period it expanded fantastically in Europe? These questions

fit together in the same way as the answers to them, and they stemmed from a primary conviction. The Communist phenomenon—taken in all its extended meaning, coming to light through an examination of the Soviet regime and the diverse Communist parties and movements that always exalted it as a model while subordinating their objectives to those of the Soviet leaders—this phenomenon could be conceived only by finding an unchanging variable [*invariant*]: the Communist illusion. Furet wrote, "This illusion did not 'accompany' Communist history; it made it. Independent of Communist history insofar as it existed prior to experience, the illusion was, at the same time, subject to that history since the truth of its prophecies was contained in its course."[10] In a few lines in the preface we are presented with the tenor of this illusion. It was a logic of history and an action conforming to that logic, a dictatorship of the proletariat whose forecasts were scientifically established, and a salvation that secured devotion appropriate for a sacred cause—that is, a last illusion requiring "a psychological investment, somewhat like a religious faith."[11] Furet reformulated each of these definitions in many ways throughout his book. Illusion thus emerged from the conjunction of many beliefs: in the theory of history, in science, in the project generating a radical transformation of society, and in deliverance from evil (following the inspiration, he eventually said, of a secular religion). The elements of the illusion did not necessarily need to be in agreement. The first derived from an idealist conception of history elaborated by German philosophy in the early nineteenth century, the second from positivist rationalism, the third from voluntarist moralism, and the last from a quasi-religious faith in humanity. Weighing the combination or, better, the condensation of these beliefs into a single belief, Furet commented, "For people lost in history, an illusion of this kind not only gives their life meaning but offers them the comforts of certainty."[12]

Nevertheless, the analysis of illusion did not stop there. Communists, we learn, showed themselves fascinated by revolution understood as the creation from a tabula rasa of a new world and a new human being. It was thus not enough to refer to the idea of an action following the logic of history, adhering to laws that governed transitions from one mode of production to another, or fulfilling the duty to transform the human condition. It was necessary that this action be a leap outside the realm of necessity. That illusion seemed, if not provoked, then at least strengthened by the image of an event—the French Revolution—that gave rise to the task of inaugurating a new path for humanity through a violence linking destruction and creation. This new illusion certainly did not involve a confusion between the respective missions of the proletariat and the bourgeoisie. Rather, it moved forward through a belief in a precedent without precedent; in other words, in the representation of a scene where the great conflict between foundational heroes, on the one hand, and conservative and reactionary forces, on the other, had already been played out. Ultimately, was the illusion of the Revolution as the great engineer of historical change spawned by historical Reason or by the scientific laws regulating the development of societies? One hesitates to answer, since Furet reminded us that the Jacobins did not appeal to a necessity that governed the course of the world, though they were the first to have made history "the only forum" (the restoration of the Supreme Being had been only an ephemeral extravagance on the part of Maximilien Robespierre). Furet furthermore reminded us that, unlike the Bolshevik Party, which "would retain absolute power for seventy-four years in what had once been tsarist Russia . . . Robespierre and his friends actually 'reigned' over revolutionary France for a mere four months."[13] However that may be, the reader ends up asking if, in the last analysis, the illusion of the Revolution should not be taken as fundamental (one entire chapter discusses "revolutionary passion"). Yet, one encounters the explanation given to the paradox that constitutes the lasting quality of the October revolution's "charm," namely, "the so-called meaning and direction of history—another name for historical necessity—which takes the place of religion for those who have no religion."[14]

Ultimately, the difficulty of defining illusion increased when Furet suddenly spoke of an "intellectual mishmash" or a "hodgepodge of dead ideas" at the end of a passage where he replaced the notion of illusion with that of Communist passion, affirming that the great innovation of the twentieth century had been the existence of ideological governments and regimes.[15] If we restrict ourselves to the history of illusion, we must first of all agree that it could be found among Bolsheviks and Western Communists alike and thus drawn from the same inventory. As I noted, it seized minds in Europe, faded in the beginning of the century, and foundered when World War I let loose nationalist passions, before it traveled to Russia, where the success of the October revolution served to rekindle it throughout a war-ravaged Europe. Even so, there, as in other continents later, the illusion split into two parts, since its object became the new Russia considered as the homeland of socialism. Thus Furet found two destinies for the illusion. Certainly he saw it persist in the Soviet Union under the reign of Leninism and Stalinism, since it was never renounced. Nevertheless, it remained in place only at the price of a lie that was believed. The more it collided with the contradictions and disappointments of reality, the less of a hold it had on the mass of the population. This is the paradox that needs to be understood: it lived better and longer in the West—"Its imaginary path is even more mysterious than its actual history."[16]

4

Marx's False Paternity

A SIGNIFICANT PART OF FURET'S analysis stemmed from a reflection on this astonishing phenomenon—Communism's imaginary course was more mysterious than its real history. By zeroing in on this phenomenon, he intended to "describe and analyze a historical consciousness common to both Eastern and Western Europe—two regions long separated by both the reality and illusion of Communism."[1] Did this project thus lead Furet to discover in Marx the first formulation of a model that would eventually subdue Russia? In fact, Marx and Engels were described in the preface to *The Passing of an Illusion* as "inventors" of the Communist idea that Lenin and Stalin would strive to realize (the latter, it is true, "exploited [the idea] . . . to his own advantage").[2] If the inventors certainly did not imagine that a proletarian revolution could take place outside Western Europe, at least they provided the principles that would guide the Bolsheviks. This passing judgment seems to go without saying. However, it is worth pausing here before we examine the reasons for the success of Communist ideology, not in order to shelter Marx from criticism but to indicate that an equivocation weighs on the interpretation. Indeed, one cannot seriously maintain that the thinker who himself refused being called the founder of Marxism advanced the premises of the theory of either the Leninist dictatorship or, even more outlandish, the totalitarian state built under Stalin's rule. Furet was too erudite and subtle a historian to confuse Marx and Engels's design with that of the Soviet leaders. Yet his problematic was such that it led him to establish a filiation that previously had been staunchly denied by the best analysts of Bolshevism.

For instance, though he had by that time largely distanced himself from the theory of revolution, Boris Souvarine in a 1983 preface to the republished anthology of his journal *La Critique sociale* condemned "the ravings of ignoramuses and second-rate minds who blame Marx and Engels for all that is wrong with existing [Soviet] society."[3] I invoke this celebrated historian of Bolshevism because Furet referred to him at length as one of the most precocious and lucid of critics of the Third International (in whose founding he had participated). Souvarine recalled in particular how he had been wrong to make the dictatorship of the proletariat a central theme of Marx's analysis:

> It was an idea among others that he only mentioned in a few lines, especially in his private letters . . . and in his *Critique of the Gotha Program* (1875), but to which he never consecrated a chapter in his works, not even a page or two. In any case, he understood by that term the political preeminence of the proletariat as expressed by universal suffrage, wage laborers being the numerical majority of the population. Engels concluded his preface (1891) to *The Civil War in France* (1871) with these words: "Look at the Commune of Paris. That was the dictatorship of the proletariat." Yet the Paris Commune was an amalgamation of Proudhonists, Blanquists, and various Republicans. It had nothing in common with the oligarchic dictatorship of a single, monolithic party that had become a dictatorship of the secretariat as soon as Lenin died.[4]

Lenin's exploitation of Marx, shored up by literal citations, is undeniable.

For their part, Stalin and his legions of scribes drew on Lenin's teachings. This fact is assuredly instructive, but it still must be interpreted. A characteristic trait of Communism, which also differentiated it from fascist totalitarianism, was that the *Text* [*Écrit*] was supposed to answer all questions emerging in the course of things. Presenting itself at once as the origin and end of knowledge, the *Text* required a certain kind of reader: the Communist Party member. Properly speaking, Lenin himself was no more than an interpreter and guide to the understanding of Marx's writings. It mattered little that he established a relation with those before him who had appealed to the teachings of the founder, since he swept them away as half-wits, hypocrites, and traffickers of the text. He appeared as the first and last reader, thus imposing the image of the only kind of Communist: the Marxist-Leninist. Actually, the falsification of Marx's works was already revealed in the institution of the party as collective possessor of the meaning of revolutionary speech. This falsification continued via the diffusion of a kind of formula according to which each person found the maxim suited to the party line. Everything in the works that invited doubt and hesitation or lent itself to interpretation was crossed out. Thanks to Lenin, Communists had once and for all perfected their approach to the text. They manipulated Marx like they manipulated the facts. Theory, like practice, became used for policing.

5

The Idea of Revolution and the Revolutionary Phenomenon

O NCE ILLUSION IS ESTABLISHED as the principle of Communism, identifying its "inventors" no longer suffices. One must ask from whence they drew their inspiration. If I am not mistaken, Furet the historian attributed this inspiration to two sources: revolutionary passion and democratic passion. The first can be dated, since it was born with the French Revolution. As I have indicated, at a first glance it seems to have furnished one of the constituent parts of the illusion: the Bolsheviks dressed it up as a *precedent* (recall that the Jacobin dictatorship lasted for only four months). From another point of view, revolutionary passion reappeared as the original source of the illusion. Furet wrote convincingly about the role played by the French Revolution within the Bolshevik movement and then outside Russia, especially in France, in debates that followed the October revolution and involved renowned historians. If those historians had not returned in their imaginations to the French Revolution, the metamorphosis of an old Russia freed from autocracy into the model of a new society would have been incomprehensible. As Furet noted, "When the known was used to explore the unknown, Russian history was returned to the Western matrix, which made it much easier to handle. Revolution, counterrevolution, parties, dictatorship, terror, planned economy were simply a series of abstract ideas, serving as parallels."[1] Reading these lines, there is no doubt that some commentators appeared under the sway of an illusion. "This is how the analogical method of reasoning worked," he continued, "relieving historians as well as contemporary or subsequent public opinion of the need to scrutinize the particularity of events and their participants."[2] In short, there was a refusal to see what one witnessed; one wanted to see what one imagined.

This was indeed one of the reasons for the "universal charm of October." And yet, affirming the effective filiation between the two revolutions had the consequence of concealing more than it revealed about the novelty of Bolshevism and, more generally, of Communism.

The French Revolution did give birth to a myth of revolution. The fact is incontestable, and with good reason Furet already grasped it in his *Interpreting the French Revolution* (1978). Moreover, the point had not been lost on numerous nineteenth-century writers. The most remarkable work on this subject remains without doubt Giuseppe Ferrari's *Machiavelli: Judge of the Revolutions of Our Time* (1849), in which the Revolution was presented as the reincarnation of the modern Prince.[3] For his part, Alexis de Tocqueville discovered in the modern world the birth of a new race of revolutionaries who everywhere seemed to him possessed by the desire to destroy established institutions.[4] As is well known, Tocqueville did not want people to confuse the effects of the democratic revolution with those of the French Revolution. The first, as he believed he had shown in his examination of American society, could lend itself to a political art that enabled taming uncivilized instincts; the second ignited a destructive passion still burning today. Furet apparently followed Tocqueville when he asked if the creation of democracy in America deserved to be called a revolution.

The work of contemporary historians such as Bernard Bailyn and Gordon S. Wood seems to me to erase this doubt.[5] Americans were themselves convinced that they were founding a society without precedent in the history of humanity, asserting universal principles in the process. The events that marked the first years of the republic were anything but peaceful. Yet, as I myself noted in commenting on Wood's analysis, "Only France saw the revolution separate from its actors. Only there was it idealized, even personified; only there was a mythology born and the character of the revolutionary hero formed."[6] I then added in terms close to Furet's, "With the French Revolution an imaginary scene was constructed on which until recently those everywhere who hoped for radical change projected their desires."

Furet did not limit himself to pointing out that the French Revolution gave birth to a revolutionary imaginary. He wanted to place the Russian Revolution back in its wake. So he was obliged to specify the French Revolution's essential contribution by recovering its trace in the principle of the Russian Revolution and, more generally, in the principle of revolutions that led to the construction of a totalitarian system. To his understanding, "What was a recent invention for the French of the late eighteenth century would later become the central and ultimately the universal figure on the European stage. It came to symbolize, above all, the role of volition in politics and was the proof and even the guarantee that people can tear themselves away from their past in order to invent and construct a new society."[7] In the same passage he went on to note, "The revolutionary passion transforms everything into politics . . . for what the French Revolution invented was less a new society founded on civil equality and representative government than a special way of bringing about change, a certain idea of human volition, and a messianic conception of politics."[8] Assuming this was the case, one must still observe that multiple revolutionary movements, programs, and utopias were born in France and Europe, even in Russia, in which one finds no trace of a Marxist or Leninist conception of change. However, Furet was interested only in the "privileged mode of change" that ensured the success of Communism. If Bolshevism alone succeeded in establishing a new regime, should one not ask about the aspirations it knew how to answer and the currents to which it knew how to give an outlet, even if one rejects the thesis of historical determinism? Must one understand that it was the only movement capable of capturing the resources of the French Revolution because it was entranced by it? To admit the latter we would have turned down the wrong road, since we learn that the myth of revolution—in the sense that it associated voluntarism, constructivism, and political messianism—also dominated fascism. No doubt one can point out that fascism was openly antiuniversalist. Yet, through its will to affirm itself as such, fascism in some sense proved equal to its adversary—bourgeois democracy—since it denounced the latter's incapacity to achieve its principles. Its revolutionary force thus came not only from its rupture with the ideal of a restoration of an old order but also from its pretension to construct an entirely new order "in the name of the political will of the masses."[9]

I am well aware that Furet was interested in the idea of revolution, in the passage that I cited and throughout his work. This topic was completely legitimate. However, the power an idea acquires and the intentions that allow it to take shape are intelligible only if one considers the ground on which the idea successfully takes root. Observing this ground, one is not led to substitute an analysis of supposedly real facts for the analysis of the idea; rather, the diversity of revolutionary phenomena appear.

The very word *revolution*, one must acknowledge, lends itself to different meanings, whether one refers to the events that inaugurated the democratic era or the revolutions of 1848 or the Italian and German fascist revolutions of the twentieth century. This last usage implied the destruction of a political and social structure and the foundation of a new regime, but it had the distinctive characteristic of having been devised and carried out by a minority benefiting from agreements with certain conservative leaders and from the active support of a large fraction of the middle classes. Fascist revolution came about by subordinating the existing state apparatus to a henceforth unrivaled party. We cannot for all that deny that the fascist conquest of power had the character of a revolution. The word was used by fascism's instigators and its victims. Nevertheless, the mode of change in that case differed from that which gave the idea of revolution its first meaning and direction. The French event, like the American one before it, was certainly different from what one previously called revolt or rebellion, but it retained the character of an insurrection. In its first movement, then, revolution consists in a popular uprising. A mass of individuals in diverse places, whose condition required them to obey superiors taken as legitimate, disobeyed those superiors' orders and affirmed their own rights as if they had the law on their side.

In Russia, as in France, "people tore themselves away from their past in order to invent."[10] I readily agree to this formula, but only in order to emphasize that these men were not moved by the "idea of revolution" and that this uprooting bore witness first of all to a collective rejection of hierarchy and a demand for freedoms. In February 1917, it took only several weeks, even several days, to topple the citadel of the state, rendering powerless the government, army, police, and courts. The forces on which the laws and the spirit of the laws depended decomposed without what one could call the motor of revolution. Insurrection spread from one source to another without orchestration, and taboos weighing on speech were lifted. Men, who even the day before had seen their existence strictly regulated within the framework of their conditions, gathered together, conversed with one another, organized themselves, and defined their common objectives. Some of them, unprepared by their authority or their competence, composed manifestos and gave angry speeches. What had so horrified Edmund Burke about the spectacle of the French Revolution—the generalized fever of innovation, the decomposition of the nation's body—was reproduced in 1917.

Astonishingly, Furet and Malia scarcely mentioned February 1917, concerned as they were only with October, when the strategy elaborated by Lenin succeeded via the conquest of the state. October is, however, intelligible only once it is resituated within the tumultuous situation that began with the February insurrection. That event had set loose a torrent of demands and given birth to a profusion of revolutionary organs. Marc Ferro devoted two remarkable works to this period, remarkable as much for the richness of the investigation as for the fecundity of his interpretation: *The Russian Revolution of February 1917* (1967, 1976) (the first of its two volumes was entirely dedicated to the first phase of the revolution) and *From the Soviets to Bureaucratic Communism* (1964).[11] I would first of all emphasize Ferro's analysis of the lists of demands [*cahiers de revendications*] originating in diverse regions of the country, which he compared with the *cahiers de doléances* of 1789 without leaving us to assume, logically, that the latter served as a model.[12] As in the past in France, popular demands in Russia testified to a remarkable convergence. They were in the beginning only weakly part of the political order; the groups that drafted them displayed absolutely no evidence of political tampering by parties. Work conditions, material security, and hygiene were the principal objects of worker protest. They were intended to expose the oppression of the population and worker exploitation, both of which had intensified since the start of World War I. No documents better dismantle the legend of a tsarist state that by its own movement would have led to the creation of a liberal regime. We discover in these documents how much the undeniable acceleration of economic progress in the years before the revolution had been accompanied by a worsening of the lot of most people. Even more important is to observe the surge of revolutionary organs that flooded the entire country from February to October. Ferro sketched a catalog of them in *From the Soviets to Bureaucratic Communism*, enabling us to understand better how events were linked before the victory of Bolshevism.

Shortly after the February insurrection, a duality of power had been set up between the provisional government and the soviet of Petrograd (prelude to the soviet of workers' and soldiers' deputies). One point stands out: the soviets sprang up spontaneously. In 1917 as in 1905, Boris Souvarine declared, the revolution began "without the help of professional revolutionaries. No socialist party had urged or guided the masses in revolt. No leader was there to give a road map."[13] Ferro made the same observation, emphasizing the willingness of parties to put their activists in the bureau and the executive committee of the Petrograd soviet, as well as the preponderant role the Mensheviks played in these organs. In the first phase of the revolutionary process, relations between the provisional government and the soviet, tense as they were, hardly evolved. On the one hand, the government, responding to the aspirations and interests of a minority social stratum whose members had absolutely no experience in public affairs, proved incapable of appreciating the urgency of the situation. Its promise of assembling a Constituent Assembly was not matched by any exactness about its deadline. It satisfied neither the demands of workers who suffered scarcity in the cities, nor those of peasants who demanded land, nor those of national communities seeking the right to self-determination. On the other hand, the Petrograd soviet enjoyed an immense prestige in the country, having democratic legitimacy but not searching to exercise authority. It resisted all measures that fettered the revolutionary movement, controlled as it was by representatives from organizations. It did not form a popular representative assembly, and its activities did not bear the mark of a political design.

In such a conjuncture, Lenin, upon his return to Russia, played a decisive role by formulating his April Theses. He realigned Bolshevik politics, assessed the weakness of the government, and set the goal of taking power. Although Souvarine considered the restlessness of the masses, he focused on the relations of force within the soviet framework and on the Bolsheviks' vacillating politics. Ferro, for his part, had the merit of displacing the perspective that privileged conflicts among political formations and tensions within Bolshevism in order to describe the space of untamed democracy [*démocratie sauvage*] that had emerged in the days after the revolution—*democracy* in the sense that the principle of election and free debate was recognized everywhere, but *untamed* in the sense that it was powerless to order itself in a system of institutions and that it was going to allow the party bureaucracy to capture a part of the energies invested in the creation of autonomous organs.

The soviet of deputies and soldiers indeed enveloped a multiplicity of local and independent soviets. Countless factory, neighborhood, sol-

dier, and (particularly active) peasant committees placed themselves under its authority. Apart from them, a powerful cooperative movement
existed, attached to the principles of liberal democracy, advocating the
distribution of land to the peasants and championing youth, women,
and national movements. Describing the activity of these organs, each
of which had its own "vision of society" and shared the desire to break
with the Old Regime, Ferro dismantled another legend (which, I should
be clear, Souvarine did not endorse) that made October a simple Bolshevik takeover succeeding by chance but attributed to Lenin's genius,
conceived from the beginning of the revolution, and guided by Marxist
theory. The art of the Bolsheviks, which in any case was not unique to
them but which they demonstrated in ways superior to those of their
rivals, consisted during this period of either placing their militants in independent committees and movements or embracing activist elements
that assisted them. Lenin's particular art consisted in adapting his strategy to the circumstances without fearing to alter either his appreciation
of situations or his guiding principles. For instance, he made the demands of the factory committees his own, touting worker control after
having opposed it. Similarly, he was late in supporting the slogan of land
to the peasants and proclaiming the right of nationalities to independence. In October, the party had the advantage of a power vacuum and
the Mensheviks' political inconsistency. It knew how to fulfill expectations and seize the occasion in order to point the revolution in a direction that made going back seem impossible. At the same time, as Ferro
showed, the party secured from all those who had become activists and
lived only by their revolutionary activity the assurance that they would
not fall back into the "old rut" of the factory, the barracks, domesticity,
or working the land.[14]

All the same, one must admit that the line followed by the Bolsheviks
after February (often provoking important divergences within the party)
was circuitous. The Bolsheviks stirred up the neighborhood committees, abandoned them, and then rehabilitated them. They were opposed
to the factory committees before finding in them a milieu favorable to
their own implantation and then taking over the committees' demands.
They denounced the agrarian policies of the revolutionary socialists before taking over their program. The soviets made them suspicious from
the beginning, but then they demanded "All Power" for them, giving up
this slogan for a moment in July under Lenin's influence, and finally, still

under his influence, reformulating it when they achieved a majority in the most important of them. Even then, Ferro observed, Lenin opposed what the insurrection had in common with the Second All-Russian Congress of Soviets (October 25–26, 1917) and thus succeeded in attributing to the Petrograd Committee of Defense—that is, the party—the paternity of the new regime. One knows the consequences of October's turning point: first the removal from the government and then the persecution of other socialist formations; the restriction of the freedom of the press, then its suppression; the destruction or subordination of all independent organs; the concentration of all means of power in the hands of the party's political bureau; measures taken intended to control all activities in the economy, state administration, justice, and culture; and the creation of the Cheka (secret police) and the exercise of terror.[15]

It is audacious to reduce the course of events to the effects of revolutionary passion, as if that passion had only one means of expression. It was expressed in Russia by the many movements opposed to the dictatorship of the party, and it was expressed outside Russia notably in the unequaled vehemence of Rosa Luxemburg's critique of Leninism. But perhaps the most significant fact is that it mobilized a fraction of the so-called Old Bolsheviks, resolute advocates in the days after October of sharing power with other revolutionary currents and of maintaining freedom of expression. This episode cannot be erased, even if one notes that those who condemned Lenin's politics and left their posts later rejoined him, participating in the construction of a bureaucratic system. Later still, they became its victims.

Realizing the change represented by the suppression of all democratic liberties, Souvarine wisely observed, "Lenin personally was not inclined to personal power or to violence; he yielded to the force of circumstances and the development of a system. That system embodied on the scale of an immense state the military idea of the closed organization of professional revolutionaries under the orders of the 'secret circle of leaders.'"[16] Was that the sole key? At least Souvarine had the merit of drawing attention to something besides the logic of an idea. He thought through the conjunction between, on the one hand, the mass movement that gave birth to multiple forms of action and largely convergent demands (a phenomenon derived from no plan whatsoever) and, on the other, the development of a party whose nucleus already contained, some fifteen years before the revolution, its fundamental characteristics.

Thus it is necessary to admit that in the wake of the revolution, beyond the contingencies of events, a finality appeared that depended on the constitution of the party. This finality seemed to impose itself on its agents, for some behind their backs and for certain others contrary to their initiatives. The party did its job, which was to tolerate nothing done outside it except out of factual necessity. This party, one will say, was Lenin's creation. Since 1903, he had decided on the principles that distinguished it from all other political formations. The imperative of organization predominated; it required a strict selection of revolutionaries capable of making a profession out of their political activity and subordinating their personal life to its practice, as well as the distribution of revolutionaries according to the imperatives of the division of revolutionary labor. The leaders, in principle chosen by the militants, determined the allocation of assignments in milieux, institutions, and regions judged strategically important according to circumstances. The application of the party line required a strict discipline of action. Militants' unconditional obedience to the orders of the center came with a feeling of identification with the party's cause. Such a model was certainly forged by Lenin. But who believed that he took it from the "treasury of his mind"? He moved forward by condensing various organizational imperatives already operating in the army, police, factories, and state bureaucracy. That the party, so small in the beginning, already contained a powerful state—this was immediately visible in the sign that all social life was, in principle, under its control.

A fact often mentioned is that Bolshevism in its first phase was not monolithic. On many occasions it was the forum for bitter debate, as much before the revolution as during its development. Not until 1922 were factions forbidden. But rather than seeing in this trait the hallmark of a democratic operation, let me point out the effectiveness of a mechanism that checked all internal divisions, following the rule that the party was above everything and everyone. It is true that, as a matter of fact, Lenin was almost always the beneficiary of this mechanism. Was it because he showed himself to be the most lucid and capable leader? To a large extent, yes. The reorientation of the party's politics in April 1917 proved his exceptional capacities to adapt. Still, on many occasions his judgment was wrong. Besides enjoying the prestige of being the party's founder—not inconsequential—he incarnated its will to exercise dictatorship or, as was often said, to organize all the forces of society. That was the constant in his leadership. Was it the result of the idea announced in *What Is to Be Done?* (1902) that the proletariat could not by its own efforts raise itself to consciousness of its historic tasks and that this consciousness had to be brought to it from the outside? But we know that Lenin here was only reformulating a remark by Karl Kautsky (citing him verbatim).[17] Kautsky, however, in no way drew the same consequences—the project of a single party—not only in the sense that it excluded the existence of other parties but also in the sense that it was confused with the people as a whole. In 1924 he would criticize the Leninist notion of the party and be one of the first theorists to discover the totalitarian nature of the regime. We should underscore again that the effectiveness of an idea is not separate from a social and political dynamic.

Nothing is more instructive on this score than Leon Trotsky's changing position. During the fissuring that led to social democracy's breakup, his opposition to Lenin was as impassioned as Rosa Luxemburg's. In *Our Political Tasks* (1904), he had denounced the "dull caricature of Jacobinism's tragic intransigence" (the French Revolution surely provided a stage, as Furet noted, but here Jacobinism merely served as a foil). Trotsky foresaw a situation of "the party organization 'substituting' itself for the party, the Central Committee substituting itself for the party organization and, finally, the dictator substituting himself for the Central Committee." According to Lenin's judgment, Trotsky continued, "the whole of the international movement of the proletariat would have been accused of moderatism before the revolutionary tribunal, and Marx's lion-like head would have been the first to fall under the guillotine." Nothing better contradicts the thesis that Bolshevik politics flowed from Marxism and that Lenin only inflected its teachings. No less significant was the critique of an unconditional fidelity to theory: "Those who deny it are to be rejected. Those who doubt are near rejecting it. Those who question are near doubting . . . the Bolsheviks represent themselves as a dictatorship over the proletariat."[18] How, then, to understand that the man, we must not forget, who played a leading role in the revolution to the point of being the architect of taking power in October had rejoined Lenin? Did he give in to the latter's arguments? Was he captivated by his genius? After 1917 was he snared by the party's trap? Did he succumb to the double attraction of a revolutionary machine and the mystical body of the proletariat?

I will not dream of trying to settle once and for all the difference between a popular "good revolution" and a movement confiscated in order to construct a totalitarian state. It was not by chance that the soviets and the autonomous organs showed themselves powerless to set up a democracy. Nor was it an accident if the party allied itself with the belief in a revolution whose objective was the creation of a society freed from all division—a strategy guided by the imperatives of the sorganization and by the absolute identification of militants with that organization's leadership. I am interested only in finding the signs of the gestation of a regime "without precedent."

Expressing his astonishment at the gullibility of French politicians and journalists, Furet wrote:

> When the Soviet regime appeared under Stalin at the beginning of the 1930s, it had no historical precedent. Nothing like it had ever existed. Never had any state in the world taken as its purpose to kill, deport, or enslave peasants. Never had one Party taken over an entire state. Never had a regime controlled the entire social life of a nation and the lives of all its citizens. . . . Not one of these characteristics of the second Bolshevism is intelligible from the examples of the past or from within a *familiar conceptual framework*.[19]

How to put it better? Although it would be pointless to underestimate the mutation the Stalinist regime marked, it was nevertheless a question of a mutation inside a new political space. That space is not identifiable as long as one makes it the product of an idea or a chain of ideas. Trotsky already had formulated this peculiar diagnosis: Stalin grabbed hold of a machine that was the product of the Bolsheviks' struggle, a struggle that was itself the product of ideas.[20] Without intending to, he led one to ask: Of what does the machine perfected by the first Bolshevism consist? Should we not agree that the first Bolshevism already constituted a party "without precedent," not comprehensible within a "familiar conceptual framework"?

6

The Jacobin Phantom

LET ME RETURN TO THE HYPOTHESIS that there was a link between the French Revolution and the Russian Revolution. Lenin had appealed to Jacobinism as an authority shortly after the creation of Bolshevism. Both Georgy Plekhanov and Rosa Luxemburg accused him of being its inheritor.[1] For his part, Trotsky appeared haunted after 1924 by the image of a new Thermidor. He announced its rehearsal or imminent arrival before declaring that it had already occurred "ten years ago" (that is, without his having noticed it at the time).[2] References to the Terror of 1793 are thus instructive, but they should not conceal what was unprecedented in the situation.[3] At the heart of the comparison, one finds the themes of dictatorship, idealization of the revolution, the people's will, opposition between representative and direct democracy, and, crucially, terror. Nevertheless, if it is fruitful to elucidate certain traits of the French Revolution in light of the Russian Revolution, does one not risk misrecognizing the originality of Communism by following an inverse path—that is, in wanting to discover its source? Furet, the author of *Interpreting the French Revolution*, had admirably attempted this comparison by showing the conjunction of ideology and the manipulation of the masses where many earlier historians had wanted to see only the drama of the birth of a nation. Certainly, Jacobinism already constituted a machine—"a terrible machine," Jules Michelet said.[4] It manufactured opinion, suppressed the Assembly's laws and decrees, and conferred an exorbitant power on Robespierre. Still, the political clubs of the French Revolution were something entirely different from the committees that emerged unexpectedly in 1917, not to mention the soviets. As Furet noted elsewhere, the successive assemblies from 1789 to 1794 spoke for [*représentent*] the people, whereas the contemporaneous clubs and the sections claimed to represent [*figurer*] them. In both cases, one found the desire to incarnate the revolution. The tension was not born in 1793; it characterized the entire revolutionary period. It remained the case, though, that it was impossible to destroy the representative regime of the Assembly. The Jacobin leaders relied on the political clubs, conforming to their will even as they continued to draw their authority from the role they played in the Assembly. Furet observed that Robespierre, more than anyone, was "always placed at the strategic crossroad where the rhetoric of the streets and the clubs intersected with the rhetoric of the Assembly"[5]

Meanwhile, the National Convention "made terror the order of the day" without sidestepping a debate on its justification. Terror was required in the name of virtue, liberty, public happiness, and the stability of laws. No doubt the principles invoked were also those of the Jacobins. But, again, it was necessary for them to be guaranteed by duly elected representatives of the people. One finds absolutely no echo in the Bolshevik universe of Robespierre's rantings on the "despotism of liberty" or Louis de Saint-Just's formal address to the Assembly along the lines: "What do you want, you who do not want virtue at all in order to be happy? What do you want, you who do not want terror against the villains?"[6] A difference of language, one might say, not of mechanism. But language is not negligible. Saint-Just was addressing men for whom it was essential to present themselves as individuals. And, by the same token, the Terror was exercised via a particular mechanism. What one calls the Jacobin dictatorship required the dissimulation of the position of a dictator—a person or group—elevated above the laws. Robespierre ruled the National Convention, and his words terrorized because he was able to make the suspicion of conspiring against the republic hang over his enemies. His ruses bore the imprint of the regime and testified to the necessity whereby terrorists leave the place of power apparently empty. In this sense, the revolutionary Terror was not sundered from a democratic principle; it called for terrorists to mutually recognize themselves as such, equals before the law—this law for which the Terror was called the double-edged sword and that had to be affirmed without restriction. Each had to assume responsibility for the Terror. What was missing was the institution that welded the people together in a block and submitted them to what Lenin called the "iron hand" of the party. From the double-edged sword of the law to the iron hand of the party—can we not recognize the change taking place in minds and actions? Jacobinism was not a stuttering Bolshevism. It mixed the syntax of democracy with that of absolutism. As soon as Robespierre seemed to want to consolidate the system of Terror, he destroyed what remained of the terrorists' unity, previously maintained thanks to their active or passive complicity but always under the effect of the representation of the law. The instauration of a cult of the Supreme Being contributed to crediting him with the plan of affirming an absolute authority founded on a doctrine. However, the Terror could be combined with neither an orthodoxy nor the dictatorship of a supreme leader.

Bolshevism's principle of the organization and incorporation of militants into the party was in place from the beginning. We do not detect in that principle the tensions between dictatorship and freedom, institutions and individuals, equality and subordination to the orders of a committee and a leader. Lenin did not hesitate to justify dictatorship and did not concern himself with the states of revolutionaries' souls. He declared, "The scientific term 'dictatorship' means nothing more nor less than authority untrammeled by any laws, absolutely unrestricted by any rules whatsoever, and based directly on force." And elsewhere he said, "The revolutionary dictatorship of the proletariat is rule won and maintained by the use of violence by the proletariat against the bourgeoisie, rule that is unrestricted by any laws." All this can be summed up by the formula of Dominique Colas (from whom I borrow these citations): "Power outside the law, or else the law of the relations of force between classes."[7]

As early as March 1918, in "The Immediate Tasks of the Soviet Government," Lenin unambiguously proclaimed the principle of the masses' unconditional submission to a personal dictatorial authority. This principle was asserted on the scale of the state and industrial enterprises. To his own question—"Is the appointment of individual persons, dictators with unlimited powers, in general compatible with the fundamental principles of Soviet government?"—he responded first of all, "If we are not anarchists, we must admit that the state, *that is, compulsion*, is necessary for the transition from capitalism to socialism," before adding this detail: "Hence, there is absolutely *no* contradiction in principle between Soviet (*that is*, socialist) democracy and the exercise of dictatorial powers by individuals."[8] Next approaching the problem of industrial performance, he stated that "large-scale machine industry—which is precisely the material source, the productive source, the foundation of Socialism—calls for absolute and strict *unity of will*, which directs the joint labor of hundreds, thousands, and tens of thousands of people. . . . But how can strict unity of will be ensured?—by thousands subordinating their will to the will of one."[9] In another section of the same text, entitled "Raising the Productivity of Labor," he sought to "pose the question of piecework and apply and test it in practice; . . . applying much of what is scientific and progressive in the Taylor system, we must make wages correspond to the total amount of goods turned out."[10]

An idea of Leninism's principles can be gleaned if one reviews the following subjects: the call for an iron hand; the critique of existing power as "excessively mild, very often [resembling] jelly more than iron" and of revolutionary and popular tribunals as "extremely, incredibly weak"; the denunciation of the lies and calumnies of anarchists, revolutionary socialists, and Mensheviks; attacks on petit bourgeois elements justified by the argument that "the nearer we approach the complete military repression of the bourgeoisie, the more dangerous does the element of petit bourgeois anarchy become"; and other attacks, even more disturbing for the intangibility of their objects, against "the petit bourgeois mind-set" and "the *small-proprietor* outlook." And, I would add, the will to oust the guilty and punish them mercilessly.[11] This text, "The Immediate Tasks of the Soviet Government," well known to all historians of Bolshevism, is interesting for the way it foresaw less than a year after October 1917 the creation of a new type of society. As Colas noted, the factory was a recurrent reference in Lenin's writings (alongside the machine, the army, and the orchestra). The organization of the party was inspired by it, but he added that the relationship between the party and the factory could be read in an opposite way: the factory appeared as a political entity.[12] Lenin never breathed a word about the oppression resulting from industrial labor. Once mass production became the principal objective of socialism, neither workers' conditions nor their worsening mattered very much. The dictatorship of the leader—and, with it, iron discipline—were the rule. Recalcitrant and wayward workers proved to be political enemies as much as the petit bourgeois or small property owners. Thus, as soon as 1918, the Stalinist phantasmagoria of sabotage, parasitism, and anti-Sovietism could be glimpsed. The image of the revolution concealed from Lenin the gestation of a new system of domination. Whereas he claimed to import from the West, especially Germany, the element of capitalist rationality necessary for the construction of socialism, in fact, by dissociating it from democracy, from capitalism, he took only a monster. It is true that this monster had not earned its name: the totalitarian state.

Let us return to the theme of the petit bourgeois mind-set. It could be found in any number of political groups or social categories. For instance, in 1922 it was discovered pursuing its pernicious work among the rebels at Kronstadt.[13] The intelligentsia provided it with another preferred terrain. To be sure, intellectuals were considered the only ones capable of raising proletarians to consciousness of their historical tasks. They imparted knowledge to the proletariat, as they had previously supplied it to the bourgeoisie. Without them there would be no revolutionary theory, and without revolutionary theory there could be no revolutionary practice—all militants knew the maxim. But these intellectuals merged with the party. In contrast, other intellectuals comprised a detestable species: people who took themselves for thinking beings. They claimed to follow their own judgments. They were "hysterical," were given to sentimentality, loathed violence, and were blind to the tasks of the revolution. Through the petit bourgeois or the intellectual, the target aimed at by Lenin and, until recently, by all good Communists was the individual. Only one characteristic of the individual was kept: indifference toward others and to the destiny of the collective. And through the individual one could grasp the ultimate target: every mode of sociability likely to escape party control, every association that might suggest independent initiative, and all relationships and communication whose effects were unforeseeable. After all, it was not extraordinary that Lenin lost no time in immediately restricting the freedom of the press, since nothing is more dangerous than the existence of a circuit of public speech.

One criterion suffices to contrast Bolshevism with Jacobinism: the Rights of Man. From February to October 1917, the freedoms of association and expression, not to mention to right to resist oppression, prevailed. The Constituent Assembly was expected to guarantee basic freedoms. Once the Bolsheviks came to power, though, this assembly, at last convened, was immediately dissolved. In France, the Rights of Man were subsumed by the Terror, but their symbolic rupture with the Old Regime was not effaced. For its part, Bolshevism—after having acquired the strength to do away with the Mensheviks, revolutionary socialists, and anarchists—not only ended political pluralism and affirmed itself as the sole party, but also arrogated to itself the authority to decide the principles governing economic life as well as the family, mores, sexuality, education, literature, or art (one would have to wait until the Stalinist era for the party to declare its competence in genetics). The image of a civil society became intolerable to it. By civil society, we understand a society in which opinions, beliefs, and divergent interests can, more than simply coexist, pit themselves against one another and possibly be transformed through mutual interaction: a society in which domains of activity can develop whose relationships elude all bird's-eye views or perfunctory glances [survol], thereby keeping in check the voluntarism and constructivism of the leaders of the state.

7

A Liberal Matrix for the
Dictatorship of the Proletariat?

I WAS ASTONISHED TO FIND Furet detecting a kinship of intention between Communism and democracy. Unquestionably, Communism seemed to him one of the two kinds of antidemocratic revolution that developed in the twentieth century. "The great secret behind the complicity between Bolshevism and Fascism," he wrote, "remained the existence of that common enemy which the two opposing doctrines would downplay or exorcise with the idea that it was on its last legs: quite simply, democracy."[1] I will sign on to this judgment without reservation, having written elsewhere, "In my view, totalitarianism can be clarified only by grasping its relationship to democracy. It is from democracy that it arises, even though it has taken root initially, at least in its socialist version, in countries where the democratic transformation was only just beginning. It overturns that transformation, while at the same time taking over some of its features and extending them at the level of fantasy."[2] Still, we must ask what democratic society means and by what route it opened the way for Communism. We must ask whether Communism, when it broke away from democracy, kept the latter's imprint. In short, we should ask if the Bolshevik revolution was antidemocratic in its consequences or its principles.

I will attempt again to reconstruct Furet's argument in *The Passing of an Illusion*. After having described the political voluntarism of the French Revolution, he went on to define what he meant by democratic society. "Here I shall be using the term [democracy]," he wrote, "in its two classic meanings: the first as a form of government based on the free suffrage of citizens and the periodic competition of parties for the exercise of power and equal rights guaranteed for all; the second, as the philosophical definition of modern societies, constituted by autonomous and equal individuals, free to choose their activities, beliefs, and life-styles."[3] Under this double aspect, democracy seems to elicit a radical rejection of Communism as well as fascism. Nevertheless, Furet imme-diately mentioned a particularity of Communist discourse: "Lenin, heir to Marx, or his disciple, saw the revolution he was trying to create as the realization of the democratic promise through the emancipation of ex-ploited workers."[4] By this we understand that the revolutionary project aimed to establish genuine freedom among men. Here, Furet was taking only Communist discourse or representation into consideration. But he went a step further by declaring: "The intellectual advantage of Leninist over Fascist discourse was to go beyond the critique of bourgeois de-mocracy and recover the pedestal of liberal philosophy. Even if regimes that laid claims to that philosophy had to be overthrown in order for their promises to be fulfilled, it remained true that the autonomy of the individual was as much on the horizon of Communism as it was at the center of liberalism."[5] Here, Leninist discourse conveyed the principles that had generated modern democracy. One finds this judgment con-firmed a page later when Furet wrote, "The second major advantage of Marxism-Leninism is, of course, its universalism, which not only allies it to the family of democratic ideas but, better yet, employs the sense of human equality as its psychological mainspring."[6] Thus it is necessary to admit that Lenin made a mistake only in believing that the hour of the proletariat had arrived: "From the start, Bolshevik universalism would bump up against the concrete conditions that had surrounded its suc-cess. Its leaders had risen to power in the most backward and hence the most unlikely country in Europe."[7] In short, it seems that one is supposed to take literally both Leninist discourse and the promise of universality rather than search for the design that reveals Bolshevik practice.

Doubts a reader may have about the established kinship between Communism and liberalism are dispelled in a later chapter in which Sta-lin appears as the successor of Leninism and of the revolutionary tradi-tion inaugurated at the end of the eighteenth century:

Through their idea of revolution, which was as different from the Old Regime as day from night, the revolutionaries of 1789 man-aged to articulate the fundamental constructivism that haunts modern society. Modern society is a contract between associates with equal rights, a contract produced by their wills and thus secondary to them. This idea is not incompatible with the dictatorship of the revolutionary state, to the limited extent that the state is conceived of, or cast as, the collective agent of citizen volition, in defiance of the powers of the past. The Bolshevik version of revolutionary subjectivism was even more radical than the Jacobin one, for two reasons. The first is that Lenin, despite his claims to the contrary, made use of the idea of the party as the avant-garde of class to develop a theory of omnipotent political will.[8]

(The other reason given was the support political voluntarism found in science.) It is true that at this juncture Furet pointed out that Lenin had aspired to something other than what he had said. But can one remain satisfied with the concept of political will characterized as omnipotence? What was it that was wanted—passionately and inordinately desired? Were the emancipation of workers, the completion of democracy, and the autonomy of the individual to be found at the end of the path toward total power? To tell the truth, the question is not so much to know whether Lenin was genuinely driven by the conviction of working to build socialism. It is more important to detect Leninism's intentionality and to decipher its signs by scrutinizing a politics entirely guided by the destruction of the autonomy of individuals, of every mode of sociability that escaped the mastery of the party, and of all opposition within the party itself. In other words, the question is not so much to know whether the difficulties arising for a revolution in a backward country more or less constrained it to use means that contradicted the ends pursued; it is more important to identify a system of thought and action articulated at the moment when the party was established and then gradually affirmed during the revolutionary period. Given the circumstances, introducing socialism by way of hammer blows had the effect of giving rise to obstacles and resistances that justified a reinforcement of dictatorship and terror.

Is the observer justified in concluding that socialism was one and the same as the regime where the party exercised its omnipotence? I have already alluded to the rallying to Leninist politics by those who had earlier denounced aspirations for dictatorship, a rallying that occurred after the rift with social democracy (Trotsky was a remarkable example) or during the era when Mensheviks and revolutionary socialists were excluded from the exercise of power. Why this rallying, despite a previously fundamental critique, unless these revolutionaries were captured by the representation of a sequence of events that left no other choice than attachment to freedoms or the Great Leap Forward. I will note in passing that the Trotskyists, confronted by the spectacle of Stalinism, never understood that they were dealing with a regime irreducible to traditional categories. They denounced the formation of a bureaucratic stratum, without ceasing to believe that it constituted a transitory, superstructural, and parasitic phenomenon destined to give way in the face of a restoration of the bourgeoisie or, alternatively, a new rise of the proletariat. Paradoxically, only their leader, Trotsky himself, at the end of his life considered the hypothesis of a totalitarian state without understanding that Lenin and he had participated in its construction.[9]

Communism is intelligible only within the framework of a world transformed by democratic revolution, but I will not go so far as to say that they were part of the same matrix. In a way, the advent of democracy marked a rupture with the order of Old Regime societies: aristocratic societies in which men were ranked and in which relations of personal dependence and proximity, as well as ties to the land and the community, predominated. Once barriers that separated people were destroyed; once the notions of natural inequality and of a hierarchy conforming either to divine will, the order of things, or custom were eliminated; and once the belief in a monarch who was steward of the law and guarantor of the nation's unity disappeared—then all societies that we call modern became in some manner democratic. It is obvious that Communism and fascism were conceivable only in a universe that had ceased to be fascinated with aristocratic values. But investigating the links between those twentieth-century movements and democracy becomes relevant only if one narrows the field of investigation and considers the characteristic institutions of a liberal regime. The features of such a regime were established in America at the end of the eighteenth century (exactly the object of Tocqueville's study), but France had to wait several decades before it entirely disengaged from vestiges of the Old Regime and drew the consequences of premises posed by the Revolution of 1789. Nevertheless, it was not only in democracy, in the broadest sense of the term, that Furet thought he had found the source of Communism. In the passage I cited earlier (on modern constructivism and revolutionary subjectivism), he did not evoke, as he did elsewhere convincingly and in ways close to Hannah Arendt, the problem posed by the entry of the masses into public life at the end of the nineteenth century. Nor, moreover, did he evoke the related contradiction of a bourgeoisie that appealed to universal principles, thus fanning the flames of social demands, but that, driven only by private interest, suffered from an indifference toward the res publica. Furet's concern was to detect the root of Communism in liberalism as much as in Jacobinism. Liberalism indeed originated in a constructivist passion—born from the entrance of the individual subject [*l'individu-Sujet*] onto the historical stage—while giving that passion a different destiny.

I believe that in Furet's argument I recognize the trace of a current of thought for which Leo Strauss's work has been a source (or at least Strauss belongs to that current).[10] This philosopher, who contributed so much to the restoration of ancient political philosophy, saw in the "crisis of our time" an ultimate consequence of the *project* that, outlined before the eighteenth century, took complete shape in the era of the rise of liberalism or of what he also called original democracy.[11] The *modern project*, as he put it, involved a rupture with the principles of classical philosophy and coincided with (if it did not derive from) the birth of a representation of nature that made nature the object of human domination. Thus science, which for antiquity required the ideal of a contemplative life, henceforth demanded the ideal of an active life. Without overstating the case, one might say that science opened the reign of constructivism and voluntarism. In the register of political thought, the change consisted in abandoning both the idea of a polity whose ends were written into the order of the cosmos and the idea of citizens whose relationships were regulated according to the needs of the community. The notions of *natural* finality, hierarchy, and order (nature meaning that which is not the product of human will) were all eliminated when two conceptions arose simultaneously: that of an entirely egalitarian society and that of an agglomerate of individuals who each had at his disposal the same knowledge and rights. In such a society, the cohesion of the ensemble was supposed to result in the majority's delegation of public authority to a small number of representatives accountable to those who elected them. As supposedly autonomous individuals were equal under the law, no matter their other virtues and vices, and nothing permitting the restraint of their civic spirit (their education and mores escaping the public authority's control), it turned out that political leaders [*les responsables*] put in place by suffrage had henceforth only to answer to people without obligations [*des irresponsables*]. Consequently, their own responsibility became fictive. Following this argument, one might believe that the modern project, founded on the unrestricted equality and freedom of citizens, testified only to an erroneous conception of political society. However, since this conception molded and fashioned the reality of human relationships, one can ask whether political society itself was not in the process of dissolution. It tended, indeed, to lose the meaning of its cohesion and limits, together with the meaning of its ends, and thus to dissolve into the heart an undifferentiated universe.

Strauss concluded not only that the distinction in our era between conservatives and liberals hid a common adherence to the modern project, but that "at first glance liberalism seems to agree with Communism as regards the ultimate goal, while it radically disagrees with it as regards the way to the goal. The goal may be said to be the universal and classless society, or to use the correction proposed by [Alexandre] Kojève, the universal and homogeneous state of which every adult human being is a full member."[12] This theme was clearly formulated in "Political Philosophy and the Crisis of Our Time," where Strauss argued that the conservatism of our age merged with what was at the origin of liberalism. "One can go further," Strauss noted, "and say that much of what goes now by the name of conservatism has in the last analysis a common root with present-day liberalism, and even with Communism."[13] Furet, it is true, limited himself to finding in Communism the sign of a pathology of the universal. But if "the universal" came to follow the image of a contract binding together individuals equal under the law and resulting from their will, one can likewise ask if it was not already the sign of a political pathology.

However prestigious the authority of theoreticians of modern natural law (beginning with Thomas Hobbes, whom Strauss always invoked), it can be acknowledged that in imagining the advent of a *society of individuals* we tend to disregard—or perhaps conceal—the great driving engine of liberal demands: the separation of political and religious authority and, in the same movement, the affirmation of freedoms of belief and opinion. Those freedoms were indeed individual ones, but they presumed the recognition of a civil life without necessarily contesting the right of public power to protect society against threats of sedition. The recognition of a civil life is to my mind essential because freedom of opinion does not transform an individual into the proprietor of his opinion; rather, it puts him in contact with the opinions of others, making possible both a diffusion of opinions in a more or less extensive, in fact indefinite [indélimitable], space and the modification of those opinions via their mutual contact. The rights to speak, to hear and understand, to read, and to write—these are indeed indissoluble. If freedom of opinion is the freedom of expression, it is also the freedom of communication. Freedom of belief involves the freedom to demonstrate one's faith and share a practice with an indeterminate number of people in places protected by law. So, although it belongs to the private realm, and as much as it escapes norms imposed by the state, freedom of belief, like freedom of opinion, is irreducible to the property of the individual; it becomes open to all, public, and recognized in a common space.[14]

Within the history of ideas, liberal thought does not, however, boil down to the critique of theological-political authority. It introduces the need to dissociate what is related to the political domain from what is in principle removed from it. In fact, this dissociation itself possesses a political signification because the origin of a form of society and style of life requires institutions, new elaborations of citizenship, and working out the status of the individual. John Milton, James Harrington, Benedict de Spinoza, and the Baron de Montesquieu—even before the American and French revolutions—made us recognize the connection between liberalism and the republican tradition, a tradition that pointed back to the era of Florentine civic humanism. A century later, Niccolò Machiavelli gave that civic humanism an entirely different inspiration. Furthermore, if one examines the ideological sources of the American Revolution, which indisputably rests at the origin of modern democracy, one finds mixed together references to the Roman Republic, the biblical emancipation story of the chosen people battling idolatry, examples of modern free cities (Italian, German, and Dutch), and the English monarchy, the last illustrating the modern species of the corrupt regime.

Nevertheless the history of ideas, though instructive, is inadequate to illuminate the genesis of modern democracy. Recall that Tocqueville paid attention to the modifications of the social state [*état social*]. This social state consisted of a configuration of relations among classes and the various categories that composed them. There is little reason to think, as Marx had claimed, that these classes were strictly determined by a system of property. The social state depended, on the one hand, on the representation people had of their mutual dependence, according to their conditions, and on the other, decisively, on the sovereign's political efforts to ensure the foundations of his power. According to Tocqueville, the democratic revolution came together with an erosion of aristocratic authority, an erosion for which the monarchy had been the agent before aspirations for political freedom and the independence of the individual developed at its expense. If I am not mistaken, Tocqueville spoke only once of a fundamental contract, when he mentioned the arrival of immigrants on the shores of what would become New England and the vow they made to form themselves "into a body of political society."[15] Still, we should not forget that they expressed their will by invoking God and that they imported to America political and religious beliefs born in Europe. "Democracy," Tocqueville continued, "such as antiquity had never dared to dream of, leapt full-grown and fully armed from the middle of the old feudal society."[16] In the same chapter he observed more precisely, "The general principles on which modern Constitutions are based—principles that most Europeans barely comprehended in the seventeenth century and whose triumph in Great Britain was still incomplete—were all recognized and incorporated into the laws of New England: involvement of the people in public affairs, free voting on taxes, accountability of government officials, individual liberty, and trial by jury."[17]

Undoubtedly, one of Tocqueville's major theses was that the social state characterized by an equality of conditions arrived slowly in Europe, giving birth to a passion for equality to which everything could be sacrificed—notably, the love of freedom. I would not dream of denying that this passion came to find an opening in the different species of socialism and that Bolshevism professed to establish an egalitarian society at the end of the dictatorship of the proletariat. But if one wants to appreciate the dynamics of democracy and the dangers that it conceals, it is worth recalling even briefly what Tocqueville believed to be the effects of the progress of equality on the individual. Certainly, it provoked everyone to want to be independent. Each person, seeing in the other only a fellow human creature, imagined himself detached from all personal dependence, thinking it possible to find in himself alone the origins of his opinions. For all that, there was no reason to think that society could henceforth be conceived as an agglomerate of individual wills. As Tocqueville wrote, "It is easy to see that no society can prosper without such beliefs [about interdependence] or, rather, that none can survive in that way, for without common ideas, there is no common action, and without common action, men may still exist, but they will not constitute a social body." This observation led him to conclude that "in any event, there must always be a place in the intellectual and moral world where authority exists. This place may vary, but it must exist somewhere. Individual independence may be great or small, but it cannot be boundless."[18] Examining the source of beliefs in democracy, Tocqueville foregrounded the threat that weighed on the individual. Once the individual was no longer subjected to a visible authority, he found only the authority of the greatest number to guide him. In other words, an invisible authority was formed: common opinion. By this I mean not that each individual imitated his neighbor, but that each regulated his judgment under the influence of the similitude of opinions. An argument of this kind explained the subjection of the individual to anonymous powers such as the state, the people, and society (the last, Tocqueville observed, was hardly imagined under the Old Regime).

Thus, without forgetting that the individual effectively acquired a new independence in democracy, one must acknowledge that his isolation and "smallness" exposed him to despotism. As is well known, Tocqueville distinguished two types of despotism in a society where a leveling of conditions occurs. In the first, which we could call classic despotism, only one commands and is free, while everyone else submits to him. In the second, the despotism of modern democracy, while the appearances of freedom are preserved and the passion for well-being is satisfied, the risk is that a despotism of a "new kind" will set itself up. Again we must recall that, in the last part of *Democracy in America* (1835–1840), the author concluded that people will not put up for long with such a state of affairs, that they will soon create freer institutions, or else that they will come to prostrate themselves once again at the feet of a master. Without denying that Tocqueville repeatedly weighed the hypothesis of a combination of democracy and despotism, I would point out that he imagined a society in which the individual would be dispossessed of that which made his independence valuable: the taste for initiative, for association (enabling him to increase his power within the circumstances of his life), and for participation in public affairs. Finally, let me draw attention to the unequivocal judgment he made in a note intended for *The Old Regime and the Revolution* (1856): "But the words *democracy, monarchy, democratic government,* in the true sense of these words, can only mean one thing: a government where the people play a more or less large part in government. Their meaning is intimately linked to the idea of political freedom. To give the name 'democratic government' to a government where political freedom is not found is to say a palpable absurdity."[19]

Furet certainly did not see in the Bolshevik dictatorship a modality of democratic government; he clearly said that its true adversary was democracy. Nevertheless, he considered that "the conception of the contract is not incompatible with the dictatorship of the revolutionary state, to the limited extent that the state is conceived of, or cast as, the collective agent of citizen volition."[20] He seems to me not only to have assigned democracy a fictive origin (the instituting of the contract), but also to have assumed that freedom was not so intimately tied to democracy that one could find something of its inspiration in Communism. Furthermore, he was of the opinion that we are in the presence of a self-same "family of democratic ideas."[21]

8

Democracy and Totalitarianism

T HE DICTATORSHIP OF THE PARTY presented itself as the dictatorship of the proletariat or, more exactly, as that of an organ expressing the will of the proletariat struggling for its emancipation and, in the same movement, the abolition of all forms of domination. Declaring itself to be transitional, it also claimed not to impose itself from above. If Lenin asserted that intellectuals brought to the proletariat the consciousness of its historic role from the outside, he thought that they succeeded only on the condition of being identified with its cause, thus transforming themselves into proletarians. Thus it was within the exploited class that the dictatorship was supposed to be born and exercised. At any rate, Lenin tirelessly affirmed that the Bolsheviks had to learn their tasks from the man of the people: one had to listen to him, since he knew that he did not know how to know [*il sait ce qu'il ne sait pas savoir*]. Lenin qualified nonrevolutionary intellectuals as foolish because they judged from the outside. Even so, to dwell on this image of the party, dedicated to acting in conformity with the will of a master who lacked the means of expressing himself, we would overlook its practices—practices that were in no way mute but, on the contrary, accompanied the express demands of the monopoly of power.

Why, then, has knowledge of these practices, exercised not only during Lenin's time but also in Stalin's with an unequaled violence and indifference toward the destiny of millions of victims, seemed not to have undermined the idea of Communism's connection to democracy? The question had already been asked by those who read Raymond Aron's great work, *Democracy and Totalitarianism*, when it was published more than thirty years ago—a book that proved to be a fortunate bombshell amid the chorus of liberal critiques of the Soviet system.[1] As we will see, Aron's point of view differed from mine. Intending to conduct a sociopolitical analysis as objectively as possible, Aron, in a chapter entitled "Constitutional Fictions and Soviet Reality," noted the signs of a fidelity, however formal, to democratic rules in the way the party and state functioned. At the same time, he attempted to disclose the contradictions in which Leninist ideology had mired itself. The interpretation he developed in this chapter, though referring to events that hardly interest the contemporary reader, deserves a closer examination since it called for reflection on the nature of Communist belief. Aron advanced two arguments: first, that the *majoritarian principle* had always been formally respected, from the creation of Bolshevism to the advent of Stalin's regime; second, that the first three Soviet constitutions that saw the light of day—the first at Lenin's initiative, the other two under Stalin—showed a democratic inspiration, especially the last, promulgated in 1936.[2] "It suffices to take seriously the constitutional texts," Aron wrote, "in order to have the feeling that there was not a difference of nature between the French and Soviet regimes."[3]

Following the first argument—on formal respect for the majoritarian principle—we cannot forget that, in the period following Lenin's death, Stalin succeeded in imposing his authority only by playing the game of majorities: first in making alliances with Nikolai Bukharin, Grigory Zinoviev, and Lev Kamenev against Trotsky and then with Bukharin against his old partners.[4] His maneuvers to eliminate all opposition were so transparent that they suggested a concern for adhering to democratic rules. "This verbal fidelity to principle," Aron wrote, "does not guarantee but can act in favor of the return from the absolute power of a single person to the constitutional game."[5] To be sure, the analyses of *Democracy and Totalitarianism* dated from the Khrushchev era, and its hypotheses were linked to the uncertainty brought about by the formation of a collective leadership.[6] But, beyond observing that the new leadership team (concerned as it was to condemn crimes committed during the Stalinist period) enforced an obedience as total as Stalin's, such that there was scarcely reason to believe in an expansion of political liberties, Aron's analysis in reality demonstrated only the existence of conflicts at the heights of power and a persistent instability in relations of force under the pretext of proclaimed party unity and the unanimous support of the people. The phenomenon in no way indicated an attachment to democracy. Without exception, the composition of delegations to party assemblies remained regulated according to the General Secretariat's directives. Aron underscored this practice, which he qualified in an understatement as "manipulation." Furthermore, the institution of suffrage was not unprejudiced. How could its practice be a sign of democracy if electors knew that their possible opposition to official candidates threatened their safety; or, to say the least, if they risked losing their jobs; or, conversely, if they knew that their obedience to the Secretariat's orders guaranteed the pursuit of their careers or a promotion? I will have the occasion to return to this last point, since we cannot understand the development of the new regime after the 1920s and the success of Stalinism without considering the formation of a new social stratum whose modes of existence and legitimation have no equivalents in a democratic society.

Finally, irrespective of objections to the idea that the majoritarian principle exhibited a tacit fidelity to the democratic spirit, and despite the manipulations it hid, how does one not recognize that this principle was radically subverted by the *unitary principle* that Aron anyway saw as preponderant? Indeed, where the idea of an opposition was rejected, absolutely no minority could take shape, even in debates that did not question the general line. If they did not follow that line, participants in those debates risked elimination; if they became the majority, they quickly made the unitary principle their own. In other words, the majoritarian principle loses all democratic significance if it does not involve the institution of pluralism, the recognition of the rights of a minority (or many minorities), and the principle of alternation. Drawing on the majority's support, the supreme ruler in a Communist regime exercised a formidable intimidation of those who were not part of this majority; he could intimidate whenever he decided it was convenient. A good example, which brings out the perversion of the majoritarian principle, occurred in 1922 when Lenin secured a majority in order to forbid divisions inside the party. From that moment forward, the so-called majority ruled; that is, power was supposed to represent it (no matter the authority of its adversaries). This is indeed a good example since, in our day, even after the experience of Communism and fascism, one can still find well-intentioned minds concluding that a terrorist power, such as an Islamist one, should obviously not be refused democratic legitimacy as long as it is derived from suffrage.

Aron's second argument—on the Soviet constitutions—presents us with an extremely interesting problem. Rapidly but precisely examining the three early constitutions, Aron concluded that they generated the image of a regime that resembled a liberal democracy. The first two, he noted, did not refer to the function of the party, whereas that of 1936 mentioned it: "Article 141 indicates that candidates for election should be chosen by a certain number of groups, among which the Communist Party figures discreetly, with great modesty, on the same level as the trade unions. . . . Article 126 declares that the most active citizens of the Soviet Union have formed in a Communist Party which is the vanguard of the workers."[7] Certainly, Aron's commentary left no room for equivocation: "We are all aware, and so are the citizens of the Soviet Union, that it is a game of illusion. . . . As the list of candidates is a single list, the choice lies between voting for or not voting at all, and for extremely concrete reasons, 99 percent or more of citizens prefer to vote for."[8] One is nevertheless surprised that, given the essential restrictions mentioned in the constitution's text, it would be judged to have had a democratic appearance. Many articles, it is true, indicated that "the governed enjoy, in theory and on paper, all the fundamental rights, freedom of speech, freedom of the press, free assembly. Individuals are sacred and dwelling places inviolable; all the demands of habeas corpus, all the demands of formal liberty, are guaranteed."[9] But these articles were accompanied by basic reservations: rights must be exercised "in conformity with the interests of the workers." Since the party alone represented their interests, how could one rely on liberal legal provisions? Nevertheless, while observing that these provisions were in obvious contradiction with Communist practices, Aron deemed that "one fundamental question remains: to what extent do those in power, doctrinaires or citizens, believe in the meaning, scope, and virtue of these constitutional fictions?"[10] In fact, the constitutional texts were not as ambiguous as Aron suggested. The Constitution of 1918, we might recall, was not the work of the Constituent Assembly. That assembly, anticipated since February, had been dissolved by the Bolsheviks the first day it met, due to their meager representation in it. The document submitted for ratification to the Third

All-Russia Congress of Soviets resulted from the work of a commission in the hands of the Bolsheviks and made room in its first part for a text already composed by Lenin himself. Its status was that of a declaration that claimed to have a force similar to the Declaration of the Rights of Man and Citizen; it was entitled the Declaration of the Rights of the Working and Exploited People.

Dominique Colas, thanks to whom we have the French edition of the Soviet constitutional texts, has shown clearly that the Constitution of 1918 was a "purifying text, a civil war text."[11] The principles stated in the aforementioned declaration, he observed, were largely already applied, notably, the socialization of land; the transfer to the state of the ownership of the means of production and transportation, mineral resources, and all the banks; and even the elimination of parasitic elements from society and the establishment of mandatory work. The second part of the document specified that "the fundamental aim of the Constitution . . . is to establish a dictatorship of the urban and rural proletariat and the poorest peasantry in the form of a powerful All-Russian Soviet government with a view to crushing completely the bourgeoisie, abolishing the exploitation of man by man, and establishing socialism, under which there will be no division into classes and no state power."[12] Colas commented: "The Constitution described the gearwheels of democratic centralism, then imposed on the state as it had been previously on the party, and which instituted the primacy of central organs where certain posts could be obtained via election. In this way democracy proved to be a method serving the concentration of power."[13] At a glance, the absence of any mention of the party's well-known role at the time is striking. Mighty Soviet power in everyone's eyes was the same as the absolute power of the party. What mattered to Lenin, it seems, was to present the dictatorship of the proletariat as the first expression of a real democracy. The terms used—"true freedom of conscience, true freedom of opinion, true freedom of assembly, true freedom of association"—attest to the implicit reference to the Declaration of the Rights of Man and Citizen, but they were each time accompanied by correctives whose meaning was unequivocal. The resources and means conditioning the exercise of these freedoms were as a matter of fact considered the property of the working and peasant class. That class, following criteria consistent with its interest, furnished the supply of paper necessary for the publication of a journal, the spaces needed for holding assemblies, and the required means for organizing parades and meetings. Even sticking to the letter of the text, one should not be surprised at the declared freedoms—they would surprise only a liberal observer. The proletariat was clearly designated as the possessor of the true and the false, just and unjust, legitimate and illegitimate.

Paradoxically, the Stalinist Constitution of 1936 seemed to justify better the hypothesis of a democratic inspiration. This third constitution was conceived not in order to define the principles of a regime functioning in a time of civil war, but rather to establish the character of the Soviet state as it stabilized and established itself as a universal model. A number of innovations attract our attention: direct universal suffrage and the secret ballot, personal ownership of earned income and savings, ownership of objects for domestic use and the associated right of inheritance, and the independence of judicial power and the affirmation of the rights of defense for the accused. One chapter enumerated the fundamental rights of citizens, including, in addition to what we in a democracy call social rights, the right to work, the rights of women, and the right of association. (The right to work and the rights of women had distinctive protections, and the right of association was a significant development since it mentioned groups—professional and cooperative unions; youth, sport, and defense organizations; cultural, technical, and scientific associations—responding to the need to galvanize both the masses' initiative in terms of organization and their political activity.) The same article mentioned "the All-Union Communist Party (Bolsheviks), which is the vanguard of the toilers in their struggle to strengthen and develop the socialist system and the leading core of all organizations of the toilers, both social and state."[14] So briefly was the party mentioned that its supremacy came to the fore. The articulation of social organizations placing unions and cultural societies side by side highlighted the importance granted a network of collectives that thereafter covered the entire society. It was never a secret that the freedoms of opinion, assembly, and association were subordinated to a political authority that alone had at its disposal the means of making them effective or not.

Looked at closely, the Constitution of 1936 did not measurably modify the already existing structure of a socialist society whose political foundation was the system of soviets and whose economic system was the collective ownership of the means of production. Nor did it modify the organizational schema of the federal state and federated republics.

This constitution was no doubt distinguished from its predecessors by the institution of universal suffrage accompanied by the secret ballot and by the guarantees afforded by an independent judiciary. These qualities were actually what led one to attribute a democratic inspiration to it. Nevertheless, the text does not let us ignore the fact that, on the one hand, candidates in elections were proposed by the party and by organizations that depended on the state and, on the other, the basic rights of citizens were not dissociated from no less fundamental duties that one could forgo only by identifying oneself as an enemy of the people.

Aron asked why one would have wanted to formulate a constitution that maintained the appearances of democracy. He distinguished two interpretations: the first, to which he nevertheless conceded partial truth, was that in the international context—the political rearmament of Germany, the necessities of the antifascist struggle, the creation of popular fronts—the Communist regime wanted to appear before international public opinion, contrary to Nazism, as a constitutional regime. The second interpretation was that the constitution had internal uses: it offered "the opportunity to create or to reveal the unanimity of the people themselves" and resulted from "a psychological technique of uniting people and rulers; [a] unity [that], even if fictitious, tends to become stronger if it is given expression."[15] Both interpretations thus summarized were judged unsatisfactory.

What was Aron's response to his own question? To be honest, one has to search for the answer. Indeed, immediately after having affirmed that, contrary to fascist regimes, "the Communist regime proclaims its faith in [democratic principles] even though it does not apply them," and then that "one must try to understand," Aron returned to the past and launched into a reconstruction of the history of the party.[16] The Bolsheviks, he told us, established a state never conceived by Marx and that they themselves had not foreseen. As a close reader of his works, Aron explained that Marx had not troubled himself with thinking through what the economic organization in a socialist society would be; in terms of political perspectives, he had expressed anarchist or even Saint-Simonian tendencies. Hence, one had to admit that the Bolsheviks were obliged to find an "ideological solution."[17] This consisted, first of all, in making the party's absolute power the expression of the dictatorship of the proletariat, a satisfying solution as long as it justified the monopoly on all the means of power, but one that became the source of difficulties as soon as the proletariat appeared to have destroyed the domination of the bourgeoisie, since the idea of the formation of a new class antagonism was excluded in theory. The affirmation of a socialist regime's existence thus ran up against the fact of the state's persistence and, further, the project of its reinforcement. Without following the argument in detail, we could say that Aron intended to underscore the contradiction into which the Bolshevik doctrine fell during the Stalinist era. This contradiction seemed to culminate when Stalin declared that the flowering of socialism had to be accompanied by an intensification of class struggle.

After having apprised us of his conviction that the Bolsheviks accomplished (for better or worse) something other than what they had wanted, and that they had become powerless to think through what they had accomplished, Aron suddenly delivered his response to the question that his readers believed him to have forgotten: "Hence, one can understand the duality between the constitutional fictions and the reality. For the time being, the Bolsheviks have not succeeded completely in reconciling their doctrine which remains, in purpose and aims, democratic with the practice of a one-party state, born of circumstances."[18] Finally, he specified that "it would be false to believe that the constitutional fictions are without significance, simply 'fool's traps' or 'Potemkin villages'; in a certain way, as long as the democratic constitution is proclaimed, there is a chance that the regime will evolve in that direction. In proclaiming this constitution, the regime itself proclaims one possible end of its enterprise."[19]

In dwelling somewhat at length on this passage from *Democracy and Totalitarianism*, I do not want give the impression that it represented all the author's thoughts on the matter. Many times he expressed great doubts about the possibility of a liberal reform of the Soviet regime. But his line of thinking strikes me as crucial because it was sparked by a reflection on ideology that is worth examining. The Aronian response to the problem of the constitution's character seems to me disappointing. Contrary to what Aron intimated for a moment, the monopolization of the state by a single party was not a simple product of circumstances. He himself knew well that it was prefigured in the practice of Bolshevism, which since its origins bore witness in its strategy and mode of organization to its inclination for the monopolization of power. He also knew how

quickly after October freedoms were destroyed, rival formations eliminated, and all institutions issuing from the revolution absorbed. These
practices, as I have said, were not mute. Lenin conceived, theorized, and
proclaimed them in the party assemblies. In truth, to make Aron's argument consistent, one would have to modify the meaning of the formula
"ideological solution" he had at one point introduced. To his understanding, the formula was appropriate only at the moment when the dictatorship of the party presented itself as the dictatorship of the revolutionary
class, but it became untenable once the elimination of the bourgeoisie
was declared, since the existence of the state had then lost all justification. However, if one admits that the ideological solution consisted of
combining the idea of socialism with that of the party's omnipotence—or
of amalgamating the two—it would be wrong to deem that solution con-
troverted by the alleged triumph of the socialist state, a triumph that,
logically, had to coincide with the disappearance of the state.

Ideology indeed eluded the criteria of rationality.[20] Adapting to or, better, feeding on contradiction, it kept thought in a vise grip by subjugat-
ing it sometimes to a principle beyond all contestation, sometimes to a
contrary principle. As a result, this ideology stated: the party commands
absolutely (the workers obey it), and, simultaneously, the party is the pure
emanation of the proletariat; the socialist state abolished class domination, and, simultaneously, the state more than ever hunts down the people's enemies. Submitting ideology to the imperative of coherence could
come to the mind of only an observer formed in the school of liberalism.
In fact, the role reserved for the party signaled not the solution of a problem created by ideology, but—what was totally different—an ideological
exploitation of Marxism. It did not introduce, as is often said, a doctrinal innovation; rather, it attended a project of state conquest by a group
beholden to the image of a collective body. The party was from the start
something real and something imaginary. We do not need to conclude
that its members, at least in its first period, were moved by an appetite
for power or material goods. It is hardly disputable that they had for their
objective the creation of a supposedly socialist society. But no more is
there reason to think that their project changed meaning solely due to
circumstances. The image of the party *above all*, its fetishization, made
its presence felt by the time the party seized the state apparatus, founding
and directing a state to which the ensemble of social life was submitted.
Let us grant only that, when this happened, ideology became completely

consistent; it circulated by enveloping all relations of force and all clashes of interest born from the differentiation of roles and responsibilities within the party as well as from the differentiation of social categories within a new socioeconomic system (the state control [*étatisation*] of production was accompanied by the formation of a new hierarchy and of material inequalities whose misrepresentation was necessary).

Doctrine and *ideology* were the terms Aron most often conflated. They were either placed side by side or substituted. However, they are not equivalent, and the use of *ideology* poses a problem that calls for a specific reflection. Thus in the chapter "Ideology and Terror," which followed that called "Constitutional Fictions and Soviet Reality," Aron, after having underscored the artful use of doctrine by Communist leaders in order to impose commands contrary to those already in place, took account of a new argument: "Here one is inclined to reverse the idea of relations between the party and ideology which I have submitted to you up to now and to say that after all ideology is perhaps merely an instrument of government."[21] The hypothesis led him to adopt, at the expense of the Communist system, the critique that Marx had made of bourgeois ideology: "Turning the Marxist method against the Soviet regime, leads to saying: the party or the few who lead it use this or that doctrinal formula according to the needs of the moment in order to remain in power and to create a society in which they hold the leading positions."[22] Without denying the relevance of this hypothesis, Aron did not champion it: "Marxist ideology is an instrument of government, in the same way that democratic ideology is an instrument of government in constitutional-pluralist regimes. But it would not be true to believe that doctrine is merely an instrument of power and that the Soviet leaders do not believe their own doctrine. The Bolsheviks are not pure opportunists."[23] It would thus be more worthwhile to speak of a "blend of doctrinal fanaticism and exceptional flexibility in tactics and practice. . . . Ideology is neither the sole end nor the exclusive means."[24]

It is important to point out that here Marx's thought was, at the very least, simplified. For him, ideology did not come down to a means of government. It originated in a social structure that no longer permitted the bourgeois class to give itself a representation of its domination, once that class was deprived of reference to an order of things conforming to tradition or a divine will. It was in the realm of ideas, in a regime of Reason, that it projected the origin and meaning of social relations instituted in the mode of production. Bourgeois ideology was thus disclosed only by observing the inversion between existence and social consciousness. This inversion went hand in hand with a misrepresentation of reality, a dissimulation of the internal division of society, and a justification of domination. But Marxist analysis gives another means of understanding that the ideology of Communist society cannot be described according to a schema analogous to that which unmasked bourgeois ideology. Bourgeois ideology found its conditions of possibility in the institution of private property, in an economic system that involved the separation of the spheres of production, and in a social order that involved the separation of the domains of the economy, politics, and culture. Thus the critique of this ideology had for its objective discovering the hidden connections among representations proper to each domain of only apparently independent activities. And yet, Communist ideology is intelligible only if one relates it to the institution of state-owned property and to a kind of society in which different sectors of activities are markedly articulated with one another—in short, to a world uniformly subjugated to the party-state. I will add that if one resorts to Marx's interpretation, it would be better, rather than simplifying it, to worry about its strong risk of reducing all intellectual creations to the modality of ideology. But I will leave aside the objections that this interpretation calls forth.

"Returning to the Marxist method" must at least lead one to ask about the nature of a system in which not only the governing but also the social strata on which they depended needed a misrepresentation of reality and a dissimulation of class divisions in order to justify a new mode of domination. It nevertheless suffices to appreciate the argument that appropriately warns us against the danger of reducing Communist doctrine to an instrument of government and, by the same token, of neglecting leaders and citizens' beliefs in this doctrine. Undoubtedly, the two caveats have weight, and the second even more so, since for a long time the Bolsheviks supported a criminal politics from which they derived no material benefit. Still, the question remains: In what did those who governed or those who supported them believe?

In truth, I have already put forth part of an answer: in the best scenario, belief in socialism was indistinguishable from belief in the party. But rather than ask what became of socialist belief, since it was ensnared in belief in the party, and try to distinguish the various modalities of the faith invested in the party (a faith that could revivify an excluded and condemned militant, or bring others the pleasures of terror), I would like to return to the circumstances in which the famous Constitution of 1936 was conceived and understood, since it was in respect to it that Aron spoke of the doctrine's persistence and its democratic inspiration. I have scarcely mentioned a crucial circumstance: the publication of the constitution coincided with the start of the Great Purges. In August 1936, Stalin put Zinoviev, Kamenev, and other former leaders on trial. They were accused of having formed a terrorist center as well as assassinating Sergey Kirov and conspiring against his character.[25] At the time, absolutely none of them any longer possessed an influence capable of disturbing the reigning powers. In January 1937, Yury Piatakov and fifteen members of a supposedly new "terrorist center" were similarly judged and condemned to death for the same motive.[26] The third great trial was launched in 1938 against Bukharin, Aleksey Rykov, and Genrikh Yagoda, the head of the Soviet security police (Narodnyi Komissariat Vnutrennikh Del, or NKVD), who had been placed in charge of concocting the first affair.[27] These were the most spectacular episodes of the Stalinist terror, given the prestige of the victims. Nevertheless, we can appreciate its dimensions only if we consider the offensive launched in 1934 against cadres in the party (members of the Central Committee, provincial and local secretaries), in industry, and in the army. The purges ended in the elimination of hundreds of thousands and the recruitment of a new mass of militants.

One must certainly be astonished by the absence of resistance by party members, notably a large number of officers, including Marshal Mikhail Tukhachevsky.[28] This absence says a great deal about the nature of the regime. In the first place, every effort to build coalitions among suspects was defeated in the climate of denunciation that emerged. Everyone saw in all others a potential informer. Second, most of the accused showed themselves powerless to oppose a terroristic politics in which they had participated before it was turned against them. Third, there was no other pole of legitimation apart from the party. To the argument that "the security police had now replaced the party as the heart of the system," Martin Malia justly objected that "Stalin now used the police to rule the party, just as he had always used the party to rule the country. But he did all of this as the embodiment of the party, not as the mere head of the police. . . . Stalin had to keep the party supreme because it was the embodiment of the ideological purpose of the regime, and therefore the basis of its legitimacy."[29] The interpretation is convincing, with the reservation that Malia confused "ideological purpose" with the conception of socialism he attributed to Marx. The arguments by Aron I have just cited refute this conflation. Let me underscore this remark of Malia's: "The purges and the institutionalization of terror thus completed the party's pulverization of civil society and the near-atomization of the population. Vis-à-vis the party-state there now existed only a pallid shadow society and a mass of isolated individuals afraid to associate among themselves and constrained even from thinking of doing so by the new culture of socialism triumphant."[30] Nevertheless, I will still raise a reservation, since the decomposition of civil society in this period was accompanied by a vast enterprise controlling culture and education, inaugurated in 1934 and culminating in 1936, the goal of which was to include so-called atomized individuals in myriad microbodies gravitating around the party.

It is in such a framework that one must appreciate the Constitution of 1936 and interpret the signs of an allegedly democratic discourse. The articles that specified the rights of citizens did not attest, as we are told, to a split between theory and practice. They were instead the product of a tremendous lie whose effectiveness was measured by the fact that no one had the possibility of denouncing it and that everyone would henceforth find no other means of naming events than to borrow the coded language of "true freedom" or "true equality." We will admit only that the power of language prompts one to believe what one says. The fantasy about Stalin using the constitution hypocritically does not stand up to an examination of his regime. I would thus like to reintroduce the hypothesis, half-neglected by Aron, of a demonstration addressed to Western opinion. It seems probable that, on the one hand, it resulted from the discovery of Nazism's threat to the Soviet Union, but it is equally plausible that the conjuncture made leaders aware of the considerable benefits they could acquire from a new style of propaganda. That style gave European Communist parties powerful means of expression. Do we not see here how valuable it would have been for them to refer to "the most democratic constitution in the world"? In response to criticisms aroused by Stalin's Great Purges, they declared that the Soviet regime had for its principal objective ensuring concrete freedoms and making a social democracy prevail and that the regime had to unmask conspiracies at the same time as it imposed a discipline of action eliminating machinations among factions. Soviet society thereafter presented itself as a universal model, meanwhile conserving its revolutionary prestige. As Dominique Colas sharply observed, the Constitution of 1936 was promulgated to teach the lesson that the period of civil war and the transition to socialism had ended. The conjunction of a terroristic politics and an exhibition of democratic principles was no less an extraordinary phenomenon and one that has largely escaped the understanding of most Western observers.

9

The Myth of the Soviet Union in the West

HOW COULD COMMUNISM, despite the turn events took from the early 1920s, have inspired so much confidence beyond Russia's borders, mobilizing masses of supporters on the European Left and fascinating so many intellectuals? This question was at the heart of Furet's book, and I have already indicated his response to it: the power of illusion. This illusion was preserved even better in Western Europe, which was not submitted to the test of reality, unlike a Communist country. Furet, though, did not assume a general ignorance about what was happening inside the Soviet Union. He took account of information that circulated, doubts born within part of the Marxist Left, and fundamental criticisms made early on by capable analysts of the Leninist dictatorship, and then the Stalinist state. But these facts led him to sharpen his question, since he had to admit that "illusion resists the knowledge of facts." Evoking at one point the cataclysm provoked by de-kulakization[1]—in fact, a veritable war against the peasantry—he noted that with this unprecedented mass terror the hour of the totalitarian state had arrived: "Most surprising of all is that something so excessive should have seemed so ordinary to Western intellectuals and to international public opinion and that something so atrocious should have been hailed as exemplary."[2] Elsewhere, after observing that Trotsky, like Bukharin, had said nothing about the horrors of the famine, he declared, "Even more astonishing was that this deadening of judgment extended to so many people outside of the Soviet Union, for the facts—at least in their massive atrocity—were not entirely mysterious."[3] The evidence and information diffused by émigré Russian newspapers as well as the analyses of Karl Kautsky and Boris Souvarine led him to conclude that "those who wanted to know could have known. The problem was that few people really wanted to."[4] To his understanding, Stalinism lost none of the mythological power that Bolshevism had enjoyed: "On the contrary, its image swelled in the contemporary imagination just when it was carrying out its most heinous crimes; instead of dissipating, the mystery of the regime's fascination only grew denser."[5]

At no moment did Furet try to downplay Soviet agents' stratagem of creating peace associations and movements that served the policies of the Kremlin. Briefly recalling the role played by Communists in Spain during that country's civil war, he showed that they set their sights on the physical elimination of anarchists and partisans of the Workers' Party of Marxist Unification [Partido obrero de unificación marxista] and the monopolization of key posts in the new republic. Despite these wrongdoings, the Soviet Union emerged from this episode with the reputation of being the sole defender of liberties in a Europe facing fascism.[6] Nevertheless, one cannot avoid challenging the validity of Furet's major thesis that "illusion did not 'accompany' Communist history; it made it."[7] This thesis, I would like to reiterate, was based on the comparative examination of the effects of the same illusion or idea (as mentioned in chapter 3, two equivalent terms) "in two different political forms, depending on whether it exerted its power through a one-party system or whether it was spread through liberal democratic public opinion, guided by local Communist parties but extending beyond them in less militant forms."[8] I have already discussed the first part of this equation, and the second now merits attention. It seems to me all the more important, since I retain a clear memory of the practices of the French Communist Party [Parti communiste français] and "progressive" intellectuals after 1945.[9]

Furet's account derived directly from his hypothesis. Once he placed illusion at the origin of Communism and affirmed its "channeling" by Western national parties, the path was already laid out. In short, it was a question of identifying events that impeded *disillusionment* while the Soviet state increasingly showed totalitarian traits. These events were situated in three conjunctures corresponding, first, to the installation of the dictatorship of the Bolshevik Party and of what is called wartime Communism (1917–1921); second, to the crushing of the peasants' resistance, mass terror, and the Great Purges throughout the 1930s; and third, to new waves of terror in Russia after World War II as well as the domination of Eastern Europe and the repression of uprisings in that region.

The first period posed fewer problems than the other two. Social and political agitation in the leading countries of Western Europe encouraged belief in the creation of a socialist state. In France, Furet observed, revolutionary hopes awakened by the Bolsheviks' success were so strong that the testimonies of Menshevik exiles—or, I would add, the nevertheless irrefutable ones of Julius Martov, Lenin's old companion—were readily greeted with suspicion.[10] Furthermore, for numerous intellectuals, reminiscences about 1789 impeded understanding the party-state's dynamics. This depiction is in general agreement with Marc Ferro's *L'Occident devant la Révolution soviétique* (1991).[11]

And yet, it was more difficult to explain the persistence of the illusion or, better, its intensification in the two following conjunctures, when events should have dissipated it. Furet dwelt on the fact that the first of these circumstances, during the 1930s, witnessed the development of antifascist ideology. The defense of the Soviet Union thus came to coincide with the struggle against Nazism. Then, at the end of World War II, the Soviet Union appeared as the country that had contributed decisively to the victory of the democratic camp, while Communist militants who had participated in the resistance in all lands occupied by the Axis acquired the image of being democrats and, what is more, patriots in each country where they fought. These arguments are not negligible. I recalled in the previous chapter the strategic turning point in the mid-1930s when the Soviet government, increasingly aware of the danger constituted by Nazism and German rearmament, worked to support antifascist campaigns and Popular Front policies. For a fraction of public opinion, the antifascist idea combining with the Communist idea shielded the reality of a totalitarian state. Already, between 1936 and 1939, the idea was asserted that all depreciation of the Soviet Union played into the hands of fascism. Later, it found renewed effectiveness during the cold war, with the exception that American imperialism had taken the place of fascism. Despite the resistance of a small number of clear-thinking people—notably Boris Souvarine in his *Stalin* (1935), in analyses published in his review, *La Critique sociale*, and in *La Révolution prolétarienne* (the testimony of Yvon [Robert Guihéneuf] prefaced by Pierre Pascal contained a detailed report on workers' conditions in Russia), later by Ante Ciliga's *The Russian Enigma* (1938) [the French title is *Au pays du grand mensonge*], but also in Trotsky's writings and the pamphlets of the Left Opposition (which Furet passed over in silence)—despite these exceptions, the idealization of Soviet socialism masked Stalinist terror.[12] This was the era when the Kremlin welcomed famous visitors from France and England. Only André Gide among them, though worried about his reputation, was bold enough to convey his misgivings upon his return from the Soviet Union, earning him Communist invective and condemnation from self-righteous intellectuals.[13]

Nonetheless, does antifascist mobilization suffice to explain what would become of the myth of the Soviet Union? More particularly, can the interdiction that, already at the end of the 1930s, forbade all criticisms of the Soviet bureaucracy be understood only through changes taking place on the international scene? Certainly, a link is missing: the action of "local" parties. Furet rightly noted that they "channeled the Communist idea." But what a peculiar image! In reality, since their creation, the parties of the Third International had been strictly subordinated to the direction of the Russian party. Their constant task was to paint the picture of a country in which the proletariat had captured power, continued to struggle to extirpate the roots of the bourgeois class, and resisted the aggression of imperialism from their "besieged citadel." One cannot disregard the fact that in interwar France it was thanks to the Communist Party that Soviet society appeared as an egalitarian and free society governed by leaders who had maintained the same course of action since the revolution. It was thanks to a crude falsification of the facts that the myth became popular.

Generally speaking, observing how the progress of antifascism benefited the Soviet Union need not distract us from the carefully mounted spectacle of the "fatherland of socialism," with which the cult of Stalin was blended (a cult the national party shared). Now, local parties, if one considers their structure and methods, were replicas of the Russian party. Without being in a position to gain power—certainly not a negligible difference—their mission was the establishment of a totalitarian state. Furthermore, to a large extent they owed their success, uneven as it was, to the model adopted from a country where socialism reigned. The power that the French Communist Party acquired in 1936 was no doubt explained by a program that distinguished it from the reformism of the Socialist Party [Section française de l'internationale ouvrière] and by its adeptness at marrying the revolutionary and national traditions.[14] However, its prestige fed on the Soviet Union's, which it ceaselessly reinforced.

Who today can seriously claim that the leaders of the French Communist Party were, at the time, victims of their illusions about the Soviet Union? They already knew and never stopped knowing, if not in detail than at least for the essentials, what the dictatorship of the party-state was. If they never perceived any monstrosity, it was not because they had faith in the laws of history (I do not doubt they had such faith, though I would point out that social democrats invoked such laws on their side in order to accuse the Bolsheviks of having violated them), but because, weighing the chances for revolution in a large, already developed country, they sought to create a regime out of the same material as the Soviet one. The distinction Furet drew between the "Communist idea in power" and the "Communist idea in a diffused state" masked the resemblances between these parties and between their forms of organization and action.

There is no doubt that the October revolution aroused revolutionary aspirations in Europe and that these aspirations were fueled by the distress of World War I and the memory of Social Democrats having abandoned internationalism. The rise of Communist parties found its point of departure here. Even so, the functioning of the Comintern teaches us more about those parties' consolidation and strategy than does the development of social and political conflicts in Germany, France, and Italy. Local parties became integrated into an organization governed by Leninist principles: strict obedience to leaders' orders, clandestine operations, "rational" division of tasks, and assignment of militants to missions when and where they were needed. It is well known that for a long time the Comintern was never a collaborative committee composed of the leaders of different parties. It constituted a supreme organ under Bolshevik authority. As Aron accurately noted, its agents were certainly not opportunists. They accepted being manipulated by the center's instructions, and they made a rule out of not knowing what the center alone was supposed to know, since it alone had at its disposal a global view of the world's workings. A very remarkable variety of the Communist species came to light with the Comintern: men sworn to tasks whose justifications they did not know; who consented to eliminating their counterparts as soon as the latter were judged to be traitors, suspicious, or simply dangerous; and who themselves consented to their own possible elimination if circumstances required it. Thus they were carried away in a sinister, sometimes ridiculous adventure in which the interests of world revolution had become for them indistinguishable from webs of local intrigue. In this respect, the story of Jan Valtin, agent of the Comintern and a longtime dedicated Communist, always doomed never to know who or what to believe, has more to teach us than many learned studies on aspects of the Communist universe.[15] The Comintern succeeded in weaving together an entire network of associations in service of the Soviet Union, thanks to agents captivated by the system's efficiency. After all, it is necessary to recall that the Hitler–Stalin pact, if it threw a certain number of national militants into disarray, hardly shook up the solidity of the machine.

Even though World War II was brought to the Communists, it seemed to put them back in the camp of democracy. I touch here Furet's second argument, which turns on the revivification of the Communist illusion. It is appropriate to consider both the observation and the interpretation. The difficulty comes from the way each encroaches on the other. In a first moment, the observation does not encounter any objection: Stalin's regime in 1945 took advantage of the Soviet people's contribution to the victory over Nazism. In a similar manner, militants of national parties everywhere benefited from their participation in resistance movements in occupied countries. In France, Communism's good image was restored. The postwar era afforded it new chances to develop, so high was the expectation of great economic and social changes and so widely shared was the critique of the institutions and practices responsible for the defeat of the country. Bourgeois democracy had previously collided with two revolutionary currents: Communism and fascism. At that time, Furet observed, "The end of World War II offered antifascism a second political wind by permanently ridding it of its fascist enemy. Thereafter, antifascism no longer had any rivals in the critique of bourgeois democracy: it held a monopoly on it. The end of World War II was thus even more of a political victory for the Communist idea than for the democratic idea."[16]

There are grounds for questioning the picture Communists had, to some extent, worked out for themselves. Although it may be indisputable that the end of the war conferred a new prestige on the Soviet Union and national parties, the role of antifascism in their legitimation depended largely on their own propaganda. The important issue is to find out why that propaganda was so effective. Moreover, after having repeated that the Soviet Union appeared among the foremost victims and victors of the war—"which sufficed to obscure its nature"—Furet all of a sudden declared, "None of this explains why the Communist idea was the greatest beneficiary of the Nazi apocalypse. After all, the contrasting American model was also available and would progressively, if slowly, make up for lost terrain in the half-century to follow."[17] A fair reflection. But why insist so much on a debt of recognition toward the Soviet Union and the Communist parties? People do not always show such memory and fidelity; they willingly forget services rendered. The response to the problem leads us back to the thesis already mentioned—the attraction to Marxism-Leninism and the theology of history—to which I will reintroduce my objection: the "idea" found itself given colossal power. Furthermore, we can admit that the path of disenchantment was once again blocked for Communists and the throng of sympathizers they had gathered around them. I will add that the new antagonism between the Soviet Union and the Western powers accentuated the demand to defend the country of socialism, considered a "besieged citadel." Should one not agree that the gap between belief in the virtues of Communism and knowledge of the facts increased considerably?

While terror reemerged in the Soviet Union in the days after the war, Eastern Europe, without having the advantage of the "illusion" of a revolution under way, fell under that country's dominance. It is probably not surprising that Western Communists and their allies were pleased that Soviet troops stayed in the lands they had liberated and that their counterparts in the East achieved preeminent positions in the new democracies soon to be called "popular." But then they were confronted in 1948 with the Prague coup. Of course, the event was not viewed as a coup; once again, many were pleased at the extension of socialism. Soon the spectacular trials took place of László Rajk and Rudolf Slánsky, renowned leaders suddenly submitted to the same treatment as the accused in the Moscow trials (the latter already usefully forgotten).[18] Then, in 1953 the worker insurrection of East Berlin exploded, at the head of which were found union members previously interned in Nazi camps. In 1956 two events took place: the uprising in the worker district of Poznań—prelude to tremendous turmoil in Poland—and the Hungarian insurrection.[19] One could not hide the fact that the latter was accompanied in all the large cities by the formation of workers' councils and their federation in Budapest. The democratic demands formulated by the Central Workers' Council were widely reported: pluralism of parties, freedom of expression, the guarantee of individual security, a parliament elected by universal suffrage, and a council composed of delegates from enterprises responsible for the management of the economy. On this occasion, the Western parties, first of all the French Communist Party, condemned the popular uprising and justified the intervention of Soviet troops. One would have to wait until 1968 for the French party, without needing to question the formula of the party-state, to protest against a new Soviet intervention, that time in Czechoslovakia.

10
The French Communist Party
After World War II

T HE YEARS BEFORE AND AFTER World War II do not merely resemble
each other. During this time, submission to Soviet power grew—a
remarkable fact, since public opinion was amply informed. Delusion and
calumny mobilized the energies of the French Communist Party. Only a
small number of Communist intellectuals left it in 1953, more often than
not silently. Edgar Morin distinguished himself by the intellectual cour-
age and lucidity he showed in sharing his experience of Communism in
his resounding *Autocritique* (1959).[1] Departures were more numerous
after the second Soviet intervention in Hungary in 1956 (Soviet troops
had helped bring the Communist Party to power in 1948), though the
reflex of solidarity continued to overcome any discord. In the context
of the Hungarian events, a minor incident illustrated the tenacity of the
defenders of the Soviet Union. In December 1956, the Committee of Intellectuals Against the Algerian War [Comité des intellectuels contre la
poursuite de la guerre d'Algérie] had convened a large assembly. Morin
read a proposal calling for the condemnation of the Soviet intervention
in Hungary in the name of a people's right to self-determination—the
same right being invoked in favor of Algerian independence. Communist intellectuals immediately resisted. Close to me, two of them, well
known but with spiteful faces, interrupted and railed against him, laying
on Stalinist vulgarities (they later left the party). At the time, knowledge
about the Soviet system had, nevertheless, greatly improved. Revelations
had been made several years before about the existence and scale of concentration camps.

I recall here Furet's point about events at the beginning of the 1930s:
"Those who wanted to know could have known." Of course, sources re-

mained rare. Still, Victor Kravchenko's book *I Chose Freedom* appeared in France in 1947 (it had been published the previous year in the United States with a wide circulation). Subsequently, in 1950 in Paris, the author sued *Les Lettres françaises* for slander. The book and the trial made a great stir.[2] The book revealed the scale of the concentration camps and the role of forced labor in the industrial system. The Communists' response was virulent. The trial permitted those who had been deported, notably Margarete Buber-Neumann, prisoner in a Soviet camp before it had been handed over to the Nazis, to speak.[3] Those testifying were defamed and ridiculed by the Communists, whereas distinguished fellow travelers like Paul Éluard (a poet on this occasion no less worried about his reputation than Louis Aragon) presented themselves as guarantors of the Soviet regime's integrity. Were these defenders of the Soviet Union acting in good faith? Were they innocent victims of the Marxist-Leninist utopia? Who would believe it today? André Wurmser, literary critic for *Les Lettres françaises*, held an abject position largely echoed in the Communist press. I do not want to say that Wurmser incarnated the full-fledged Communist type, but I also do not want to leave intact the myth that all sorts of Communist intellectuals lived bewitched by theory. Kravchenko, one might object, appeared as a renegade. Hadn't his book been published in the United States? This alone would have been enough to render him suspect. Still, whoever had read Ante Ciliga's *The Russian Enigma*, published a dozen years earlier, could not doubt the veracity of information about the role of forced labor.[4] Ciliga (mentioned in the previous chapter) had in his way chosen freedom by following an opposite direction in his youth, and his fidelity to Marxism had won him a long stay in Siberia. Perhaps Kravchenko's attackers ignored a book with such a disturbing title. However that may be, his account came out of the gulag. Two years later, David Rousset, author of an unforgettable book on the Nazi camps, divulged the corrective labor code of the Russian Federation of Socialist Soviet Republics and the scale of the Soviet concentration camps.[5] It is true that he wrote in the right-leaning *Le Figaro littéraire* and seemed to launch an anti-Soviet campaign. He was thus mistrusted in left-wing circles and suspected of wanting to conceal the crimes of colonialism and the Greek dictatorship(!).

This kind of attack was common at the time. The most important thing was to know what ends an author was pursuing and "from where" he was speaking. Meanwhile, the Economic and Social Council [Conseil économique et social] published the Soviet corrective labor code and the results of an investigation that estimated the population of the gulag at no fewer than 10 million. Consequently, the journal *Les Temps modernes*, which had since its creation treated Soviet Communism cautiously, published an editorial evaluating this investigation and drawing a stern conclusion, from which I will quote a few lines: "If there is in the USSR one saboteur, spy, or idler for every twenty inhabitants, even though more than one purge has already 'cleansed' the country, and if today it is necessary to 'reeducate' ten million Soviet citizens while the children of October 1917 are in their early thirties, it is because the system itself endlessly re-creates its own opposition."[6] This drive toward truth would not last. Two years later, as is well known, Jean-Paul Sartre, who had cosigned the editorial with Maurice Merleau-Ponty, leaped to the aid of the Communist Party, which he judged the victim of a bourgeois plot. For Sartre, the proletariat existed as a class only to the extent that it identified itself with the party.[7]

The delusional arrogance shown by French Communists in the decades following the liberation of France had the advantage of the protective cover many intellectuals gave it. Without dreaming of joining the party, many considered it the representative of the oppressed masses and the Soviet Union the country that, against the whole world, maintained the path toward socialism. Without overestimating Sartre's role, one could judge him as exemplary. Although his dialectical tours de force no longer impress our contemporaries, one cannot forget that there was a master thinker, if not for a generation then at least for all those who sought to become or to remain "right-minded people" of the Left. Furet dedicated only one ultimately severe note to Sartre at the bottom of one page. This was not very much in view of his long passage in the first part of the book on writers adrift in political waters—first of all Romain Rolland—who set out for the Kremlin and tasted the emotion of welcoming a few precious words from Stalin's mouth.[8] One note was not very much indeed, since we cannot say of Sartre, as of others, that *he did not know* or that *he did not want to know*. With an astonishing perversity, he assigned himself the task of explaining, better than Communists themselves, the French Communist Party's politics and the Kremlin's strategy.

It is true that, generally speaking, Furet scarcely pursued his investigation of the intellectual milieu once he reached the period when, as he noted, "the mystery of the [Communist] fascination deepened." Thus he

unfortunately deprived himself of the opportunity to examine a new species—what I have called the progressive intellectual (an analogue to the
American species Harold Rosenberg called the couch liberal). This type
proliferated at the beginning of the 1950s in the press, journals, and associations controlled by Communists. Its representatives were reticent
about facing the evidence about the Soviet Union once Russian dissidents
began making it known, and they were similarly reserved when Solzhenitsyn's *The Gulag Archipelago*, a book considered the work of a mystical and
reactionary Russian, appeared in French in 1974. Finally, thanks to the
positions and status they held, the non-Communist Left developed analyses that did not escape the confines of small circles. Should one imagine
"right-minded intellectuals" under the sway of illusion? Subjugated by
Marxism and the theology of history? They seemed to me to have been
fascinated by the force emanating from the Communists—not just the
force that secured for the party the support of part of the working class
but also that shown by their capacity to use or accept the use of violence
without soul-searching, to put to the test an inflexible conviction, and to
disdain those, even among their allies, who were hesitant or lukewarm.

Communist intellectuals who came on the scene after the war turned
out to be made of the same substance as their predecessors, but their
number and influence grew significantly in Western countries, notably
in France. There they were implanted in the world of publishing, letters,
theater, and art; in cultural centers and the university; and sometimes
(who remembers this today?) in the small world of psychoanalysis. From
belonging to the party of the working class they gained the feeling of being historical actors, and in a number of cases the advantage of creating
in various places a separate milieu, an elite whose members, in good class
consciousness, were eager to help one another out. There is no reason to
confuse apparatchik intellectuals, simple adepts of a Marxism stamped
with the party's approval, for whom faith was possibly rewarded by benefits to one's career, with militants dedicated to a cause they had decided to
defend at the price of sacrificing their interests and possibly their lives. It
remained no less true, though, that both together exercised a formidable
intimidation on the non-Communist Left, Marxist or Marxisant, libera-
tional or liberal. In their eyes, all criticism of the national party, the Soviet
Union, or Marxist-Leninist doctrine strengthened the class enemy.

I recall an incident that illustrates the habits of French Communists
when the designated target was a philosopher who was far from defining

himself as their adversary. In 1955 the French Communist Party (again, who remembers this?) organized a meeting at the Mutualité auditorium in Paris to denounce Merleau-Ponty following the publication of *The Adventures of the Dialectic*.[9] In this book, he analyzed shifts [*déplacements*] in the interpretation of Marxism. He returned to Marx himself in order to reflect critically on the idea that the meaning and direction of history could never be invested in an empirically determined class. He furthermore dismantled Sartre's arguments before concluding his investigation with the impossibility of either lining up with the Communists by granting them the benefit of the doubt or joining the anti-Communist camp. Under the name of "a-Communism," he reclaimed for the intellectual the freedom to judge through the examination of events. In front of the kind of large crowd the French Communist Party was capable of assembling, the following figures appeared at this meeting: Georges Cogniot, a prominent apparatchik; Roger Garaudy and Jean Kanapa, appointed the role of guardians of orthodoxy; and the honorable philosophers Jean-Toussaint Desanti, Henri Lefebvre, and Maurice Caveing, who shamelessly brought their confident intellectual authority to a comedy of a trial.[10] Yet the Stalinist-style ceremony allows one to imagine what the fate of the accused would have been if the party had had state power. Rather than accuse French Communists of blindness when they were confronted with facts that might have destroyed the illusions inspiring their attachment to Soviet socialism, one might point out that many of them were disposed, if circumstances were favorable, to employ methods used in Eastern Europe. I am not suggesting so much that they were cynical; they did not lack conviction. Their model was of a society—defined by them as socialist—perfectly regulated and delivered from its parasites.

Still, in order to emphasize the relentlessness with which French Communists pursued deviant Marxists, I need to make room for the myth, directly imported from the Stalinist mill, of Trotskyist conspiracy. A particularly ludicrous episode I witnessed is worth recounting. During the first electoral campaign in France after the war, a recently reconstituted Trotskyist party with no more than six hundred or seven hundred members presented a small number of candidates. Although very young, I was charged with introducing one of them at a public meeting in the thirteenth arrondissement of Paris. The candidate was a postman, well known in his neighborhood, a conciliatory man who had been an antifascist for a long time and whose convictions were shaped by reading

Trotsky's *The Revolution Betrayed* (1936) and texts by the Left Opposition. His knowledge of the history of the workers' movement impressed me. I had just finished my brief speech in front of the room, which to our pleasant surprise was crowded, when chairs started flying at the podium and a fight broke out. The incident was not unforeseeable. And yet, I found myself thrown into a scene that, when it was over, left me confused. Noticing a young woman being mistreated by some angry young men, I went to her aide. They had grabbed her, yelling in her face, "Hitlerist-Trotskyist!" She kept shouting back at the top of her lungs, "I was at the Ravensbrück concentration camp!" "Lying bitch," they continued to bellow at her. The moment I reached them, she was waving a card. "The proof, the proof!" she cried, "My deportation card!" The card was taken from her hands and torn up, the pieces thrown at her face before I succeeded in shielding her from the hysterical band. I had known about Stalinist violence from books, and I knew what had happened to anarchists and militants from the Workers' Party of Marxist Unification in Spain. But things that are seen become indelible. If I still had doubts about the methods of French Communists, my apprenticeship was being completed. Although the "comrade" had left this incident physically unharmed, and, as one says, "she had seen it before," all the same, a question haunted me: Why such relentlessness against Trotskyists in the thirteenth arrondissement of Paris when we had at last rediscovered peace and democracy? Why did a small group matter so much to Communists?

Much later, I discovered the subtle pages Hannah Arendt had dedicated in *The Origins of Totalitarianism* (1951) to the Communist, which she compared with the Nazi, fiction of conspiracy. She showed well that both had an essential role in the constitution of totalitarian ideology. Jewish and Trotskyist "conspiracy," she said in substance, were invented thanks to an exploitation of "real" facts capable of inflaming the collective imagination: the enhanced role Jews played in public life or Trotsky's opposition to Stalin's reign. The fiction of conspiracy, she went on to say, contributed to producing an apparently coherent vision of the world: a new order won against the work of malevolent powers. But the analysis did not stop there. She followed the persistence of the fiction when it lost all anchor point in reality—that is, after the Nazis proceeded to exterminate Jews and after Stalin assassinated Trotsky and then liquidated the Left Opposition in Russia. Arendt's idea was that "once these propaganda slogans are integrated into a 'living organization' [an expression borrowed from Hitler], they cannot be safely eliminated without wrecking the whole structure."[11] Her arguments about totalitarian ideology were not always as clear, but in this passage, it seems to me, she reached the heart of the matter. She discovered the bond that united ideology and organization:

> The point was that the Nazis *acted* as though the world were dominated by the Jews and needed a counterconspiracy to defend itself. Racism for them was no longer a debatable theory of dubious scientific value, but was being realized every day in the functioning hierarchy of a political organization in whose framework it would have been very "unrealistic" to question it. Similarly, Bolshevism no longer needs to win an argument about class struggle, internationalism, and unconditional dependence of the welfare of the proletariat on the welfare of the Soviet Union; the functioning organization of the Comintern is more convincing than any argument or mere ideology can ever be.[12]

Arendt thus suggested that the construction of reality is inseparable from the construction of a collective body.

To return to the event I evoked, the lunatics who attacked the young Ravensbrück survivor were neither fanatics nor madmen. It is doubtful that they had any knowledge of what Trotskyism or even Marxist theory was. But it is probable that they did more than execute orders given by a boss and that they believed firmly in the party, and *because they were members of it*, believed in the logic of their reasoning and action.

Communist violence does not allow itself to be separated from Communist belief. But one would no doubt be mistaken to conclude that those who exercised violence always acted under the influence of belief. This notion has led great minds astray; it could be found, for example, behind the desperate efforts to explain that the infamous Moscow trials had been mounted and carried out with the intention of eliminating those who opposed policies defined by the party leaders and judged by them as conforming to the revolutionary project. On that occasion,

so great was the intellectual repugnance at acknowledging violence—I will not say gratuitous violence but, instead, violence intended to demonstrate Stalin's total power—that Andrei Vyshinsky was presented as a Bolshevik theoretician, whereas he was nothing but a boorish scoundrel dragged out of obscurity by Stalin and throughout his career given the task of concealing the latter's intentions in judicial verdicts.[13] It can furthermore be admitted that the staging of the trials galvanized the imagination of Western observers in the humanist tradition. On the other hand, to attribute illusions to the secret police (Gosudarstvennoe Politicheskoe Upravlenie, or GPU) or the gulag's functionaries, one would have to surpass the limits of naïveté. Bearing these reservations in mind, the problem of belief deserves to be reconsidered, so much has it been invoked to point out the sincerity, if not the noble intentions, that led to terroristic measures or their acceptance. Thus, in a general fashion, one has been able to picture at the origin of Communist engagement, notably in Western countries, either a faith in Marxist doctrine or a desire for social equality shared by millions of people and so powerful that it rendered them indifferent to all facts capable of tarnishing the image of the socialist homeland.

Furet did not invent this interpretation. I find a trace of it in the *Temps modernes* text already mentioned, "Les Jours de notre vie," which Merleau-Ponty had partly written in evaluating David Rousset's revelations on the Soviet concentrationary system. As I indicated, Merleau-Ponty in no way minimized the phenomenon. On the contrary, in the first part of the article he denounced Communist denials of its scale to the point of concluding, "There, no doubt, is how the best Communists are deaf to ten million prisoners."[14] But he immediately began an argument that, without exactly being antipodal, tended to rehabilitate the Communists. "In looking for the origin of the concentrationary system," he wrote, "we assess the illusion of today's Communists. But it is also this illusion that bars confusing fascism and Communism. If our Communists accept the camps and oppression, it is because in them they await a classless society via the miracle of infrastructures. They are mistaken, but that is what they think. They are wrong to believe in obscurity, but that is what they believe."[15] As a contemporary reader might remark, the problem posed by the comparison of Communism and fascism is not new—it had been formulated much earlier. In a long passage, Merleau-Ponty lamented Communist illusion, but without ceasing to intimate a kind of sympathy for it: "Nazis never burdened themselves with ideas like the recognition of man by man, internationalism, and a classless society. It is true that these ideas only find in today's Communism an unfaithful bearer and that they serve more as *decoration* than *motor*. Still they remain."[16]

The tone of Merleau-Ponty's and Furet's propositions barely differed. Bearing in mind the values they held, the former had concluded, it is true, that Western Communist parties remained "sane."[17] He wrote in 1950, unaware of how those values would evolve. On the other hand, Furet, knowing the history of the intervening forty years, suggested nothing of the sort. But both made illusion into Communism's driving energy. Merleau-Ponty does not seem contradicted by Furet when he asserted that the (unhappy) illusion that concealed from Communists either the fact or the scale of the concentration camps flowed from a first (generous) illusion, according to which the transformation of the mode of production, regardless of the calamity of terror, would ensure the success of socialism. Was it because his argument happened to be squeezed into an article? Regardless, Merleau-Ponty revealed the weakness of the interpretation that privileges the power of illusion. Acknowledging that Communists' humanist ideas (which "are ours") served in his day "more as decoration than motor," he said nothing about the "motor"—a term that, like a Freudian slip, makes the ears perk up—or what the "decoration" concealed.[18] In the end, what did the persistence of noble ideas matter if they had only an accessory role? The major question, however, is this: What was the motor? What made Communism start moving? What sustained it in Russia with so much power that it spread to Western parties? In remaining with the image of the motor, I will ask yet again: What made the great totalitarian machine of the Soviet Union turn? The machine of the Comintern? Those of the satellite states and the Western parties? Undoubtedly, illusions were not negligible. Yet they displaced one source for another and merely orbited around a power generating a new type of society.

It remains necessary to investigate not only the nature of the illusion or illusions that Communism generated but also the limits within which the very notion of illusion is relevant. Obviously, whoever compares Communist and fascist values does not have difficulty judging

them inassimilable. Only a right-wing anti-Communist, in his fanatical way, would want to conflate them. But once this distinction is acknowledged, must one conclude, like Furet, that Communist illusions
emerged from the Procrustean bed of democratic ideas or, like Merleau-Ponty, that they expressed values that were "the same as ours"?
At the time, such ideas and values were not the exclusive preserve of
Communists: most non-Communists on the Left shared them, even if
they were never driven to mythify the Soviet Union and rationalize terror. The assessment of Communists of "good faith," which considers
only the radicalism of their involvement and their determination to act
according to the ideal of a classless society (no matter the obstacles
that ideal encountered)—this assessment fails to appreciate the traits
that distinguished Communists: their love of the discipline of action
and thought; their love of authority, culminating in the cult of the supreme leader; their love of order, for which the system provided them
the criteria; and their love of uniformity, which they fulfilled already in
the spectacle of their unanimity. It was through these traits that, even
before they began to forge their new world, they invented a new kind of
person: a man endowed with the capacity to not let himself *be affected*
and therefore surprised by *what happens*. Such a man was characterized by something besides his illusions. For illusions are inadequate to
explain a capture of the individual, such that he became caught up in
the Communist *we*; a capture of thought, such that knowledge [*savoir*]
became separated from the exercise of understanding [*connaissance*]
and judgment; and a capture of sensibility, such that all compassion
disappeared as soon as victims of oppression or even torture were not
counted in the good camp.

The critique of Communism, it is true, felt itself reduced to silence
when facing the spectacle of militants who had sacrificed everything
for their political engagement and who had given everything, including
themselves, to the party. It seemed improper to confuse these militants
with the minor or prominent apparatchiks, arrogant intellectuals, or
executants of dirty work. Nevertheless, this critique could not neglect
the phenomenon of capture. In it, the memory of the bond established
by Étienne de La Boétie between the domination of the One [*un seul*]
and voluntary servitude returned: the strange inversion of freedom
into servitude he saw accomplished under the charm of the name of
the One [*le nom de l'Un*]. For the most respectable militant—who had

taken a stand against poverty and the condition of the proletariat in capitalist society, against colonialism and the despicable forms of oppression that accompanied it, and against fascism—the name of the One regained its power of enchantment by clinging for a while to Stalin's power and, from the beginning until the end of the adventure, to the name of the party.[19]

11

Utopia and Tragedy

U NDER ANY ASPECT that one imagines it—regime, party, type of personality—Communism is conceivable only within the horizons of the modern world. Martin Malia, in recounting what he called the Soviet tragedy, analyzed it as a regime, intending to reveal its origins and explain its development, attrition, and collapse. Early in his book, he rejected arguments that saw the prolongation of the tsarist Old Regime in what would become a new despotism. The Communist phenomenon seemed to him essentially a product of modernity, with the reservation that despite the creation of a "new politics, a new economics, and (almost) a new Soviet man . . . [the Soviet Union] was neither a developed nor a modern nation."[1] One of his deepest concerns was to discredit a fiction legitimated by Western Sovietology that made Russian history a variant of the histories of developing countries: "It has been, rather, the extraordinary adventure, for the first time in Western history, of attempting to put 'utopia in power'" (the formula was borrowed from Mikhail Heller and Aleksandr Nekrich).[2] He noted the failure of such utopias by specifying that "through the law of unintended consequences, they lead, rather, to the emergence of a monstrous caricature of reality—a surreality."[3] To this paradox was added another: "Never before in Western history has such a monumental failure been such an irresistible success."[4] Malia's main thesis followed in short order: "Yet the solution to all of these paradoxes is surprisingly simple. The utopia that October put in power was the ideological common property of the modern age, and the experiment was conducted not just for Russia, but for all mankind."[5] Why, he asked, was it necessary that the experimentation take place in a country that remained in many ways on the margins of the modern world? For the moment, I leave that question unanswered in order to point out that the utopia with which we are presented was of a thoroughly egalitarian society, a utopia that fed on belief in the constant progress of humanity and the ultimate reign of Reason. It had its source in Marxism but was derived more distantly from the philosophy of the Enlightenment.

Is there not cause to be wary of solutions of a surprising simplicity, especially when analyzing great events that shocked the physiognomy of a society and that invite a new reading of the twentieth century—when, as here, it is a question of explaining the birth and duration (seventy years) of a regime qualified as without precedent? To be sure, Malia seemed aware of what was paradoxical in his approach when he claimed to dispel all paradoxes. On the one hand, he dissolved Communism into utopia to the point of denying the former all stability in reality. Hence, in light of Communism's failure, he affirmed—even more severely than Furet, who had made Communism a parenthesis in the course of democracy—that "if in the end Communism collapsed like a house of cards, it was because it had always been a house of cards."[6] On the other hand, Malia dedicated all his assuredly considerable competence to reconstructing a long chain of events, not only paying attention to the "unintended consequences" of leaders' politics, but also pointing out their hesitations and improvisations—first of all Lenin's, in the years preceding the revolution, but also Stalin's, notably in the late 1920s, either before the start of the First Five-Year Plan (1928) through the early 1930s or on the eve of the offensive he launched against the peasants. The two outlines—Communism as utopia and detailed historical reconstruction—actually overlapped once it was acknowledged that all decisions by Soviet leaders, as peculiar and rash as they seemed, testified to a *logic*: that of the "partyocracy" and "ideocracy," which themselves issued from primitive utopia.

Conceding that the adventure's vicissitudes had to some extent escaped the forecasts of its actors, Malia believed he had detected the inflexible direction introduced by the idea of socialism (at least socialism conceived by Marx, he said, since taken in its general meaning the term makes little sense). Without wanting in any way to succumb to an idealist or a materialist theory, he intended to demonstrate the necessity that derived, moment to moment, from one unprecedented situation to the next, from a choice: either upholding or abandoning the revolutionary project. In vain, he declared, would one want to find in the creation of the Bolshevik Party the sign of a rupture with Marxism. Either Lenin would have remained within social democracy and, as shown by its getting bogged down in parliamentarianism in Europe, renounced revolution, or he would forge the instrument capable of implementing Marx's program at the cost of making the theory inflexible. By the same token, he thought that one would be wrong to split hairs between Leninism and Stalinism. Is it true that Lenin would not have consented to the war conducted against the peasants? Circumstances [*la conjoncture*] were such that Stalin was obliged to draw the consequences of a work that had already been accomplished: the destruction of a class whose interests opposed those of the proletariat. The errors committed in estimating peasant resistance, the excesses of repression, or the preparation and execution of the First Five-Year Plan—these mattered little. The essential thing was to recognize the necessity of the choice between a decisive alternative: socialism or ruin. At the end of his reconstruction of the Soviet tragedy, Malia drew the conclusion that the experiment did not turn into totalitarianism in spite of socialism, but that socialism "is the ideal formula for totalitarianism."[7]

If *The Soviet Tragedy* fortunately distinguished itself from other studies with similar ambitions, it was to some extent because the *logic* Malia detected in the history of the Communist regime, considered in all its dimensions (by means of a construction that proved unknowingly idealist), permitted him to free himself from an explanatory framework in which either relations of force on the world scale, the play of circumstances in Russia, or the intentions and personalities of actors were privileged. Above all, Malia's book is notable because the project of reaffirming the primacy of the political and ideological over the social and economic prompts us to reexamine the very notion of the political.

One can, without conceding anything to his major thesis, admire the incontestable merits of the work. Malia did not hesitate to qualify the Soviet regime as totalitarian: "The rude experience of the twentieth century has given us such a [separate and distinct] term. It is *totalitarianism*. To use any lesser, diluted name is to denature reality and to misrepresent what we are talking about."[8] His appreciation was based on a factual analysis that showed the extent of control over the economy as well as over social and cultural life. It was not important to him, as it had been for Carl J. Friedrich and Zbigniew K. Brzezinski, to establish the criteria according to which the totalitarian model was identified.[9] To their static vision of the phenomenon, Malia opposed a dynamic vision that allowed one to grasp the constancy of the enterprise, despite changes in the government's methods, the abandonment of mass terror, and the withering of ideology. Thus he denounced in particular the fable of a passage from totalitarianism to authoritarianism after the death of Stalin. We should be grateful to him for recalling, without ceasing to recognize the coherence of the system, that totalitarianism was never entirely achieved in reality. He also usefully denounced the illusions of Western Sovietologists who had believed that totalitarianism could be reformed. Better still, he questioned the categories of the social sciences that had led some to find in Soviet society an opposition between an economic infrastructure and an extraneous ideological or political superstructure.

These merits are not negligible. Nevertheless, they do not make up for the fact that totalitarianism was reduced here to a product of a utopia and that Malia relied on a schema of mechanistic interpretation playfully peppered with references to Marx. "The Soviet system was an 'inverted world,'" he wrote, "a world 'standing on its head.' That is to say, it was a world where (contrary to Marx's own sociology) ideology and politics formed the 'base' of the system rather than its 'superstructure,' and where socioeconomic arrangements derived secondarily from this party base."[10] In the end, he went so far as to affirm that "in the world created by October we were never dealing in the first instance with a *society*; rather, we were always dealing with an ideocratic *regime*."[11] This last proposition leaves me perplexed. How can one conceive of a regime separate from a social organization? Or, one might as well ask, how can one conceive of a society whose internal differentiation and cohesion do not bear the mark of a formation [*mise en forme*] regulated tacitly or openly by laws or norms, a society in which an organ of power is not differentiated and set apart, whether or not it has the means of coercion at its disposal?

12

The Political and the Social

MARTIN MALIA'S ANALYSIS of the Soviet system was in some respects so close to Raymond Aron's justly celebrated one that it is worthwhile to identify the source of their divergences. According to Aron, a totalitarian regime "gives to one party the monopoly of political activity"—that is, a party armed with an immutable ideology and impervious to contestation.[1] Aron had thus already expressed Malia's later ideas of a partyocracy and an ideocracy. Nevertheless, one must recall that the Sorbonne course called "Democracy and Totalitarianism" (published in the book of the same title) had been preceded by two series of lectures on economics and class relations.[2] Aron the philosopher-sociologist was careful in the beginning of the course on democracy and totalitarianism to reestablish his trajectory, pointing out that he had not changed direction and did not intend to substitute for a unilateral determination of politics by the social or economic an opposite determination of society and the economy by the political.[3] It seemed to him impossible, though, to stop at an investigation of economic and social relations and to neglect the nature of the regime in which these relations were integrated. Justifying his new project, he indicated that the concept of the *political* [*le politique*] was used in many ways. Here I want to emphasize only one of his arguments. In a first meaning, this term designates a particular domain of the social ensemble; it delimits the source of authority, the conditions and means of its exercise, and the range of its competences. In a second meaning, the *political* refers to the social ensemble itself, for the entire collectivity is affected by conceptions of the nature of power and the mode of the exercise of government. Aron made clear not only that decisions made at the top have repercussions in all domains of social life but also that the representation of authority in the particular sector of politics circulates in some manner throughout the social ensemble. It is in this second sense that it becomes relevant to affirm a "primacy of the political," no matter the society under consideration. In other words, *regime* and *political society* are equivalent notions. "'Politics,'" Aron wrote, "is a translation of the Greek term *politeia*. Politics is essentially what the Greeks called the way in which the city is run, that is, the method of establishing command, taken as characteristic of the method by which the entire community is run."[4]

After having demonstrated the "politicization of the economy" in the Soviet Union—as Malia later did—Aron concluded, "If the Soviet economy is the outcome of a given policy, Western economy is the outcome of a political system which accepts its own limitation."[5] In truth, the last formulation does not seem to me well chosen, since the democratic principle of the limitation of politics did not derive from the establishment of a new type of government. This principle attested instead to a mutation in the symbolic order whose cause remains elusive. Liberal democracy was born from the rejection of monarchical domination, from the collectively shared discovery that power does not belong to anyone, that those who exercise it do not incarnate it, that they are only temporary trustees of public authority, that the law of God or nature is not vested in them, that they do not hold the final knowledge of the world and social orders, and that they are not capable of deciding what everyone has the right to do, think, say, and understand. On the other hand, Aron saw clearly that the distinction between the political and the nonpolitical characterizes the liberal regime, a characteristic that itself has a political signification. Its effacement or denial is a sign of the formation of a new type of society.

The Aronian analysis in no way led to dismissing analyses of economic and social facts; of class, group, and individual relations (especially with respect to a system of property); or of representations made by people in different circumstances of the legitimate and illegitimate, good and bad, and truth, falsehoods, and lies. I am not twisting Aron's thought here, for after having conceded that politics, in the limiting sense, does not determine all relations among people in the collectivity, he specified, "However, even if we do not agree with the Greek philosophers who held that human life is essentially politics, it remains true that the way in which authority is exercised, the method by which leaders are selected, contributes more than any other relation to mold personal relations."[6]

To keep to the problem posed by the nature of social relations, I would like to observe that in his chapter on the constitutive traits of the Soviet regime, Aron mentioned, first of all, "the domination of the single party and the maintenance of ideological orthodoxy of which the party is the sole interpreter"; second, "centralized planning, directed by a bureaucracy"; and third, "the existence of a bureaucratic hierarchy that constitutes a principle of discrimination within the society itself."[7] How, indeed, was the leaders' omnipotence practiced, and how did their decisions become efficacious, if they did not rely on a large social stratum and satisfy collective interests and aspirations? Referring to a principle of social discrimination, Aron showed that bureaucracy is something besides an administrative organ whose characteristics are set by the requirements of the rationalization of tasks. He furthermore thought that Soviet society was, like Western society, heterogeneous, and that the former differed from the latter only in the attempt to conceal its hierarchy and internal divisions: "A Western society is, in its essence, a class society in which groups are distinguishable, oppose each other, and compete. A Soviet-type society is composed of separate groups, all enclosed within a bureaucratic hierarchy, within a state hierarchy."[8] On the whole, although social division (by which I mean the division of groups and also of spheres of activity) is found throughout society, especially in an industrial society, "bureaucratic absolutism" looks to cancel its effects.

Is it therefore appropriate to speak of classes in Soviet society? At the beginning of his course, Aron declared, "The problem of social classes cannot be treated in the abstract as an abstract reality of the political regime. It is the political regime, that is, the constitution of power and the idea that those who govern have of their authority, which decides on one hand the existence or nonexistence of classes and above all their self-awareness."[9] *On one hand, above all*: the language was cautious. And yet, in the chapter I have cited, where he frequently spoke of bureaucratic absolutism, the step was taken: "As the whole privileged class has a feeling of solidarity with the state, the creation of centers of independent forces becomes almost impossible."[10] Aron was too conscientious a sociologist to believe that bureaucratic hierarchy in Russia came down to the small number of those who carried out orders under the direction of a supreme leader. Even so, the term *class* was addressed only in passing in

order to show the pointlessness of expecting that a stratum whose interests depended on its insertion in a state could give birth to reformers. He
lucidly remarked that "the privileged are not divided into factions which
can be compared to Western parties. It is ridiculous to imagine a party
of technicians against a party of ideologues or a party of soldiers against
a party of the police."[11]

While discerning the importance of bureaucracy as a social stratum,
the Aronian analysis did not hesitate to look for what the totalitarian
regime owed to its formation. If it is important to link the Soviet process of bureaucratization to that which developed in Western societies, we should not confuse them. Aron noted that "a bureaucrat, in the
sociological sense . . . is the representative of an anonymous order. He
does not act as a person, but as an individual defined by his function,
with a set place in the hierarchy." He then recalled that the great American companies possessed bureaucracies like Soviet public enterprises
and that it was plausible that all had reached the "Administrative Age."[12]
But the similarity between the characteristic processes of the modern
world's two species of regime was clarified in order to underscore their
contrast: "What does authorize us to speak of bureaucratic absolutism
is that the labor organizers, engineers, and managers are all part of one
administration, instead of being spread among autonomous companies,
each with its own bureaucracy."[13]

Thus Aron suggested that Soviet bureaucracy did not mark the last
step in an evolution that had already appeared in the West but that it
signaled the formation of a new kind of society in which the principle
of pluralism and the distinction between civil society and the state, constitutive of democracy, found themselves abolished. In short, bureaucracy cannot come to constitute a class in the West because it is fashioned within a society in which the dominant stratum makes room for
divergent interests and the administration of large businesses remains
distinct from state administration. On the other hand, bureaucracy became a class in the Soviet Union at the moment when, paradoxically, it
integrated itself entirely into the state.[14] To use a language that was not
Aron's, I would willingly say that one attends the double birth of a party-
state and a class-state. The imbrication of the political and the social
seems to me to be essential.

When "this unification and state control [*étatisation*] of bureaucracy"
were achieved, Aron wrote, "we find a *privileged class* composed of men

who owe everything to the state—their work and their income—and who stand to lose everything if they are dismissed or purged. There is only one way to reach important positions and it is through the state bureaucracy, with all the servility that this entails."[15] I will observe in passing that this unification and state control helps explain a phenomenon mentioned in chapter 8: the absence of resistance by the regime's cadres, notably the most prestigious military leaders, when the Great Purges took place during the 1930s. As individuals, these men were nothing; they had no power other than what they held due to their insertion in the bureaucracy.

Again, we should not forget that the unification of bureaucracy was never entirely realized or realizable. Anchored as bureaucracy was in the party, myriad satellite organizations, the state administration, enterprises, the collective farms (kolkhoz), cultural institutions, and universities, not to mention disseminated in the multiple republics of the Soviet Union, it was certainly entirely dependent on political power. Yet bureaucracy did not cease being linked in each of its parts to particular interests and being subject to local constraints. Moreover, it was undermined by rivalries that intensified, since the hierarchy never objectively stabilized. The integration of bureaucrats of all species and ranks into the state went hand in hand with a centrifugal process that obstructed the power of the supreme leader. This also helps clarify the Stalinist purges. One of their objectives was the redistribution of posts to a host of new elements. The promotion, authority, and privileges those elements acquired had the effect of welding political power and state administration. But for the operation to be possible, it was necessary for the ground to be prepared, something already outlined at the end of the 1920s with the position of the cadres—minor or important leaders who were servile and prepared to secure for the regime its social "base" while profiting from the system of state property.

Trotsky had clearly formulated the "position of the cadres" in *The Revolution Betrayed* (1936): "The notorious slogan: 'The cadres decide everything,' characterizes the nature of Soviet society far more frankly than Stalin himself could wish."[16] No doubt his mind was clouded by the idea of a bourgeois restoration, but Trotsky not only gave an incomparable description of social inequality, from which power [*pouvoir*] secretly drew its strength [*puissance*], but also went so far as to declare in a passage that, it is true, abundantly contradicted his own interpretation and in which the concept of bureaucracy slipped from one meaning to another:

> The Soviet bureaucracy has expropriated the proletariat politically in order by methods of *its own* to defend the social conquests [of the proletariat]. But the very fact that its appropriation of political power in a country where the principal means of production are in the hands of the state creates a new and hitherto unknown relation between the bureaucracy and the riches of the nation. The means of production belong to the state. But the state, so to speak, "belongs" to the bureaucracy. If these as yet wholly new relations should solidify, became the norm and be legalized, whether with or without resistance from the workers, they would, in the long run, lead to a complete liquidation of the social conquests of the proletarian revolution. But to speak of that now is at least premature.[17]

Trotsky hid from himself the truth for which he had gathered all the elements. He could have discovered that truth only by seeing the role he himself had played in the creation of a monopolistic party. The so-called conquests of the proletariat—the nationalization of land and the collective ownership of the means of production—became, in fact, those of the bureaucracy.

Although Malia's objective had been to reaffirm the primacy of the political and, in another formula, "to rehabilitate a history from above at the expense of a history from below," his work scarcely treated the changes that took place in Soviet society (given the restrictive sense he gave the term *society*). The working class and what he called the new "oligarchy" had no other history than that which transpired through decisions made at the highest levels of the party. We learn that the party was in the beginning composed of intellectuals who were then later overpowered—before being for the most part eliminated—by a mass of elements issuing from the lowest tiers of the people. However, Malia was interested only in the *regime* and its formation, rise, attrition, and final decomposition. To his understanding, the regime was reduced to a formula of government derived from a small minority's ambition to implement the Marxist theories of the dictatorship of the proletariat and of a classless society. Describing its evolution consisted essentially in showing how this ambition collided with obstacles it encountered in reality, and how each time it pushed back it gave rise to a universe of fiction, a "surreality." *The Soviet Tragedy* took events seriously; it did not disregard the slippages that occurred from the Leninism of the revolutionary period to the Leninism of the post-revolutionary period, from the later Leninism to Stalinism, and, in the Stalinist period, from the phase of the conquest of power to the phase of absolutism. Nevertheless, the concept of *unintended consequences* always provided the key to change. It was this perspective that led Malia, aston-ishingly, to ignore the February revolution. In fact, as I have indicated in chapter 5, the Bolsheviks never played any role in triggering the Feb-ruary revolution or in the sudden appearance of countless committees (factories, neighborhoods, soldiers) and the soviets. On the other hand, they profited from the withering of those committees and, during this process, from the spontaneous choices of activists looking to integrate themselves into a state apparatus—in short, the phenomenon that Marc Ferro adroitly described as a "bureaucratization from below."[18]

Malia was additionally not inclined to appreciate the effects of what Ferro called the "plebeian-ization of the party" during the early 1920s. No less surprising was Malia's analysis of the conjuncture that opened with the "second Russian revolution"—that is, forced collectivization and industrialization "full steam ahead."[19] He dedicated an entire chap-ter—"And They Built Socialism"—to this revolution in which he showed the breadth of the upheaval between 1929 and 1933 and the violence of the means that brought it about. But in that chapter, he did not consider either the support Stalin found in a fraction of the population for launch-ing his economic offensive or the rise of a social stratum benefiting from the change, and who brought to power a considerably enlarged base.

There is no doubt that, at the time, Stalin took the decisions and chose the means. Still, his power came in part from the prestige he enjoyed as leader of the party. Malia himself noted an incident that was eminently significant: Stalin declared on the twelfth anniversary of the October revolution that 1929 would be the year of a substantial turning point. One month later, his own birthday was celebrated with great ceremony, and the cult that had been centered on Lenin since his death henceforth referred to Stalin (for the first time called supreme leader). The coinci-dence among the offensive against the peasantry, the launching of the First Five-Year Plan, and the first signs of the idolatry of Stalin was not fortuitous. The staging [*mise en scène*] of an infallible power incarnated in the person of its leader signaled an enslaving of minds that unquestionably surpassed the circle of the party's petty tyrants. The terrifying initiative of expropriating the peasants—ending with millions of victims massacred, reduced to famine, or deported—leaves the observer stupefied. How can one imagine that this initiative had not mobilized a great deal more than small militarized groups under the orders of the general secretary or fanatics dedicated to making Marxist doctrine triumph? As for the politics of industrialization, if it had been decided on high and accompanied by an unprecedented exploitation of labor, how can one still imagine that it did not benefit from the assistance of part of the working class, whether newcomers to industry or elements who had abandoned all hope in collective resistance and were henceforth more preoccupied with their own destinies than class solidarity?

Malia noted in passing that "whereas Stalin's collectivization was an unrelieved disaster for the country, his industrialization drive—for all its inordinate cost, brutality, and wastefulness—was a significant historical accomplishment. It was indeed the Soviet experiment's only real achievement."[20] Why this success? one might ask. He added, "It was a source of genuine pride for much of the urban population . . . it endowed the country with a bare bones modernity that irreversibly transformed peasant Russia into an urban society, or at least the simulacrum of an urban society. And, finally, it was the supreme feat of Bolshevik voluntarism."[21] Despite the last proposition, which stressed the *revolution from above*, we glimpse here one of the reasons for the enterprise's success: part of the population adhered to Stalin's policies because they satisfied expectations from below. That adherence represented *possibilities* already designed in a universe where all on-ramps to positions of authority and material advantages passed by way of insertion into a sector of the bureaucracy. While it is difficult to discern the motives for this adherence, undoubtedly, at an extreme, it merged with resignation about changes from then on taken as irreversible. It furthermore fed on fascination for mechanization and modern products, and it satisfied ambitions for authority and appetites for privilege. Although signs of them had appeared in preceding years, a great disturbance in society, a mixing of conditions, and a deployment of new hierarchies accompanied the collectivization of lands and the whirlwind unleashed by industrialization.

Few testimonials are as precious in this respect as Ante Ciliga's, whose convictions led him in 1926 to Russia, where he stayed until 1933.[22] When I learned of his book *The Russian Enigma*, at the end of the 1940s, I glimpsed for the first time the conjunction between what Ferro later called bureaucratization from above and bureaucracy from below, between the power of the party and the aspirations of new social categories. Thoroughly aware of the drama unfolding in the countryside, Ciliga did not hide the consequences. "The new economy," he wrote, "upset all routine, elevated the lowest levels of the population, and absorbed part of them into the administrative staff. For a middle peasant it was an undeniable rise in the world to become president of the kolkhoz, or even a brigade- or field-leader. Vast possibilities of action rose before him and his organizing faculties were developed."[23] Likewise, he described the accession of a few workers to positions of authority and their rupture from the milieu in which they had been raised. Recalling his students at the university in Leningrad (where he briefly taught) who were supposed to form "the elite of the proletariat," Ciliga noted their careerism and even their cynicism, especially their indifference to the lot of workers suffering from hunger in the city during the terrible winter of 1929/1930, while the students never lacked anything.[24] He pointed out the satisfaction they felt in parroting official slogans about the sacrifices necessary for the construction of socialism. Ciliga's judgment on his students was telling: "By their social position and their ideology, they were identified with the bureaucracy. In the end I was forced to accept the belief that they represented not a workers' elite, but a 'young guard' of bureaucracy."[25] The itinerary of Victor Kravchenko—son of a revolutionary worker, singled out by Sergo Ordzhonikidze, and a brilliant student who became director of a combine before "choosing freedom"—accurately fulfilled this description.[26]

Rather than worrying about testimonials of this kind, Malia was not afraid to write that "defense was not the primary motive at the outset of industrialization; that motive clearly was to put an industrial and proletarian 'base' under the existing 'superstructure' of the party, and thereby make the party viable within the country as the vehicle for building socialism."[27] He must have been so preoccupied with his relentless discrediting of Marxism that he uncovered a *proletarian infrastructure* where a new class came to secure its foundation in the regime. The interpretation is even more disconcerting since Malia in no way concealed the reinforcement of labor exploitation, the fettering of the worker to the factory through the institution of the work registry, the establishment of wage labor, and the birth of a frankly inegalitarian discourse. Nor did he hide the new modes of social discrimination, even repeating Stalin's 1935 slogan whose significance Trotsky had grasped: "The cadres decide everything." Malia went so far as to decide that "this system could give rise to a veritable caste."[28]

Caste? Malia appropriated a concept introduced by Trotsky and popular in the literature of the Fourth International. The use of this term had not prevented the author of *The Revolution Betrayed* from thoroughly analyzing the component elements of bureaucracy in the various Soviet republics and from evaluating the stratum on which the party and the high administration of the state depended—12 to 15 percent, if not 15 to 20 percent, of the population, if one counted the beneficiaries of privileges that set them apart from the masses (supplementary remuneration, access to vacation spots, hospitals, rest homes, cultural centers, and sport associations).[29] Although he had previously spoken of a new caste, Trotsky underscored the great characteristic of the bureaucracy: not to appear as a class. To his understanding, its members could convert their de facto condition into a publicly recognized status only by reestablishing private property. They took care not to do this out of fear that the proletariat would mobilize to defend social gains. That is to say, this interpretation (which Cornelius Castoriadis showed so well in one of his first important texts in *Socialisme ou Barbarie*) derived from the refusal to admit that the collective ownership of the means of production could cover up an appropriation of surplus value by a minority of the population.[30] At least Trotsky made his readers aware of the contradictions in which he caught himself. On the other hand, with Malia, the concept of caste was deprived of all sociological meaning and used instead to evoke a system of discrimination founded on an ideocracy that took the place of religion. This was, indeed, a strange rapprochement at the very moment when the aforementioned ideocracy was supposed to have derived from an egalitarian utopia.

I would not dream of substituting the concept of bureaucracy for that of "partyocracy." After 1947, Trotsky's analysis seemed to me vitiated not only by its representation of the collective ownership of the means of production and the fetishization of new economic institutions but also by its representation of the party, the fetishization of an organization that had constituted, no matter its founders' intentions, the matrix of a totalitarian regime. Thus my claim is not, by calling attention to the process of bureaucratization carried out in the depths of the social, to minimize the function of the party in the creation of a new form of society. Rather, the dislocation of organs coming out of the revolution of 1917, the convergence of currents of activists under the attraction of a single pole of authority, and the subsequent establishment of new social discriminations—these became possible only because the Bolshevik Party appeared as a party altogether different from others and as the embryo of a new state.

13

An Intentional Movement

I HAVE ALREADY SUGGESTED the term *intentionality* to clarify that the rise of Communism was neither accidental nor due to the will of a small number of Marxist prophets who imparted their belief to the masses and mobilized them. One must instead situate the rise of Communism at a conjuncture where the destabilization of a system of domination in place for centuries made a historical alternative possible. Could this intentionality be detected in the observation that Communism tended to represent fully what democracy keeps in check? At the source of democracy can be found the rejection of a number of things: power detached from the social ensemble, law that governs an immutable order, and a spiritual authority possessing knowledge of the ultimate ends of human conduct and of the community. However, it is not enough to say *at the source of democracy*: this rejection has been democracy's permanent driving energy. A force of negativity inhabits it. Largely under the influence of this negativity, the image of a people emerges whose sovereignty is actualized in the will of the majority; the power of an immense state administration with a constantly expanding capacity for control is constructed; and an increasingly advanced integration of human activities takes place in a society subject to changes that seem to escape human willpower. Tocqueville had already observed the link established in a democracy between the development of freedoms and the development of anonymous powers such as the people, public opinion, the state, or society (the last, as I indicated in chapter 7, had barely been envisaged in the past, when men lived in a milieu dominated by relations of personal dependence such as the guild, commune, seigneury, or kingdom). Tocqueville failed only to grasp the force—capital—that was going to bring an entirely new stability to what he called *social power*. In sum, what democracy keeps in check is both the unleashing of the forces it enables to emerge and the danger of their conjunction.

Should one therefore think, in the spectacle of the Soviet regime once it attained maturity during the 1930s, that Communism captured currents borne by democratic society and provided them a singular outlet? The new regime had the following distinctive characteristics: an actualization of the will of the people, confused as it was with the proletariat in the unrivaled organ of the directing party; the constitution of a unanimous opinion; the fusion of political power with state power; the integration of all domains of activity and knowledge through norms handed down by the party and, consequently, the blurring of the boundaries between the political and the nonpolitical; and, finally, the imposition of a universal model of organization together with a model for incorporating individuals into "multiple collectives" to be linked together within the great society. Could one object that Communism destroyed capitalism? Certainly. For although the hypothesis of state capitalism is tempting, it hardly seems tenable. As Aron and Trotsky before him correctly noted, it is futile to separate capitalist development from the existence of a market that involves both competition among entrepreneurs and the preservation of free labor. Still, one cannot ignore the fact that the new regime involved a scission between the ownership of the means of production and the labor power at the origin of modern capitalism. In a sense, the regime aggravated this scission, since the majority of the population, deprived of all means of resistance, became subjugated to the authority of those who, at different rungs of the hierarchy, participated in the management of the economic system.

Placing Communism against the backdrop of modernity does not, however, give us grounds to conclude that totalitarianism rose up from within democracy. Identifying the processes by which each tended toward a standardization of human conduct does not lead one to conclude that, as if by a natural inclination of democracy, their convergence could establish a new form of political society. I have recalled that the idea of such an inclination is found in Tocqueville. But besides the fact that he abandoned that hypothesis, the democratic despotism he imagined did not resemble Communism. It is an inescapable fact that Communism, whether one considers the new structure of the party or that of the regime, took root in Russia (moreover, its second home was China). Russia was a country where democratic institutions and mores had not taken root and where the introduction of modern capitalism, regardless of the intensity of its development in limited sectors, had not altered the general physiognomy of society. It is true that the dictatorship of the Bolshevik Party had been preceded by the formation of a government responding to the wishes of a liberal elite, and by a revolution that gave birth to multiple autonomous organs. However, the incapacity of that elite to implement political reforms and the failure of the popular revolution were signs of a social state in which the ideas of limited political power, a civil life independent of the state, and rights to oppose the power of the sovereign had not matured and spread. For its part, Bolshevism inherited an autocracy, an omnipresent bureaucratic administration, and customs of servitude—all of which severely inhibited the development of modern industry and a bourgeois stratum. One does not need to fall back on the fiction of a continuity between tsarism and Bolshevism to gauge the considerable burden brought to bear by such an inheritance on institutions emerging immediately after the revolution as well as on the mentalities of those who created those institutions and those who submitted to them. I have said (chapters 5 and 6) that in this way the Russian Revolution is not comparable to the French Revolution. They differed as much as did the respective old regimes of both countries. By using the term *Old Regime*, one thus risks conflating two different forms of society. In both cases, the fate of the revolution was to some extent guided by the nature of the regime it destroyed.

In a chapter of *The Soviet Tragedy* discussed earlier—"And Why in Russia First?"—Malia disputed the validity of a contrast between Russia and Europe. To his understanding, such a contrast led one to conceive of Europe as a "fixed geographical entity" that was homogeneous. In fact, Europe had seen many changes of a structural order since the Middle Ages, and in the twentieth century it remained divided between countries of the West and East.[1] This perspective allowed Malia to treat in an offhand way the thesis of Oriental despotism or an Asiatic mode of production. Nevertheless, Malia's scruples as a historian led him to demonstrate the very opposition between Russia and Europe that he had denied. At one point, he mentioned the transformation of the hereditary nobility into a "service gentry" after the sixteenth century and the reduction of peasants to the status of serfs attached to the land and trapped in subsistence living. He wrote that Russia "has always been quite separate and apart from Europe or the West," while adding, to be sure, that it extended to a part of Central Europe beyond the Elbe.[2] But this qualification did not add up to much, since the distinction between two historical schemas of development had always been formulated by taking Western Europe as a reference point. Furthermore, this distinction was fully illustrated in a passage that confirmed the views of Marx, Weber, and Karl Wittfogel: "Until well into the nineteenth century there were, in effect, only two classes in Russia, or at least only two that mattered. There was the service gentry (*dvoriantsvo*), which constituted 2 percent of the population, and the peasantry, which until the 1890s was roughly 95 percent. The gentry possessed most of the wealth, monopolized all privileges, staffed the state bureaucracy, officered the military forces, and dominated culture."[3] Malia drew a specific conclusion from this balance sheet: "The introduction of the post–French revolutionary concept of democracy into such a society could only have a devastating effect."[4]

No doubt one might balk at the idea of an Asiatic mode of production in Russia or, more exactly, a semi-Asiatic one, since this was the term used by Marxists to describe autocratic systems. One might furthermore object to the interpretation of Wittfogel, who thought he had detected in Oriental despotism the expression of a "hydraulic society" (whose constitution stemmed from the necessity of huge irrigation projects and the control of water that alone could provide large-scale manpower and a state bureaucracy).[5] Yet, more important than how one defined a type of society unprecedented in Western history was its identification as a form of society in which the resources of the dominant class came from an integration into the state, and their authority—the stability of their prerogatives—from their submission to a monarch endowed with a sacred power. Malia reminded us that the idea of an Oriental despotism had already appeared in antiquity with Herodotus, who had applied it to Persia. It also appeared in Montesquieu's comparative analysis of political systems. Malia might also have pointed out that, before Montesquieu, Machiavelli had contrasted despotism in which a master had only land and his subjects at his disposal (the Ottoman model) with European monarchs whose strength remained limited by that of their lords (the French model). No one believes that the discovery of the idea of Oriental despotism dates to the nineteenth century, but its antiquity does not discredit it. It becomes fecund, however, only if the sometimes considerable differences among societies fashioned by despotism are not erased. It is true that Malia noted that in Russia the land and its inhabitants were not the property of the sovereign: "Autocracy had been in theory an extreme form of despotism; it recognized the existence of noble property and a small class of merchants. Furthermore, the state apparatus was not very developed and did not directly govern most of the population. The peasants, as serfs, broadly governed themselves in communes or were under the control of nobles. The state played absolutely no economic role other than the classic one of levying taxes."[6] Although fair, these reservations cannot make us overlook the fact that the system was arranged in such a way that, in spite of market activity and aristocratic property, the interests of the bourgeoisie and the nobles were never able to assert themselves against the state. The weight of the autocracy and the efficiency of the bureaucracy not only were gauged by the effective interference of government agents in the minutiae of social life, but also were found in the inhibition or restriction of initiatives capable of setting in motion dynamics escaping state control. If it is thus meaningless to speak of a proto-totalitarianism in the time of tsarism, it does make sense to detect a despotico-bureaucratic social formation underpinning the Communist regime.

It is astonishing that Malia, after having rightly reproached Western Sovietologists for persistently interpreting the evolution of the Communist system according to categories taken from their own experience of the world, proved in turn susceptible to a kind of Eurocentrism. He did underscore the distinctive political, economic, and social characteristics of the empire constructed by Peter the Great, but always with the intention of showing a process of *Westernization*. He did not hesitate to call this process a "revolution from above" whose objectives, after having been basically military (the goal being to rival the great European monarchies), became economic, political, and cultural: "The pattern of revolution from above as the response of backward Russia to the challenge of the West would be maintained down to the end of the Old Regime in 1917."[7] Thus Malia went so far as to attribute the collapse of the Old Regime to its powerlessness facing the challenge of a Europe that never stopped advancing while Russia tended to play catch-up. This was the case because the abrupt imposition of change encountered considerable difficulties: "More and more, the resources of society had to be mobilized by society itself, which eventually took over the task of modernization from the state."[8] (Let me mention in passing that this judgment became more nuanced when Malia considered the social upheaval brought about by World War I and thus introduced the hypothesis that in the war's absence the regime might have experienced a liberal evolution.)

"Revolution from above": the same formulation thus characterized the tsarist enterprise and, as it was led by Lenin, Stalin, and their successors, the Communist enterprise. Yet we learn that the latter no longer had modernization as its driving energy; it tended instead toward the realization of the Marxist utopia that was derived from the philosophy of the Enlightenment. In truth, the last phrase I cited could have led to an entirely different conclusion: since society proved too weak to take over the reigns of the revolution directed by the state, the Bolshevik Party could seize them. But Malia wanted to establish a break between the old and new regimes and thus to distinguish the traces of Westernization on two different paths. On the whole, what Bolshevism borrowed from the West were not the methods that ensured its success but the myths it had produced—notably, the myth of equality. Following the alternative conclusion that the party seized the reigns of revolution from society, one could, however, certainly recognize Bolshevism's Russian filiation. Since the mid-nineteenth century, Malia tells us, the Russian intelligentsia had been fascinated by the theories of European, especially French, revolutionary thinkers. The more destructive these theories became, the more Russian intellectuals found themselves excluded from all participation in public affairs. Thus did two revolutions "from above" go their separate ways.

In Russia, the Social Democrats and the Bolsheviks themselves did not, nevertheless, ignore the problem posed by a proletarian revolution in a society they judged economically backward and subjugated to despotism. They repeatedly identified the structure of society as an Asiatic or semi-Asiatic mode of production or an Oriental despotism—definitions that invited comparisons of Russian history with Chinese or Indian history. Wittfogel emphasized, in particular, Georgy Plekhanov's influence in debates leading up to the Stockholm Congress of 1906. Plekhanov had opposed the Leninist project of land nationalization, objecting that it risked leading to an Asiatic restoration.[9] Lenin took this argument into consideration for a long time. Until 1916, he made room for the concept of the Asiatic mode of production or *asiatchina*—the latter term more generally designating a kind of civilization. The important fact was that Lenin, in the last period of his life—that is, after the Kronstadt revolt—drew attention to the danger posed by the development of a bureaucracy whose mind-set remained precapitalist. There again, he made new use of the concept of *asiatchina*. In the mid-1920s, as Wittfogel reported, David Ryazanov and the economist Eugene Varga paid new attention to Marx's work on Asiatic society.[10] For his part, Trotsky published in *Pravda* in 1922 a study called the "Peculiarities of Russia's Historical Development." He took up those arguments in the first chapter of his *History of the Russian Revolution* (1934) and republished the earlier article as an appendix to the first volume of that book.[11] His observations on the comparative development of European and Russian cities since the end of the Middle Ages were remarkable. So, too, was his treatment of the weakness of the privileged classes in Russia (a phenomenon that justified comparisons to China and India) and of the reduction of the clergy to a civil service. No doubt the theoretician of "combined development" supported the idea that the destruction of the old and already decaying medieval edifice made possible a revolution so radical that "in the course of a few months [it] placed the proletariat and the Communist Party in power."[12] Yet, taking issue with historians interested only in the progress of industry since the beginning of the century, he noted that "backwardness . . . continued not only up to the moment of liquidation of the old Russia, but as her legacy up to the present day."[13]

As is well known, Marx began a debate that troubled socialist theoreticians until the imposition of Stalinist dogma in 1931. His interest in an Asiatic mode of production, or a type he called Oriental despotism, emerged several years after the publication of *The Communist Manifesto* and became prevalent after 1853. If it is plausible that reading Montesquieu and Hegel prompted him, it is certain that the account of François Bernier, who had traveled in the Middle East and India during the seventeenth century, and the work of classical economists from Adam Smith to John Stuart Mill convinced him of the existence of a stagnant universe—in other words, societies whose common characteristic, despite their differences, was to keep in check any danger of social opposition. It would be beyond my interest here to describe the oscillations in Marx's thought examined by Wittfogel and Miklós Molnar, though I would point out, following Molnar, that the theoretical problem Marx confronted was combined with a political problem.

It was indeed during the period when he discovered and explored the Asiatic mode of production and Oriental despotism—phenomena problematizing his conception of history as progressive accumulation—that Marx developed a passionate interest in international relations, both British colonial policies and Russian expansion (the two subjects were linked, since the United Kingdom was accused of playing into Russia's hands).[14] Molnar demonstrated that Marx grasped all situations in terms of the chances they gave to European revolution. Thus, despite his concern to denounce British exactions in India, Marx determined that colonialism ultimately had positive effects, since only the influx of foreign capital could allow colonized countries, especially India, to escape stagnation.[15] Russia seemed such a threat to Europe that from 1853 to 1856 he tended to emphasize an antagonism between barbaric Russia and the civilized West, believing that the fate of the proletarian revolution depended on its outcome. He reformulated this belief in 1867, declaring that "there is only one alternative left for Europe. Asiatic barbarism under Muscovite leadership burst over her head like an avalanche, or she must restore Poland, thus placing between herself and Asia twenty million heroes and gaining breathing-time for the accomplishment of her social regeneration."[16] It is true that Marx amended his judgment after the abolition of serfdom and then again when he learned of the progress of the Russian socialist movement and its rallying to the International. Additionally, the success of his works in Russian revolutionary circles and his contacts with revolutionary leaders, notably Vera Zasulich, led him to imagine the possibility that "the Russian Revolution becomes the signal for a proletarian revolution in the West"—a claim made in the 1882 Russian edition of *The Communist Manifesto*.[17] He even admitted that the rural peasant communities could offer a base of operations for socialism. Nevertheless, his doubts, like those of Engels, lingered until the end. As Molnar observed in a meticulous analysis, "If certain of our two authors' writings expressed the hope of seeing a revolution, even a 'tremendous and inevitable social revolution,' explode in Russia, they never envisioned that this revolution's path toward socialism could be brought about in an autonomous fashion."[18] Molnar wanted to say, first, that a revolution in Russia could not achieve its ultimate goal without the support of European revolution, which in any case the Bolsheviks later admitted before Stalin imposed his thesis of socialism in one country. But Molnar's point was also that Marx never stopped making a full development of productive forces, possible only in capitalist societies, one condition of the emergence of socialism.

Thus, in the early twentieth century, theoreticians of the proletarian revolution referred to Marx when they assessed the situation in Russia. Boris Souvarine suggested that Lenin was particularly attentive in his early writings to the specificity of the Russian world. He wrote in one article, "Hopeless poverty, ignorance, inequality, and the humiliation of the peasant give our whole regime an Asiatic stamp." Tsarism seemed to him "the most powerful rampart of European reaction . . . and of Asiatic reaction," and he portrayed Russia as "a state politically enslaved in which 99 percent of the population is completely perverted by political servility."[19] According to Souvarine, from whom I take these citations, the picture Lenin painted clarified his project of constructing an organization that would oblige men to liberate themselves from their servitude. Lenin therefore appeared as a leader at once lucid and blind. On the one hand, he knew how to reappropriate Marx's statement that "the tradition of all the dead generations weighs like a nightmare on the brain of the living"; on the other, he did not foresee the consequences of a politics that entrusted to a small group of professional revolutionaries the task of motivating and leading the masses. One could say of both Lenin and Trotsky (the latter being the first to conceptualize the notion of combined development, which permitted bypassing the stage of bourgeois democracy) that they concealed what they knew, or even that what they knew did not diminish their attraction to governing men with an iron hand. Theirs was a revolutionary government, of course, but one determined not to give way to unbridled desires for freedom.

As early as 1918, Karl Kautsky, for a time the uncontested heir to Marx and Engels, was the first to denounce this sham dictatorship of the proletariat born of a despotic regime and suddenly empowered with the capacity to create a socialist society. In 1931, confronting the first developments of Stalin's reign, his judgment was fully formed:

> A characteristic of the Russian aristocracy was the contempt shown by its representatives for the people over whom they ruled, and whom they knew only as trembling slaves without any will of their own. For this reason the rulers continually imagined that they could equal or even surpass rich and powerful Western Europe, by adopting technical methods without that freedom which alone made the

success of the pioneers and organizers possible, and which alone encouraged the existence of those hard-working, efficient, and highly skilled workers on whom the superior technique and economic organization of the West are based. Not one of the autocrats who desired to give Russia a superior position in the world, from Peter the Great to Lenin and Stalin, has realized this.[20]

To some extent, this judgment fits well with Malia's, who had questioned whether Soviet society had ever successfully become a modern society. Kautsky, however, differed radically, since for him it was the contempt for freedoms and not the utopia of equality that lay at the origin of the Soviet adventure and its failure.

We would be led up a blind alley if we looked to tsarism for anticipatory signs of totalitarianism or to totalitarianism for signs of a restoration or rebirth of despotism. The rupture between the old and new regimes was obvious. Still, one must admit that, in the passage from one to the other, the principle of limitless domination persisted. Yet Malia neglected or underestimated this fact, since he found in the establishment of a totalitarian system only the "unintended consequence," however unavoidable, of applying Marxist theory or, more generally, of executing a utopia specific to Western democracy.

The history of Communism cannot be deciphered by focusing only on Russia. That much is obvious. All the same, that history took shape in a certain place in the world and bore its marks. Observing the spectacle of postrevolutionary France, Tocqueville had called attention to the lasting effect of the absolutist state and its administrative centralization on institutions and mentalities. Edgar Quinet, witness to a new Bonapartism, observed even more severely, "What we call order, in other words, obedience to a master and peace in the arbitrary, is for us carved in stone and infallibly reborn from itself and from immemorial tradition. Order thus understood is protected by the centuries; its antiquity labors for and secures it."[21] Both Tocqueville and Quinet exaggerated: the French monarchy had never been a despotism; it had been supported by an edifice of rights with the help of a theologico-political elaboration. Although the king had turned his back on this edifice, he had never destroyed it. Reading them today, one has the impression that Tocqueville and Quinet had been speaking of Russia. Yet, although carried away by their judgments, they bore witness to a sensibility that exemplifies the persistence of the past in the present and the attachment of history to place. Shortly after the revolution, Russia revealed the inheritance of a political system and a culture that had never made room for rights. The October insurrection and subsequent events showed the will of the Bolsheviks to exercise an exorbitant power and, at the same time, make it appear.

Marc Ferro pointedly observed that we need to pay attention not only to the attack on the provisional government but even more so to Lenin's move to immediately deprive the Petrograd soviet—the only organ capable of claiming legitimate power—of paternity of the new regime. Instead, he attributed that paternity to the defense committee put in place by the party.[22] The Constituent Assembly was not even allowed to debate its role and possible dissolution; its members, as I mentioned in chapters 6 and 8, were evicted by armed men the day they met for the first time. No less remarkable were the conditions under which the tsar and his relatives were executed. The new masters of power amassed all symbols that marked the end of the tsarist era and the emergence of a state of law. The French had launched a trial against the king that was also a trial against the monarchy; the Americans had risen up against the English in the name of the same rights the English themselves had demanded; and the English, in their own revolution, had solemnly executed Charles I after accusing him of having attacked the monarchical institution in wanting to destroy the link that tied it organically to Parliament. On each of these occasions, the idea of law was in play, whether the advent or the restoration of its rule. Could we say that the Russian Revolution was not bourgeois and that, led by the Bolsheviks who relied on the landless, worker, and peasant masses, it gave free reign to a limitless violence? But this would be to overlook the fact that in a first phase of the revolution such violence was accompanied by the creation of institutions, such as the soviets, that claimed legitimacy. It would also be to overlook the considerable resistance to the Bolsheviks' monopolization of power—a resistance by Mensheviks, revolutionary socialists, anarchists, union sections, and groups of workers in the large factories. These groups demanded the guarantee of fundamental freedoms within the framework of socialism. It is true they proved powerless in the face of a dictatorship that exploited the support of a fraction of the population and that won over those who saw careers for themselves in the framework of state organizations. Nevertheless, it is a myth that the Bolsheviks were the only radical revolutionaries. Should anarchists be taken as moderates? Could one say that the *worker opposition* that materialized within the party was not as committed as the party leadership to pursuing revolution? Once more, the facts have been misrepresented by the Communists.

Bolshevism marked a rupture with the principles that drove the ensemble of revolutionary movements. This rupture becomes clear when one observes the methods of the new party, its idealization of violence, and its plan to seize power—all of which had something in common with a specifically Russian terrorist tradition, even if, it is true, the Bolsheviks repudiated it. Souvarine seems to me again to have been one of the first to bring attention to the genealogy of Bolshevism. In the conclusion to his brief analysis of the anarchist *Revolutionary Catechism* (1866), as prepared by Mikhail Bakunin, he wrote, "No résumé can give any idea of the tone of cold hatred and explicit cynicism of the famous anonymous *Catechism*, which *no study of the origins of Bolshevism can afford to neglect.*"[23] He evoked the figure of Sergey Nechayev, who "was the first genuine 'practitioner' of subversive organization in Russia, and the first *professional revolutionary* for whom the desired ends justified the use of any means."[24] In the groups formed around 1875 by Petr Tkachev, a populist converted to Jacobinism, Souvarine saw the idea of a coup d'état affirmed for the first time, a coup that would be the "work of a conscious minority" requiring "a centralized, carefully chosen, disciplined, and hierarchical party."[25] He then cited Tkachev, who had declared that "the people, deprived of leaders, is not fit to build up a new world on the ruins of the old" and that, in contrast, this role and vision belonged exclusively to a revolutionary minority.[26] Souvarine determined that Tkachev's small group heralded terrorism and the future Bolshevism. He emphasized the history of the first socialist and revolutionary party in Russia, Land and Freedom (Zemlya i volya), which already possessed a central committee, sections, and a military organ and which multiplied attacks and fomented conspiracies (including one that cost Lenin's brother his life).[27]

It is scarcely necessary to explain that Souvarine in no way underestimated Bolshevism's originality. However, relating it to the succession of conspiratorial and terrorist groups that marked the second half of the nineteenth century also makes us recognize how Bolshevism differed. Coming out of social democracy and claiming the Marxist legacy, it broke with a long tradition of populism. Its primary objective was the organization and mobilization of the Russian working class, which it saw as destined for the same future as the working classes in the West. Its ultimate objective (no matter how it was achieved, either following the footsteps of "bourgeois revolution" or at the end of its development) was the installation of a dictatorship of the proletariat, the prelude to a classless society. But this obvious and indisputable filiation is inadequate to explain Leninism's great innovation: it seized a doctrine and converted it into a *body of ideas* and, simultaneously, required militants to have a discipline of action that made them members of a *collective body*. This action made it break with the Social Democratic tradition. Thus the search for the component elements of Bolshevism—the nucleus of the future totalitarian state—leads one to consider it the product of an extraordinary condensation of heterogeneous processes that coexisted in the same space and at the same time.

14

The Party Above All

I T IS FIRST OF ALL the methods, organizational machinery, and program perfected by Lenin that draw one's attention. But these factors
alone do not enable us to appreciate the event that constituted the birth
of a new type of party and then its transformation into a party-state.
The first critics of Leninism saw in the institution of democratic centralism the danger of a dictatorship of a supreme leader over the ensemble
of militants, a danger that magnified the danger of the party's dictatorship over the proletariat. Nevertheless, they could still only guess that
something besides a tyrannical power was emerging: a recasting of social relations related to the representation of a unified mass of people
whose harmful elements had been removed. It was only after the fact,
with the spectacle of a society restructured by Stalinism, that certain of
Bolshevism's distinctive traits—the strict separation between members
of the party and all those, even sympathizers, outside it; the claim to circumscribe within the boundaries of the organization access to the truth
of revolutionary doctrine; the resulting certainty of an alternative that
left no other choice but to join the army of the proletariat or be catego-
rized as an opportunist, petit bourgeois, or even traitor; the idealization
of the party, the representation of a collective being above militants and
leaders themselves and, at the same time, including them—emerged in
all their significance. This last trait was perhaps the most remarkable:
even when he held all the means of power, Stalin would remain, as Lenin
before him, an executor of the party's will.

The mythology of the revolution, one might observe, was not born
with Bolshevism, but Bolshevism was at the origin of the mythology
of the party. The revolution became, so to speak, embodied. To want

to be a revolutionary was henceforth to admit that nothing was possible or thinkable outside the party. The Social Democrats had said that "the safety of the revolution is the supreme law."[1] These were Georgy Plekhanov's words at the Stockholm Congress in 1906. Even he considered, once the proletariat was in power and if circumstances required it, the hypothesis of limiting the political rights of minorities hostile to the regime. After October, one might recall, Lenin used another formula: "The party above all." Thus it was supposed to incarnate the supreme law while possessing exclusive knowledge about the march of history.

Undeniably, from the initial structure of the party to the structure of the society that emerged during the 1930s, much more was involved than a change of scale. However, the system of representations that governed the party likewise governed society. All seemed, step by step, organizable and incorporable. The model of a society without divisions made its presence felt. This society was not expected to include any opposition among class interests once the old mode of production had been destroyed. Political power and state power were merged. The notion of a civil life was wiped out, as were differences of principle among modes of human activity and paths to knowledge. Each person had to give proof of the so-called Communist spirit and place himself in the framework of a general mobilization in the service of common ends.

15

Disincorporation and Reincorporation of Power

H ISTORIANS WHO DO NOT HESITATE to recognize Communism as a totalitarian system nevertheless tend to view it as the result of political will. Yet this system eludes all purely political (in the strict sense of the term) analysis, just as it escapes purely economic or sociological analysis. How, indeed, would one delimit the element of political action where political boundaries were obliterated together with the boundaries of law, economy, social organization, and mores? To speak of politics' encroachment on all areas of existence is still to give in to the idea of a hypertyranny, a hyperdictatorship, or a hyperdespotism, even if these references are ultimately found wanting. Yet it is necessary to recall that the power of the tyrant does not undermine society in its depths. It looms over and threatens, being exercised in an arbitrary fashion. The power of the dictator in modern societies is established as a result of exceptional circumstances: when the interests of the dominant strata can no longer be maintained by peaceful means. The dictator thus secures from his intervention the semblance of legitimacy (usually the army, the alleged guarantor of the nation's integrity, secures this legitimacy). The power of the despot is placed beneath the higher rule of God or the gods. In Russia, the tsar had heaven above him; whereas the earth, of which he was the sovereign possessor, gave his subjects the feeling of a perennial natural order. Communist power was entirely different. It was anchored in a collective organ on which all institutions and bonds among individuals and groups depended. Or, more exactly, that organ was supposed to bring those institutions and bonds to life and, by the same token (to use a term completely foreign to Communist vocabulary), be their soul.

It is tempting to contrast appearance and reality. We might observe that, far from being abolished, the distance separating those who command from those who obey was evident inside the party itself and throughout the reach of society. The ruling organ, with an entirely new species of master at its helm, monopolized public speech as well as the means of decision, coercion, and information. Furthermore, the position of the leader was exhibited at all the echelons of the hierarchy. However, merely opposing the regime's effective truth to its appearance risks underestimating the effectiveness of representation and not seeing how it shapes behavior. We touch here one of the most difficult points in reflection on Communism. In one sense, we can speak of a symbolic effectiveness; in another sense, of an expropriation of or a hold on the imaginary. These two terms—*symbolic* and *imaginary*—seem to contradict each other. However, the symbolic makes us recognize the instauration of a system in which settled relations among groups and individuals are articulated, and in which shared notions of the real, true, and normal are established. The imaginary makes us understand that the vision of the One is supported by a frantic denial of social division and depends on a phantasm. If language fails us in characterizing the totalitarian phenomenon, is it not because that phenomenon leads to the limit of the nameable? How, indeed, can one be satisfied with the notion of a phantasm when faced with a system of institutions through which men discover the terms of their insertion into a shared life framework? And how can one hold onto the notion of a symbolic order when access to a language allowing each person to name the distance separating him from others and to form an idea of the law beyond the factual constraints to which he is submitted—when access to such a language is blocked? The enigma of the Communist totalitarian system that confronts us certainly does not disappear, but it at least becomes more specific if one sees in it a new mode of domination that blurs the opposition between the dominating and the dominated or, more generally, between *top* and *bottom* and that simultaneously effaces the principle of a separation among the *sites* where action, knowledge, and imagination are practiced in testing limits. Such domination tended toward a petrification of the social in its depths or toward a kind of closing [*bouclage*] of the social around itself, even though that domination was accompanied by a discourse on the creation of a new world and a new man (notably thanks to the demonstration of record industrial production) and by incessant calls for the mobilization of collective energies.

To some extent, the phenomenon escapes the perspective of the historian, sociologist, or economist. Its causes are not precisely localizable. Neither the scope of changes nor the recasting of social relations can be gauged only by examining either government methods—the scale of its coercive means and the doctrine it professes—or the system of property or even new forms of social discrimination. It is inadequate to speak of a turning point in history or a detour in the path pursued by modern society—for as much as we can reconstruct the past over the long term, that past included many other digressions. After all, wanting to define the new model according to several well-chosen criteria, in order to situate it within a typology of the modern world's characteristic regimes, runs the risk of concealing the profundity of the rupture it introduced.

At one point in *Democracy and Totalitarianism*, Raymond Aron gave in briefly to the temptation of typology and even of relativism. Nonetheless, he estimated that the difference between the regime of the monopolistic party and the constitutional-pluralist regime was "essential." That difference pertained not only to lifestyle and modes of governing but also to "the very modality of community."[1] Perhaps one should go further and ask if the totalitarian regime did not undermine what had previously appeared as the very foundation of political society. It is indisputable that one of the distinctive characteristics of the totalitarian regime was the party's monopolization of the means of coercion, information, and indoctrination. Be that as it may, to stop with this characteristic is once again to avoid a question: Was this not the very first time that the dimension of the Other found itself, if not abolished (how could it be?), then at least effaced? The question deserves to be asked as soon as one considers the power the directing organ and its leader had at their disposal. Still, in order to address it, we must acknowledge that, no matter the society considered, there is no power that comes down to domination and the control of a state whose distinctive trait would be the monopoly on legitimate violence (to borrow Weber's formula). Pole of authority, agent of society's cohesion, reducer of its real or virtual conflicts—power is simultaneously guarantor of a law that surpasses communally respected rules and of a permanence that does not derive from the simple factual coexistence of groups sharing the same territory, usually the same language, and linked by reciprocal obligations stemming from the imperatives of a common life. The delimitation of a site of power bears witness to and represents an asymmetry in social space, whether that site exerts a coercive force or even if such force is forbidden it (as we see in the case of many so-called primitive societies). Thus, even if we attribute power a predominant function, we cannot conceptualize it as an institution among others and situate it *in* society. No doubt it appears in society through the visible presence of someone or several persons who are supposed to incarnate it or be its stewards. Yet the signs of power and its distance are always rendered visible and open to all by means of myths, rituals, ceremonies, or a religious elaboration. This is the paradox: from the interior of society, power points to a site that surpasses the limit of society. It signals toward a *beyond*, while it makes clear that it communicates with itself through the variety of its institutions, and possible internal antagonisms. Put differently, we could say that there is no power durably anchored in a community that does not have a symbolic function, in the same way that there is no political society whose constitution does not have a symbolic signification.

Political society does not in itself provide standards of agreement as a consequence of kinship rules or rules that stem from an organization of the production and distribution of goods. Those standards depend on the way in which power is presented, and they bear the trace of an incommensurable, no matter the name used to describe it or the form it takes. Even in the case of an extreme despotism in which the monarch has the status of a demigod, the image of the tremendous power concentrated in his person does not erase this trace of incommensurability. Actually, it is often in his very status that he is seen to be subject to the strictest obligations and, notably, the object of taboos that must be followed as a condition of the maintenance of the social order. The European monarchy's dramatic art since the Middle Ages, whose transformations Ernst Kantorowicz so astutely analyzed, drew from Christianity and, more specifically, from the representation of God's prince-vicar entirely new resources for a spiritual foundation of temporal sovereignty.[2] But such a dramatic art did not move beyond the ancient forms of sacred kingship in which the supernatural and mundane worlds were at once separated from and imbricated in each other. To recognize the many instances of representations through which the dimension of the Other appears is thus to admit a heteronomy of the social. Bearing witness to that heteronomy are both the impossibility of a reabsorption of power in and by society and, at the same time, the impossibility for power to assert itself at a distance from the ensemble of subjects or citizens without gesturing, beyond the scene where it occurs, toward an unrepresentable.

Are we therefore to believe that modern democracy opened the era of autonomy? The disincorporation of power—the fact that those who are entrusted with it depend on popular suffrage and enjoy only a legitimacy granted to them—does not mean that the site of power is limited to the interior of society.[3] If it becomes forbidden to occupy that site, it is always from it that society acquires a representation of itself, as differentiated as that society may be and as manifold the oppositions that shape it. In a sense, as I have repeatedly emphasized, democracy requires that the site of power remain empty.[4] The result of this imperative is that the distinction between the symbolic and the real finds itself tacitly acknowledged, whereas it remained obscured as long as belief in the power, will, and wisdom of a suprahuman being was vested in the image of the monarch. Contrary to a widespread interpretation, power does not become mundane. In fact, those delegated the exercise of public authority (or those who participate in or claim to participate in that authority; that is, those whose calling or career is political action) run the risk of making it appear. One can even observe that once belief in a natural foundation of social inequalities disappears, power both feeds on the unprecedented expectations of citizens with conflicting interests and comes to be regarded simultaneously as an arbiter and instigator of social change.

I therefore speak of the *disincorporation* of power, whereas the sociologist might prefer to restrict himself to the notion of a limitation of politics. This is because politics is not only the result of a juridico-functional apparatus. In order for it to become institutionalized, for the distinction between political authority and state administration to be precisely defined, and also for the space of civil liberties on which that authority should not encroach to be delimited, it is necessary that the sovereign have ceased to incarnate the community and that he no longer appear above the law. In this respect, the phenomenon of the monarchy under the Old Regime is significant. It would be careless of me to let stand the impression that the monarchy was only a version of sacred kingship, for it already involved a certain limitation of and on political power, even if it ended up violating that limit. If the sovereign had the advantage of a divine election, and if he arrogated to himself the status of a mediator between humans and God, consequently finding himself above the laws of the land, he nevertheless possessed temporal power by being subject to a higher law. It was by recognizing this law that the sovereign's authority was recognized by the community of his subjects. The division between the terrestrial and the celestial was so radical that it checked the sovereign's pretension to monopolize spiritual omnipotence. He was denied this possibility as much as the pope was denied temporal omnipotence. On the one hand, the monarch occupied himself with concentrating in his hands the means of dominating the ensemble of his subjects; on the other, the image of a *singularity* [*un seul*] imposing itself on all provided a model of order according to which each person was inserted into a network of dependences and gradually into a substantial community. Only the dissipation of this image gave birth to a new conception of the political.

The disincorporation of power did not only have the effect of undermining the representation of an organic society. By the same token, the source of the law became unlocalizable. To some extent, the law made itself known in the interdiction confronting anyone who attempted to possess it. We would thus we mistaken to conclude that it sank to the level of an artifice or that it fell into the orbit of a society dominated by a class whose representatives had the means of government at their disposal. No doubt the law was thereafter expressed in the work of legislators mandated by the people, and it thereby bore the mark of capricious opinions and conflicting interests. Yet that legislative work still had to distinguish between the legitimate and the illegitimate. For what is the criterion of legitimacy, however formal, if not the obligation to free oneself from the arbitrary and contingent? Similarly, the fact that none could present themselves as having a monopoly on knowledge of the social order and the ends of human conduct resulted in the disintrication of the theological and the political. This was a significant event, since it led to admitting the legitimacy of diverse and even conflicting beliefs, opinions, and interests, provided such conflict did not imperil public safety. Rather than effacing the dimension of the Other in the experience of life, democracy unveiled it. In reducing dogmatic beliefs, whether theological or philosophical, to the status of particular beliefs, democracy lent a kind of visibility to discord within the framework of a common world. Lastly, the disentanglement [*disintrication*] of power and knowledge precipitated a new legitimacy to the process of the differentiation of modes of understanding. It was always in the particular field where it was exercised that the activity of consciousness grappled with the principles according to which it guided itself, finding the impetus to return to its presuppositions. Far from being reducible to the exclusive effects of the division of labor characteristic of economic systems, the constraint that makes a rule out of taking a *route* [*passage*] in order to face the question of the true and false, or even of the imaginary and the real, testifies to the apprehension of a world that escapes a bird's-eye view or perfunctory glance [*survol*]. On the contrary, access to that world supposes that one learn from it the very means of orienting oneself in it.

16

Hannah Arendt on the Law of Movement and Ideology

I N THE LAST CHAPTER OF *The Origins of Totalitarianism* (1951), Hannah Arendt emphatically expressed the view that the totalitarian regime undermined the foundations of political society and tended to obliterate what I have called the dimension of the Other. The line of thinking I am pursuing comes close to hers. Nevertheless, it seems to me that her attempt to grasp the essence of the regime, elucidating what was radical and deranged about it, failed to meet the expectations her book raised. Toward the beginning of her final chapter, Arendt asked, on the one hand, whether the totalitarian regime—Communist or Nazi—could be considered the product of a combination of despotism, tyranny, and modern dictatorship that had profited from the failure of traditional political forces or, on the other, whether it was necessary to acknowledge that totalitarianism had its own nature or essence.[1] Not satisfied with calling it "unprecedented," Arendt declared that it invalidated a fundamental alternative recognized by political philosophy since antiquity "between lawful and lawless governments, between arbitrary and legitimate power."[2] By detecting the status of law in totalitarianism, one touched its *essence*.[3]

Arendt's central idea was that totalitarianism did not constitute a new political type definable within the framework of the classical problematic of lawful and lawless regimes. It was incomparable due to its "monstrous, yet seemingly unanswerable claim . . . [to go] to the sources of authority from which positive laws received their ultimate legitimation" and, consequently, to sacrifice everything to a supreme Law: the law of history in its Communist version or the law of nature in its Nazi version.[4] Following this argument, we first discover the abolition of the distance always maintained in a regime founded on a *consensus juris* between positive laws and the supreme Law at their source. Within the bounds of social life, positive laws express a supreme Law. Arendt noted, "Totalitarian lawfulness, defying legality and pretending to establish the direct reign of justice on earth, executes the law of History or of Nature without translating it into standards of right and wrong for individual behavior."[5] Put another way, one could say that the absolute affirmation of the law involves a dismissal of the subject's [*Sujet*] position. Phrased differently yet again, one could say that unconditional obedience to the law of history or nature abolishes the faculty of judgment. Arendt thus used the strong formula of the "identification of man and law" or the vision of man as a "walking embodiment of the law."[6] Second, after the abolition of the distinction between positive laws and the supreme Law at their source, we discover that the laws of history and nature are laws of movement and, further, that neither nature nor history is any longer the source of projects that stabilize the actions of mortals—history and nature are themselves movements. Third, she showed us that this new notion of history or nature stemmed from theories or ideologies (Arendt used the two terms interchangeably) propagated in the nineteenth century, notably by Marx and Darwin. Those two thinkers were not foreign to each other, since Darwin introduced history into nature, while Marx, a great admirer of Darwin, made class struggle reflect productive forces to the point that man's labor power ultimately seemed to him a natural-biological force. Thus, with Marxism and Darwinism, law changed meaning, becoming "the expression of motion itself."[7] Finally, we learn that in following the "recipes" of these ideologies, totalitarian politics unveiled the true nature of movement: it involved an endless work of eliminating either beings that were unfit to live or imperfect or else classes destined to disappear.[8] Terror flowed from the law of movement—the "law of killing." The final part of her argument led Arendt to formulate several striking judgments that remain well known. Terror, she said, has for its ultimate end

the fabrication of mankind[; it] eliminates individuals for the sake of the species, sacrifices the "parts" for the sake of the "whole." . . . It substitutes for the boundaries and channels of communication between individual men a band of iron which holds them so tightly together that it is as though their plurality had disappeared into One Man of gigantic dimension. . . . In the iron band of terror, which destroys the plurality of men and makes out of many the One who unfailingly will act as though he himself were part of the course of history or nature, a device has been found not only to liberate the historical and natural forces, but to accelerate them to a speed they never would reach if left to themselves. [9]

Nevertheless, if terror is, as it were, only the execution of sentences handed down by the law of movement, or else if "the inhabitants of a totalitarian country are thrown into and caught in the process of nature or history for the sake of accelerating its movement," a principle that guides action is again necessary.[10] In other words, the law of movement or obedience to a movement that carries people away is not enough to explain the regulation of human conduct. Arendt added, "The process may decide that those who today eliminate races and individuals or the members of dying classes and decadent peoples are tomorrow those who must be sacrificed. What totalitarian rule needs to guide the behavior of its subjects is a preparation to fit each of them equally well for the role of executioner and the role of victim. This two-sided preparation, the substitute for a principle of action, is the ideology."[11] Thus at this stage in the argument, the problem of ideology returns. The reader already knows that nineteenth-century ideologies appealed to a law of movement and that totalitarian ideologies differed from them by relying on a law of killing. In a sense, Arendt vigorously underscored that discontinuity, going so far as to say that Communism and racism were no more totalitarian than other ideologies. But in another sense, she tried to demonstrate that ideology as such, no matter its content, was the "logic of one idea."[12]

Let me evoke in passing the three characteristics she recognized in ideology: the pretension to explain everything, the indifference toward experience that has nothing to teach, and the deduction of all ideas from a premise taken as an axiom. More important is to observe that ideology itself appeared either as the law of thought's movement or as a movement of thought that is law. Insofar as it is applied to history, the result "is not a body of statements about something that *is*, but the unfolding of a process which is in constant change. The ideology treats the course of events as though it followed the same 'law' as the logical exposition of its 'idea.'"[13] Or, as she again wrote after having noted that history became material to be "calculated": "What fits the 'idea' into this new role is its own 'logic,' that is a movement which is the consequence of the 'idea' itself and needs no outside factor to set it into motion." She reformulated this judgment in these terms: "The movement of history and the logical process of this notion are supposed to correspond to each other, so that whatever happens happens according to the logic of one 'idea.'"[14]

Arendt's subtlety was profound. No one before her had grasped so well the formation of a new regime of thought. One should be surprised, though, that she believed she could give a general definition of ideology, while in fact she had in mind only the spirit of Communist or Nazi ideology. Indeed, it would be absurd to apply this definition to Marxism. One's astonishment increases in seeing Arendt, after having placed herself in the difficulty of accounting for the changes introduced by totalitarian ideology, provide a disappointing answer:

> The device both totalitarian rulers used to transform their respective ideologies into weapons with which each of their subjects could force himself into step with the terror movement was deceptively simple and inconspicuous: they took them dead seriously, took pride the one in his supreme gift for "ice cold reasoning" (Hitler) and the other in the "mercilessness of his dialectics," and proceeded to drive ideological implications into extremes of logical consistency which, to the onlooker, looked preposterously "primitive" and absurd.[15]

In short, from the notions of unfit individuals and races and of the existence of dying classes, Hitler and Stalin came to the conclusion of their necessary extermination. I am not overlooking the fact that they discovered political benefits from this "ideological operation," but that argument falls short of Arendt's reflection. The totalitarian phenomenon, at first judged incomparable, finally was seen to be derived from an ideology that carried to its ultimate conclusion the process of the alienation of thought in logic. To tell the truth, the entire argument I am trying to summarize hides slippages or twists of thought that reveal a desire to rush to produce an ultimate explanation.

What was law in the totalitarian universe? The question Arendt asked at the end of her book in 1951 contrasted strongly with the debate about

Communism and Nazism already under way before her contribution and fully developed afterward. Defining the totalitarian regime according to empirical criteria was judged inadequate. Nor did she want to keep to the justificatory machinery it produced and the manifest content of its leaders' discourse. Nor, finally, was she satisfied in locating its "origins." She asked instead: What was the supreme authority that generated a power capable of requiring and to a large extent obtaining, independently of the means of coercion at its disposal, the obedience of the majority? A philosophical question, one might say, often in order to discredit it, but a question that comes closest to the astonishment one feels when confronted with a society in which violence of an unprecedented intensity was unleashed, a society that nevertheless seemed not to have capitulated to the arbitrary but to have been entirely and incomparably regulated. Although the state of law was destroyed, the cohesion and integrity of the community were fully affirmed. Not content with presenting themselves as regimes superior to liberal democracy, Nazism and Communism promised the resolution of conflicts that were tearing apart the modern world and that had always, in other forms, divided humanity. Arendt noted that the alternative constantly formulated since antiquity between societies subject to law and those without laws seemed to have been abolished. She could have added that the classical choice between a regime conforming to nature and a corrupt one likewise seemed eliminated. While the idea of a preestablished order, in whatever way it had been conceived, disappeared, the task of bringing corruption to an end was indispensable. This corruption was not simply a matter of the reign of money or the malfeasance of demagogues produced by the party system. It designated the sickness of the social body. Making the social body germfree was the condition for the formation of a new man and a new world.

No doubt as a consequence of discerning affinities between Nazism and Communism, beyond the obvious signs of their antagonism, Arendt came to look for the source of authority from which the totalitarian regime flowed. On that account, the scandal provoked by her approach—a scandal that continues—permitted evading the question of law. Even so, we might observe that this question remains entirely relevant to the examination of Communism as well as Nazism—in other words, to the abstraction Arendt made from comparing the two regimes. Taking pains to ascertain what in the Communist regime gave it its foundation, Arendt believed she had found the answer in its professed "law of History." It is hardly necessary to point out that, in her eyes, such a law did not really exist. We learn that, though nothing was done that was not inspired by belief in this law of history, the notion of it revealed only that "monstrous, yet seemingly unanswerable claim . . . [to go] to the sources of authority from which positive laws received their ultimate legitimation."[16] It was only a supposed law: Communist politics were guided by a fiction.

This point deserves a closer examination, for when Arendt evoked the law that has guided humans, whether in so-called traditional societies, Greek city-states, or Christian Europe, she took care not to present it as a supposed or fictive law. The reason no doubt was that law in a general way resists definition. One can detect the sign of its definition only under a number of conditions: where it is taken for the generator of relations that humans maintain among themselves and with the world in which they live; where a limit that exceeds all factual limits encountered by human desire and power is tested; and where duties and rights are simultaneously interwoven. In short, the reluctance to judge as fictive the law under which communities are organized whose positive laws or even customs, beliefs, and modes of conduct have become to a great extent foreign—this reluctance had something to do with what we have acknowledged, even tacitly: that law cannot be reduced to a human artifice and simple convention. Moreover, when Arendt referred to the Communist law of history, one expected her to stand by the assertion that it denoted a perversion of the very idea of law, and above all to indicate the effective authority that became capable of constructing a law of history above humans, instead of simply denouncing a "monstrous pretension" to return to the sources of authority. For this effective authority clearly resided in the Communist Party. But the argument that the new regime was actually assembled according to a law of history becomes as unconvincing as the argument that made the regime materialize as a dictatorship of the proletariat evolving toward a classless society. Both arguments attest to a confusion between ideology and the effective operation of the regime. Arendt appropriately tried to dispel this confusion when she asked us not to stop at the manifest content of Communist leaders' discourse. But why, then, did she refrain from treating the law of history, while judging it fictive, as a product of totalitarian ideology?

Arendt's formulation of the law of history as the law of movement is inadequate. According to this view, history itself seems to become (as nature does for Nazism) *movement,* thrust upon humans to the point of plunging them in a direction they had not determined, as shown by how the regime was carried away by terror. Thus, after having noted that "total terror, the essence of totalitarian government, exists neither for nor against men . . . [it] is supposed to provide the forces of nature or history with an incomparable instrument to accelerate their movement," Arendt added that "this movement, proceeding according to its own law, cannot in the long run be hindered; eventually its force will always prove to be more powerful than the most powerful forces engendered by the actions and the will of men."[17] Later, we learn (I have already cited these lines in part) that "the inhabitants of a totalitarian country are thrown into and caught in the process of nature or history for the sake of accelerating its movement; as such, they can only be executors or victims of its inherent law."[18] Ultimately, ideology alone permitted regulating citizens' conduct and supplying the principle of discrimination between executioners and victims. Again, one must recognize, beyond the doctrine's content, a mechanism for binding ideas. The function of this mechanism was to endlessly assimilate the shock of new events. For the analysis of terror, which by its own movement knew no stopping point, was substituted the analysis of ideology, whose movement can never be stopped by experience. Moreover, a measure of Arendt's fascination with movement is found in the use she made of this term to qualify Bolshevik organization, as she had Nazi organization. She usually avoided discussing the party.

Arendt did not distinguish the notion of movement from that of process, the latter being determined from beginning to end in such a way that nothing could take place that was not continuous with what came before. For that reason, she neglected what Communist ideology took from movement: the formidable attempt to enclose history and thought at the same time. More exactly, she did not so much ignore this attempt as point out signs of it in passing: the "logic of one idea" went hand in hand with the negation of the event; "what happened" and overturned the existing state of things came together with the negation of the unpredictable and unknowable. Nevertheless, Arendt no longer considered these observations when she claimed to unmask the essence of totalitarianism. The regime in which movement revealed itself, continuously providing the spectacle of the production of a society, was organized under the sign of a refusal of history. It excluded the idea that the outlines of the future were not already imprinted in the present and the idea of a world surpassing our vision of the possible and impossible (that is why, we may note in passing, contrary to Malia, utopia was foreign to the Communist mentality).

Why, then, did Arendt forget that, under cover of idealizing the movement of history, the Bolsheviks in Russia and then their followers tried to enclose themselves in a stronghold sheltered from the assault of time? I assume that in denouncing the law of movement she aimed not only at the totalitarian enterprise and, beyond that, at Marxist (or Darwinist) doctrine, but also at the new mode of temporality that characterizes modern societies. For Arendt, this temporality testified to the birth of the philosophy of history, only the latest version of which had been elaborated by Marx; and, more generally, it referred to the diffuse representation of humanity's progress or even changes in time that made sense in themselves—all these were signs of a belief in a rupture with the ancients' conception of history as a signifying narrative, calling to memory and wresting from forgetfulness *actions* not registered in any process, but that on the contrary escaped necessities imposed by life and technology and thus constituted the most properly human and most fragile part of existence. This new mode of modern temporality illustrated for Arendt the fact that political institutions were ascribed a historical meaning and became subordinated to a state of economy and technology. As a result of the thought of an irreversible time and an attraction for new things, this new mode of temporality ultimately proved the forgetfulness of the permanence of the human condition.

I take these conclusions from reading essays published after her great work on totalitarianism, "Tradition and the Modern Age" (1954) and "The Concept of History: Ancient and Modern" (1956).[19] In the epilogue to the second essay, she explicitly referenced *The Origins of Totalitarianism*. After having recalled her work on the totalitarian phenomenon, she faithfully recapitulated her argument. "The totalitarian systems," she wrote, "tend to demonstrate that action can be based on any hypothesis and that, in the course of consistently guided action, the particular hypothesis will become true, will become actual, factual reality."[20] She then repeated her claim that "the axiom from which the deduction is started does not need to be, as traditional metaphysics and logic supposed, a self-evident truth; it does not at all have to tally with the facts."[21] The entire argument denouncing the illusion of process and the deception of deduction (as soon as the ends and meaning of the practice of thought were made abstract) fed on the critique of the modern mentality and, more specifically, on the critique of the natural sciences, whose criterion has been that "what works" measures the real and true and whose driving energy has been that "everything is possible."[22] The totalitarian phenomenon, precisely founded "in the last analysis on the conviction that everything is possible," thus "tend[ed] to demonstrate" a change of the broadest scope.[23] It was not the initiator of that change.

It is outside my interests here to discuss the Arendtian concept of modern science and technology. Nor can we ask if, notwithstanding her perspicacious critique, she agreed to the freedom to question putatively acquired experiences in ways that, far from being led by deduction, showed signs of movement as exploration and risk. It is enough to say that the critique of totalitarianism extended the critique of modernity, whether one located the origin of modernity in the Industrial Revolution or the turning point marked by the advent of the natural sciences. It would do violence to Arendt's thought to ascribe to it a deductive schema she rightly sought to avoid. Nonetheless, it seems that in her eyes the new regime precipitated a movement (or an attraction for movement) by setting it in law or submitting itself entirely to it. That movement (or attraction) derived from the loss of a need for stability that had formerly been essential to every well-constituted society. In the chapter of *The Origins of Totalitarianism* I have been discussing, this need appeared to emerge as a consequence of the threat to the community's continuity posed by the ceaseless succession of generations. The stability of laws thus responded to the perpetual movement of human affairs, a movement that can never cease as long as humans are born and die. "The laws," she commented, "hedge in each new beginning and at the same time assure its freedom of movement, the potentiality of something entirely new and unpredictable; the boundaries of positive laws are for the political existence of man what memory is for his historical existence: they guarantee the pre-existence of a common world, the reality of some continuity which transcends the individual life span of each generation, absorbs all new origins and is nourished by them."[24] Thus a division seems to develop between the order of the beginning and the order of permanence. The crude fact of birth accounts for both of them, since each man's appearance in the world guarantees the possibility of political foundation or refoundation, and yet his detachment from the succession of beings imperils the continuity of the group.

In any case, this reasoning rested on a triple abstraction: an individual who from birth was not already taken into a network of relationships imprinted by culture; laws that came to stabilize a *natural* change, while they were constitutive of every mode of coexistence; and a society not submitted, within time, to tensions capable of both altering its equilibrium and undermining the legitimacy of laws to the point that a reconfiguration of the political order was required. This triple abstraction permits one to evade the question of history. That is, one avoids the gestation of new modes of legitimacy and new styles of existence brought about within the density of the social and under the juridico-political surface. This gestation can be deciphered only after the fact and without one's being able to attribute it to a single order of factors. In short, although the theme of *natality*, or the ability to begin, enchanted a certain number of Arendt's readers, what it hid were certainly not objective processes but changes always at work in society. The effects of those changes, when they converge by means of unforeseen circumstances in order to produce a mutation, reveal their *meaning*; that is, they convey significance and indicate a direction.

Arendt clearly wanted to refute the thesis according to which the movement of history controlled the passage from one form of society to another and led to a final state. But no less did she want to denounce the belief of modern humans in a movement that, regardless of its finality, would have value in itself. She associated the everything is possible, as it were, in the major key, opening the way to total domination, with the everything is possible in the minor key, masked by the appearance of political freedoms, serving as a maxim for science and technology, disrupting mores, and undermining the work of laws. I would first observe that her apt critique of the theory or ideology of history in favor of a reevaluation of the political led her to idealize the *beginning*, whose virtue, as she said in an obscure formula, was that it "absorbs all new origins and is nourished by them."[25] Since one of these beginnings, obvious to all in her eyes, was the French Revolution, there is reason to be astonished at the fact that she overlooked Tocqueville's efforts, first, to retrace the movement or movements that, at the heart of the Old Regime, lay at the origin of the formation of an entirely new society; and second, to detect in this society, once established, all that it inherited from the world it had destroyed. More astonishing still is to read her praise for someone she took as one of the great political thinkers of modern times. Without a doubt, no one was as relentless as he in conceiving of (even if it entailed his not fearing to contradict himself in the details of his analysis) continuity and rupture, inheritance and innovation at once—this while continually brushing aside all representation of history *in the singular* and challenging every form of determinism.

One of Tocqueville's major intuitions was that American democracy was a regime in which *movement* was freed and a restless activity in all domains of social life developed. It is true that he highlighted the function of law and found in the role played by jurists the sign of a conservative (in the literal sense of the word) power that served as a counterweight to the restlessness of society. Yet it remained the case that he found in this movement and restless activity a deployment of energies in all directions, an exuberance and vitality known nowhere else. This observation deserves all the more attention, since it invites a comparison of American society or, more generally, Western democratic societies with twentieth-century Soviet society. The spectacle of frenzied industrialization and collectivization in the name of the construction of socialism is indeed not enough to conclude that Soviet society was carried away by movement. The nature of its institutions made it appear as a blocked society incapable of having movement that escaped party control, the party itself determining norms in all sectors of activity.

One might object that I confuse two notions of movement: that which designates history, insofar as it is supposed to follow a direction or even obey a law of development, and that which characterizes a type of society established, if I could put it like this, within the element of mobility in such a way that changes in individuals' condition, modes of activity, class relations, laws, ideas, and mores are tacitly acknowledged. I believe that it was Arendt who brought together divergent and heterogeneous phenomena under the concept of movement. By movement, she meant sometimes the uninterrupted flux of generations; sometimes the history of humanity (fictive in her eyes, since what is properly human comes to light thanks to narratives capable of restoring the radiance of *action* that stands out against the foundation of a sociobiological continuity); sometimes, more specifically, progress conceived without a definite end; sometimes the strictly regulated sequence of forms of class struggle described by Marxism; sometimes the movement, this time effective, that destroyed the framework of positive laws and spawned terror; and sometimes the species of movement that captured minds in the Western world as a result of the loss of the ideology of progress and of the purposeful ends of action. Arendt did not say that the virtue of laws is to block movement; rather, they permit its channeling. But her arguments about movement provide a glimpse of the great opposition between stability and instability. Nothing here leads one to believe that movement can be a generator of meaning by which men locate the capacity to find their bearings.

17

The Perversion of the Law

THESE REMARKS LEAD ME BACK to the analysis of totalitarianism. I have tried to explain why one would be wrong to look for its foundation in submission to a purported law of history or movement, whereas such a law constituted only a theme of official discourse. One would furthermore be mistaken to think that the Bolsheviks in the Leninist and then Stalinist eras became *in actual fact* carried away by the movement they had constructed in theory. But I have left Arendt's first question unanswered: What was law in the Communist regime? This is a question that—if one does not abandon the very idea of history—might be better phrased in another way: What happened to law under Communism? For we are concerned with an event: a perversion of the idea of law. I would like to return to this term *law* in order to clarify that, unlike tyranny and modern dictatorship—which did not undermine the idea of law because they clearly revealed the intrusion of force into political space and which had neither the intention nor the means to destabilize the structure of society and change the mores of their citizens—the Communist regime was ruled in such a way that citizens, no matter their position, those in charge like those who obeyed, were subjected to a supreme authority that did not reside in some person or persons.

How was the perversion of law expressed in the nature and functioning of institutions, in the conduct of and relationships among citizens, and in a common mode of existence? As I observed, Arendt drew from her notion of a law of movement, or of a movement that was law, no other consequence than a headlong rush toward terror, for which ideology alone secured a kind of regulation. At the end of *The Origins of Totalitarianism*, she paid no attention to the mechanisms that ensured the cohesion and longevity of a new political system. In her eyes, the idealization of movement, or else the subjugation to movement, precluded the instauration of a new mode of legality. She noted of totalitarian politics that "its defiance of all, even its own positive laws implies that it believes it can do without any *consensus juris* whatever, and still not resign itself to the tyrannical state of lawlessness, arbitrariness, and fear."[1] Still, if it is certain that the notion of *consensus juris* disappeared with that of legality, in the sense that the latter is understood in all civilized states, we should not disregard the constant concern to make the semblance of legality (called socialist legality) consistent. I am not thinking so much of the elaboration of the three constitutions, especially that of 1936 (discussed in chapter 8), whose function was nevertheless not negligible even if, contrary to what many Western observers believed, it bore no traces of a democratic spirit. What seems more significant to me instead were, first, the juridical apparatus set up to serve the actual terror and, more generally, though their objectives had something in common with terror, the strict control of economic and social life, the use of the administration of justice, and the persistence, even into the camps, of the simulation, at once monstrous and burlesque, of a definition of the legal and illegal. So much has been written on this subject that it seems needless to sketch a description of the Soviet judicial and penitential system. Still, if we are investigating law, we cannot neglect confronting the paradox of legalism in a regime whose leaders denounced the formalism of law as a bourgeois mystification (beginning with Lenin, who, in 1918, vilified intellectuals distressed by the disregard for law). This is indeed a tremendous paradox, and Arendt neglected it when she saw in terror only a process of elimination determined by a law of history having become a "law of killing."

As we know, terror has many modalities. It became particularly devastating when it struck, on the one hand, peasants—either directly through military means or indirectly via measures condemning them to famine—and, on the other, peoples of whom it was a question of breaking national resistance. No matter its manifestations, terror lent itself to interpretations that highlighted the rationality of the regime's framework and, more exactly, the framework of policies useful to the consolidation of the party-state. In this way, the objective had been to eliminate representatives of the Old Regime and the bourgeoisie as well as political opponents associated with groups that had participated in the revolution. Then peasant property was wiped out, since it stood in the way of the proletariat's interests. Finally, there came the struggle against nationalities whose demands imperiled the Soviet Union. Raymond Aron, for example, saw in the purges targeting the bureaucracy and the party itself only the sign of an "irrationality" attributed to Stalin's madness. One might think that the purges served both to subvert a hierarchy whose stability threatened to impede initiatives by the party leadership and, by the same token, to promote a new class of completely submissive cadres. Yet the scale of the gulag population, mixing prisoners from all social conditions, most of whom having been condemned for the widest variety of reasons, belies this kind of interpretation. Even if it were true that the camps became a reserve of forced labor satisfying the needs of industry, it would nonetheless be pointless to locate their origin in a project deriving from economic rationality. The terror that struck all strata of the population was the sign of an incessant search for or, better, an incessant fabrication of the people's enemies. The series of trials against industrialists, Mensheviks, and revolutionary socialists in the early 1930s, and then against former Bolshevik and military leaders, was situated in the context of the formidable operation that since Lenin's time had developed under the name of the hunt for *harmful elements* and of social prophylaxis.[2]

Although important, the task of counting the terror's victims is not sufficient.[3] Also inadequate is merely acknowledging that the hunt for the people's enemies characterized the essence of the regime. One must still identify the body of legislation, the codification of penalties, and the procedures of judicial investigation, even when one is tempted to consider only the signs of the pretense of law. It is true that in the period between the revolution and the end of the civil war, the reason of the party was not concerned with law. On Lenin's recommendation, the violence that broke out in the countryside or in city slums was recuperated by the Bolsheviks to benefit the dictatorship of the party. Without the dictatorship, it seemed neither expedient nor desirable for the party to trouble itself with juridical artifices. And yet, a penal code was promulgated in 1922 and a new version was designed in 1926, shortly before the trials intended to show the treachery of the revolutionary socialists—events that set off the alarm bells of international public opinion. In a modified form, the penal code remained in effect until Khrushchev's rise to power. Not a brief document, it comprised 148 articles, one of which—article 58—brought to the fore the new spirit of the law. Through the variety of charges it enumerated, the fourteen paragraphs of this article effaced the distinction between political and common-law prisoners. Thus, as Solzhenitsyn later showed in painstaking detail, all citizens to be eliminated were drawn into the same net.[4] Never before had such a combination of law and the arbitrary been imagined.

We might ask what purpose was served by this itemization of all possible offenses and, beyond offenses, of all suspicious behaviors, an inventory eventually culminating in conferring limitless authority on a commissar-investigator. But to ask this question is to imagine that the raw exercise of violence in the name of the proletariat, which the party claimed to incarnate, was sufficient unto itself. Such a hypothesis does not consider the repression that was visited upon workers and that required, beyond bombastic speeches on the tasks of the supposedly ruling class, universal criteria of the legal and illegal as applicable to workers as to the rest of the population. In general, the hypothesis of a self-sufficiency of violence does not explain a new imperative that emerged at the end of the civil war: structuring the ensemble of social relationships. The elaboration of a penal code indeed coincided with the construction of a state that had to provide signs of both its effectiveness in controlling all sectors of activity and its permanence. Let me add that if the judicial organ was limited by legislation—a circumstance, of course, that in no way involved the principle of the separation of powers—it was so as a result of the formation of a significant bureaucratic stratum. Under the supervision of the leadership apparatus of the party, and conforming to its instructions, this stratum was able to take on precisely differentiated tasks both within and outside the party. Without in any way ceasing to be practiced in its primary aspect (as Solzhenitsyn observed, the practice of the "bullet in the back of the head" was never abandoned under Stalin's regime), terror thus became imbricated with the process of bureaucratization.

Of a terroristic inspiration, article 58 provided the commissar-investigators with an interpretive grid that allowed them to catalog crimes (even if all crime was reduced to a common denominator of *harm*), to assign the accused to a category or several categories simultaneously, to assess punishments, and to assemble "dossiers." All these activities gave the commissar-investigators the assurance of having a vocation. We know that nothing is more foreign to the bureaucratic spirit than to act without instructions or records. Thus, as aberrant as the catalog of crimes seems to the outside observer, the agents of terror possessed the means to "see themselves" in their classification of random victims having become ordinary men in the eyes of the law [*justiciables*]. Solzhenitsyn described these commissars well when he wrote that "they could not seriously say to one another or to themselves that they were exposing criminals. Nonetheless they kept right on producing depositions page after page to make sure that we rotted."[5] If they enjoyed the authority to accuse anyone of anything, it was still necessary that this *anything* have a name. The law gave it to them. The commissars' authority and competence derived from the law, while they themselves were bound by it through the shared obligation to "frame" [*cadrer*] their investigations. In short, their power came across as being exorbitant only in the eyes of the accused. Everyone acted only as members of an organ that itself obeyed the party's directives.

It would therefore be wrong to see in the elaboration of law, as expressed in article 58, merely the pursuit of terror by new means. This law was not entirely instrumental. It was constitutive of a social order, and considering it from this point of view, one can ask about the foundations of the totalitarian regime without appealing to a purported law of history or to the belief in socialism. Article 58 clearly revealed the destruction of the positive laws that, as Arendt rightly noted, stabilize human relationships in a state of law. But there is no reason to conclude from this claim that the notion of legality itself was abolished or became unimportant. Without any reference to legality, the system of domination would have been unviable. Broadly speaking, relationships among members of the bureaucracy would have become unintelligible if those bureaucrats had not been bound by a web of obligations in the exercise of their duties. As for the administration of justice, it is unsatisfactory to speak of a simple misrepresentation of violence. That administration could sometimes be extremely bizarre; the instructions taken by commissar-instructors at face value, in their literal meanings, paradoxically became sources for arbitrary interpretations. The reign of violence was thus combined with the reign of formalism. The latter emerged not only within the framework of investigations but also, as illustrated by the testimonies of former deportees, including those in the gulag, despite the inhuman conditions to which prisoners were subjected. Those prisoners remained bound to their dossiers by strings that were invisible to them.

Nonetheless, we will not stop with this sole aspect of the penal code. Considering its effects on the entire population, one sees that it constituted the perverse equivalent of a fundamental law. Article 58 indeed outlined a model of society by designating actions, admissions of lack of expertise, intentions or presumptions of intention, and failures to report that came under crimes against the state, the people, or the party. According to this model, conduct, arguments made in private, writings, and modes of communication were not neutral. Accordingly, one could conclude that every person became a potentially guilty party, for the boundary between the legal and the illegal was never guaranteed. On the reverse side of this picture, one glimpsed the power of being together [*être-ensemble*], and the imperative of obeying the norm of the collective, itself derived from the norm of the party.

In all regimes, the administration of justice involves much more than an ensemble of procedures; it corresponds to its guiding principles. In a democracy, the presumption of innocence; the right of the accused to a defense; proceedings to establish facts and the veracity of testimony; and the authority granted the judge as a *third* above the parties, independent of all extrajuridical power and possessing a competence earned by his judicial training—these rules flow from the nature of the regime. In a democracy, the exercise of sovereignty is not separate from public debate that brings rival political groups together and presupposes the permanent rights of an opposition as well as the guarantee of rights of movement, opinion, expression, and information—in short, a civil life and interchange [*communication*] carried out laterally among citizens and groups of citizens. For its part, the administration of justice in a Communist regime likewise signaled a conception of the foundation of social relations. Of course, one can remain satisfied with observing that the party monopolized the means of decision, coercion, information, and propaganda. But that monopolization was neither a factual given nor the sole consequence of a theory of the dictatorship of the proletariat. Within the framework of the administration of justice, a dual relation between the commissar and the accused was established, while in all registers of social life a dual relation between the representative of public authority and the citizen was instituted. It is in considering this phenomenon that one can speak of a perversion of law, for law merits its name only if in its application it makes the figure of a *third* materialize.

Why speak, though, of a perversion of law rather than its destruction? Why say that the law still "gave itself," however monstrously, in a dual relation? This relation, I have suggested in chapter 15, was not the equivalent to the relation established between those who dominate and those who submit. In contrast, it required that those who submitted interiorize an obligation not ordered by the commissar, the latter presenting himself and in numerous cases seeing himself as an executant of the law. (That the dual relation required this interiorization did not mean that it succeeded in achieving it, especially throughout the regime's entire existence.) The judicial investigation provides well-known examples of this situation. Here, I can evoke only the practice of obtaining [*extorquer*] proof of guilt from the accused. Following Solzhenitsyn's expression, it behooved the accused to "fabricate his case." That this practice was accompanied by various means of blackmail and the use of torture did not diminish its symbolic force. Factual proof was unimportant or inadequate, since it entailed making use of something real that escaped the dual relation through which the totalitarian principle of the law was brought into play. It was thus the role of the accused to receive the law's blows.

I have noted that all neutral action was excluded. It is worth insisting on this point. Arendt rightly observed that, in a state of law, the law says what one should *not* do, but it does not say what one *must* do, even if concluding that humans need principles to guide their behavior. No doubt. But no less remarkable is that, within such a framework, the law ignores many human actions (not to mention intentions) that depend on neither the licit nor the illicit. And yet, in a totalitarian regime, everything was likely to fall under the law. Thus one understands how easy it was to produce the people's enemies, regardless of the reasons invoked to qualify them as such. And if it was necessary that the accused declare or demonstrate his guilt, failing to do so (which sometimes happened) opened a fissure in the regime's bulwark. His self-denunciation was required. At the very moment he found himself in the position of the accused, it was incumbent on him to identify with the agent of the law in order to condemn himself—that is, to reproduce in himself the dual relation. Once detected, the so-called antisocial element was reintroduced into the circuit of the law and compelled to participate in the operation mounted against him. In legal vocabulary, this was called showing one's *cooperation*. The formula "No one is supposed to ignore the law" mutated into another:

"Everyone is supposed to speak the language of the law." In other words, the same phantasmagoria ordered the social body's extirpation of its enemies—*internal* enemies—and then their conversion into foreign operatives (they became agents of a center led by an imperialist power, or at least objectively guilty of working to destroy the state). Finally, that same phantasmagoria reintroduced those enemies into the system by making them take on the roles prescribed for them. There is hardly any need to point out the effects of the perversion of law throughout society. Soviet law did not have at its disposal only the instruments of the police, commissar-investigators, prosecutors, and judges. Denunciation, one might say, was granted a kind of legitimacy, to which was joined the benefits one hoped to gain from informing on others out of hate, vengeance, or envy. Although we know that, under Stalin, the party hierarchy instructed local organs as to the number of arrests to carry out in territories under their jurisdiction, one cannot underestimate the role a certainly inestimable fraction of the population played in the success of the terror campaigns.

18

The Fabrication of the Social

H OW CAN ONE ASK ABOUT LAW in the Communist system if one loses sight of the fabrication of the social? For as soon as one pays attention to that fabrication, its central institution comes to the fore. Under the pull of the party, a new kind of bureaucracy crystallized. Surrounding this bureaucracy and connected to it, a network of collectives in all fields, from the economy to culture, was constituted. Individuals were assimilated into and organized by these collectives. For all that, ought one think that law emanated from the party? Doing so would prevent one from understanding that it swept down on party members themselves, notably but not exclusively during the years 1936 to 1939. Indeed, this period saw the elimination of many Communists from all ranks as well as the engineering of spectacular trials. But, then, should one simply adjust the interpretation that law emanated from the party and say instead that it emanated from the party's leadership or supreme leader? But this would be to empty the notion of law of all meaning and return to the image of Stalinist tyranny. Furthermore, we can note in passing, this second interpretation (the law emanating from the leader) cannot account for the reproduction of purges and trials in other countries where Communist regimes were set up. It is difficult to imagine that the leaders of these regimes blindly applied instructions from the all-powerful master of the Kremlin only because they were afraid of him. Finally, and this argument suffices, this interpretation would render unintelligible the fact that accused Communists, with a few exceptions, consented not only to confessing their crimes but also to demonstrating their guilt. The scenario of judicial investigation, which I cursorily evoked in the previous chapter, yielded even more information when it placed party members face to face. The characters of those who became victims were already hardened, since more often than not they had participated in the hunt for the people's enemies. One cannot think that these men maintained any illusions about the legality of their trials. Although they were violent, the methods obtaining proof of their treason were not enough to account for their capitulation. Thus, far from their cases contradicting the idea that Communism put in play a new relationship to the law, they furnished the best confirmation of that idea. The law was imposed on them on the condition that it was impossible to leave the framework of the party's thought and action. If they did leave, they would lose their bearings on (supposed) reality and on their own identity. Only a hero could challenge the impossible by resisting his accusers to the end. (Still, we know that he sometimes remained loyal to the ideal of the party while considering that its leaders were criminals.)

In *The Gulag Archipelago*, after first evoking Nikolai Bukharin's torment when he felt he had become Stalin's target, and then his trial, Solzhenitsyn promptly laid out the argument behind trials against Communists: "It was all that same invincible theme song, persisting with only minor variations through so many different trials: '*After all, we and you are Communists!* How could you have gotten off the track and come out against us? After all, you and we together—is *us!*'"[1] As a matter of fact, he had previously shown, in his investigation of the commissars' motives, that the sought-after objective was no longer repentance but rather the annihilation of the subject [*Sujet*]. In the previous chapter, I mentioned a passage in which Solzhenitsyn reported a commissar's remarks to a Communist director of a combine who was sent for the second time to a camp. Solzhenitsyn had the commissar say, "You think we get any satisfaction from using *persuasion*? We have to do what the party demands of us. You are an old party member. Tell me what you would do in my place?"[2] The two protagonists were joined by an indissoluble bond, but the relationship was not personal. The party no longer appeared as a power far above them, since circumstances could have made them exchange places. The accused did not cease to be included in the *we* that excluded him.

19

Voluntary Servitude

O NE COULD SAY THAT Communist law allowed taking one step further the phenomenon of *voluntary servitude* that Étienne de La Boétie had described in the sixteenth century. According to the celebrated author of the *Discourse on Voluntary Servitude* (1552–1553), subjects of a monarch or a tyrant (the two terms designating the power of the One [*d'Un seul*]) appeared ready to hand over their property, their parents, and themselves, captivated as they were by the image of the Prince or the very name of the One [*le seul nom d'Un*]. Addressing himself to these subjects, La Boétie declared, "This ruin descends upon you not from alien foes, but from the one enemy whom you yourselves render as powerful as he is, for whom you go bravely to war, for whose greatness you do not refuse to offer your own bodies unto death."[1] Party militants accepted an even stranger condition: they consented, for the party, to be condemned by the party. They gave and denounced themselves to the point of passing themselves off as its enemies out of fear of losing their bond with it. La Boétie had already suggested that men were caught in the phantasm of a body of which they were members:

> He who thus domineers over you has only two eyes, only two hands, only one body, no more than is possessed by the least man among the infinite numbers dwelling in your cities; he indeed has nothing more than the power that you confer upon him to destroy you. Where has he acquired enough eyes to spy upon you, if you do not provide them yourselves? How can he have so many arms to beat you with, if he does not borrow them from you? The feet that trample down your cities, where does he get them if they are not your

own? How does he have any power over you except through you? How would he dare assail you if he had no cooperation from you?[2]

Although one is tempted to assign to Stalin the power of this faith, as I have insisted, he appeared as the incarnation of the party. One cannot say that the party itself was a tyrant, for its body did not offer itself for view. It had the extraordinary new property of giving consistency to the One in the guise of a collective individual.

I am not brushing aside La Boétie's argument. It prompts one to break with a traditional representation of tyranny that Hannah Arendt continued to share. In the regime La Boétie described, something appeared besides the will of a master unconstrained by any law and to whom the people submitted out of fear. The tyrant awakened or precipitated the people's desire to appear to themselves as united [*tout un*]. Furthermore, not content to show, like Xenophon, that the tyrant installed in the position of the One had no friends, the author of the *Discourse on Voluntary Servitude* described a system that destroyed *friendship*—the capacity of citizens to connect to one another by mutually recognizing one another as equals—throughout the entire society. Indeed, he detected a mechanism of identification with the tyrant that was practiced by degrees from top to bottom on the social hierarchy. This observation was so important in his eyes that he introduced it with these words: "I come now to a point which is, in my opinion, the source and secret of domination, the support and foundation of tyranny."[3] How, indeed, would the tyrant govern a country if he did not have means of relay at his disposal? So, close to him, some five or six people eager to serve him oppressed the masses in his name. Below them one finds innumerable servants behaving in the image of those who dominated them. La Boétie added, "The consequence of all this is fatal indeed. And whoever is pleased to unwind the skein will observe that not . . . six thousand but a hundred thousand, and even millions, cling to the tyrant by this cord to which they are tied."[4] Probably the traits of the schema of domination sketched here could be found in different times and places, but it is noteworthy that La Boétie revealed a mode of the structuration of social relationships such that, to repeat a formula by Solzhenitsyn, *the people become their own enemy*.[5]

There is no doubt that Stalin was the object of a cult, that in turn some of his close associates—Genrikh Yagoda, for example—gave rise to subsidiary cults, and that countless petty tyrants were devoted to him.

Merle Fainsod found in the Smolensk archives "whole galleries of So-viet provincial types—the little Stalins who ruled the oblasts [provinces] or the raions [districts]" and who benefited from the servility of func-tionaries, officers, kolkhoz (collective farm) directors, local aristocrats, professors, students, and even workers recently arrived in the country-side.[6] Nevertheless, Solzhenitsyn was convinced that Communist-style domination involved a new driving force. He found it in ideology when he described the commissar-investigators who in good conscience sent innocents to the camps. "Thanks to *ideology*," he wrote, "the twentieth century was fated to experience evildoing on a scale calculated in the millions."[7] However, the argument does not live down the fact that the agents of terror were—as he himself showed so well—embedded in an institution and incorporated into an *organ*, itself incorporated into the party. More important than their convictions was their submission to the law from which they drew the certainty of being within their rights.

It would be fruitless, not to define what law is, but to delimit features of a conception of law separated from the conception of the party. If it is agreed that law as such—that is, beyond formulated laws likely to be modified—appears as that which cannot be violated and as that which imposes itself absolutely—barring a revolution and a destruction of the foundations of the social order—how would one dissociate it from the framework of the party that exists *absolutely*, that is, does not exist in the way that all things are subject to space and time? No doubt the party could change its policies, and its ranks could vary according to circum-stances, growing inordinately or being scaled down. No doubt it could become the scene for rivalries among leaders or even replace those in charge. But the party always expressed the power that society is sup-posed to exercise over itself, without which society would fall apart. In order to qualify the shock introduced by the totalitarian regime, Arendt used a gripping formula: the regime turned on an "identification of man with the law."[8] But would it not be better to speak of an identification of the Communist body with the law, under whose effect each person felt himself summoned to want, think, and act in the same way?

This last remark returns us to the Arendtian characterization of ideol-ogy as a "stringent logicality as a guide to action" or "compulsory pro-cesses of deduction."[9] These formulas emphasized both the pretension to possess a total explanation of history and, furthermore, the separation of thought and experience. In spite of their relevance, though, they risk misconstruing the fact that the supposed logic (which, after all, adapted to the theoretical line's sometimes considerable oscillations according to circumstances) was supported only by the injunction for everyone *not to think* anything that contradicted or betrayed official theses—an injunction whose efficacy presupposed that, since it was a matter of thought, it would be interiorized by a subject [*Sujet*]. *Do not think* implies an extreme command, in a sense even more worrisome than the directive to confess crimes one has not committed, since such a confession can at least come with the consciousness of not having had guilty intentions. Thus in the very exercise of thought (in which Arendt saw the fulfillment of the reign of logic), the imprint of the law was found again.

For the party member, "do not think" signified *wanting not to think*, and this wanting resulted in a duty. Acknowledging this allows us immediately to discern the relationship maintained between obedience to the law and voluntary servitude. We return to La Boétie's subtle descriptions of the benefits that *some people*, and then a great number of them, draw from their enslavement. Among these benefits, one must count the power won by self-righteous minds to pose as master thinkers facing a mass of ignorant or irresolute people. And, by the same token, we return to the image concealed by the supposed tyranny of logic advanced by Arendt: a party to which everyone was fettered. In short, one must always return to the interweaving [*intrication*] of power, law, and knowledge in the party. Yet, I must insist, the party is only the concretion of the social, the motor element of the exclusion of plurality and division. One can no more delimit what depends on ideology than one can delimit what depends on law. Both are inseparable from a model of organization and incorporation. Law becomes immobile while, simultaneously, imprinting itself in a network of rules that places everyone squarely under its guillotine blade. Thought is compressed within the limits of a faultless knowledge. Power accepts nothing outside itself.

20
Impossible Reform

I T IS ONE THING to grasp the principal traits of what I have called the fabrication of Communist society; it is another to observe how its principles failed and only could have failed. First of all, they failed due to the impossibility of a central management of all social projects, a management that required the cooperation of party organs and multiple state administrations (from ministers to the directors of enterprises). Although supposed to provide means of relay for that central management, these organs and administrations each sought to expand the field of its own prerogative and to consolidate its authority in its area of expertise. The principles of Communist society, furthermore, failed due to rivalries that tore the bureaucracy apart, even inside the party. Finally, its principles failed because local administrators found it necessary to come to terms with the elementary needs of the population and their forms of resistance—the most persistent and intractable being the workers' refusal to submit to norms of production. The progressive weakening of the regime and futile attempts at reform leave no doubt as to the flaws of its constitution.

In 1956, during the Twentieth Congress of the Communist Party of the Soviet Union, new leaders denounced the scission between state and society, the inefficiency of ideology, the intrusion of politics in the economy, the sickness of bureaucratism, and the parasitism of party activists unaware of industrial and agricultural problems, seeking refuge in mountains of red tape and incapable of taking the initiative ("busy idlers," Khrushchev had said).[1] We learned in 1956 that the norms of planning had been only apparently or not at all followed, for the cadres implemented them only with the help of illegal procedures and private bureaucratic arrangements. We learned that centralization tended to fetter the initiatives of regional and local administrations and that ongoing attempts at decentralization ended up amplifying bureaucratism, from the Soviet republics down to the local level. Far from marking the end of the totalitarian regime and its replacement by some sort of authoritarianism (a thoroughly inconsistent concept, introduced by Sovietologists shamelessly claiming the mantle of political science), the post-Stalinist era enables us to perceive more clearly traits previously dissociated only with difficulty from Stalin's exorbitant power, the reign of terror, and the efficacy of ideology. Thus, indeed, after Stalin a collective leadership was founded (even if the figure of a supreme leader remained separate from it); the use of extensive violence was abandoned, and masses of prisoners were liberated from the gulag (even though a strict surveillance of the population continued, and new methods for removing adversaries and deviants appeared); and the arsenal of ideology from which slogans had constantly been drawn in the service of the creation of a new man—this arsenal was at last junked. And yet, the armature of the system remained unchanged.

One must recall the Twentieth Congress and the reports made by Khrushchev and his associates—Nikolai Bulganin, Mikhail Suslov, and Anastas Mikoyan—in order to grasp the widening gap between the representation of a society unified under the leadership of the party and the factual disorderliness of the political, economic, and cultural system.[2] The Twentieth Congress demonstrated that, despite reformers' pretensions, the regime's foundations were not questioned. What conclusions were taken from the vast inventory of the Soviet system's flaws? More than ever, militants had to mobilize themselves in the service of building a society dedicated to surpassing the level of the most advanced Western countries. They had to roll up their sleeves and take on the role of organizers while not getting in the way of agents of the production process. The state, whose apparatuses were judged plethoric, was not to leave to regional institutions and the republics the freedom to determine the composition and functioning of their own apparatuses. Not only was the party's power not limited, but, as Khrushchev noted, the "party has henceforth to play a still greater role in the affairs of the state, in the country's entire political, economic, and cultural life."[3] The reform's success required reinforcing the control of citizens' activities to the point that, as Khrushchev continued, "it would be wrong to think that only workers who are remiss have to be checked. It is necessary to check up also on the work of conscientious people, for control is, first of all, system."[4] As a matter of fact, this last citation suffices to demonstrate the permanence of the system. We should not presume that only the sector of production was involved. Khrushchev cautioned those who waited for a moderation of the Cheka (secret police), and he insisted on the need to "strengthen the state security agencies."[5] When he touched on questions of literature and art, his warning became more general: "The party has combated and will continue to combat untruthful depiction of Soviet reality."[6] All this to say that the turn taken in the direction of "realism," which so deceived complacent observers, meant that reality, at last freed from ideology, had to remain what the party defined it to be.

I would not think of denying the scale of changes under way in 1956. The new course proved irreversible; the danger of a return to mass terror was pushed away; the dominant class was delivered from intimidation by the egocrat;[7] the hierarchy was strengthened; and the necessity of confronting problems posed by the crisis of agriculture became clear, as did the necessity of considering the needs of a population whose indispensable participation in the development of production one could not hope to obtain by violence alone. Nevertheless, the ambiguity of Khrushchev's diagnosis and his prescribed remedies left one supposing that all efforts to make the regime flexible, to ameliorate the management of the economy, to restore leaders' prestige, and to stimulate the initiatives of political and administrative cadres—all this ran up against a limit, since the party's domination and the imperative of control at all echelons had to remain intangible. Actually, the inefficiency of measures adopted during the two decades following the Twentieth Congress would clearly demonstrate that the persistence of the image of a social power condensed in the party (and its supreme organ) went hand in hand with a degradation of the cadres' behaviors and mentalities, with a general propensity to submit themselves to norms, and with an increase of corruption. Planning not only suffered from being a government instrument; the fact that decisions were made at the top was not adequate to explain its failure. The malady turned out to be much more serious. It became painful enough to provoke new, extensive reforms in 1979, more than twenty years after the turning point of 1956. But they failed in turn, for the sickness that undermined economic life was the same that struck social life; it revealed what I have called the perversion of the law.

21

Planning and Social Division

I N AN ILLUMINATING STUDY published in the journal *Libre* in 1980,
Gérard Duchêne challenged the thesis of Sovietologists who argued
that the development of a second or "parallel economy on the margins
of the official economy characterized a new conjuncture."[1] This thesis
presupposed a clear dividing line between legal and illegal practices. Yet
Duchêne emphasized the priority of the juridical elaboration that un-
derlay the management of planning. An array of rules, many of them
codified, defined "the obligations and rights of every element in the productive hierarchy," from enterprises to the directing authorities of the
state. In his scrupulous dissection of a system supposed to guarantee
"the circulation of information and directives throughout the hierarchy,"
Duchêne showed that, at each level, actors were not only tempted but
actually forced to disobey the operative rules and leave the framework
of legality in order to give the appearance of following the instructions
of the Plan. If the basic vice was a belief in the possible control of all economic operations (beginning with enterprises' evaluations of their own
objectives and labor needs), it did not amount to the arbitrary imposition of norms by the directing organ. Whereas planning was backed up
by law and all violation of norms was subject to sanction, "legality was
incoherent because it required of all ordinary men in the eyes of the law
[*justicables*]—that is, everyone—to leave its framework and place themselves outside the law."[2] Duchêne was right to say *everyone*, since, as he
went on to make clear, this phenomenon could be found in all economic sectors, all echelons of the hierarchy, enterprises, and intermediary
agencies (local or regional councils and the ministries of the republics).
It was also found within the government and the party leadership—that

is, within the milieu of so-called lawmakers, since they themselves were forced to not apply their own policies. It is for these reasons that one could observe "a practical effacement of the distinction between the legal and illegal." Certainly, this depiction seems to contradict the idea of a totalitarian state, since it highlights the fractionating of economic institutions and the relative independence of each of them. And yet the "monopoly on ideas about economic life"—expressed by a kind of miring of the law in social organization—nevertheless remained.

Examining the split between theory and practice (which, anyway, no one on the ground could have ignored), Duchêne introduced the hypothesis of a will toward "social culpabilization." He observed that "the authorities have a great advantage in putting citizens outside the law" and that "the interiorization of repression is a dimension infrequently mentioned in economic studies of Soviet citizens' daily life."[3] Nevertheless, Duchêne abandoned this hypothesis for the reason that the state and party themselves suffered the effects of the degradation of law. But perhaps this argument was borne only against the thesis of a plot by the authorities (a "poorly administered Machiavellianism," he noted) and left room for the idea, already formulated in our discussion of the Stalinist penal code (chapter 17), of a conjunction of law and social power, whose consequence was to *objectively* convert every citizen into a *potentially guilty party*. From this point of view, we should admit that the phenomenon was beyond the scope of the state and party leaders' consciousnesses; those men noticed neither the degradation of the law nor the fact that their own power was being undermined.

Duchêne gave a second explanation of the persistence of "an official economy that rang false, apparently resonating with nothing," which was that it "constituted a *guarantee of social unity*, as much by its content (it was the discourse of unity and rationality) as by its *compulsory* and monopolistic character; it signified the *existence* of Soviet society." This judgment, which served as his conclusion, seems to me to have reached the heart of the matter. Duchêne added, "Existence and unity [are] affirmed against all chauvinism and other national struggles, against all forms of *social division*."[4] Again, we should point out that official discourse was that of the party and that social unity—the duty of unity—as well as the very existence of society (and, more generally, the socialist bloc, as Duchêne mentioned) derived from the unity, existence, and law of the party.

The reader can assay the relevance of such a study. Focusing only on the field of economic analysis, Duchêne showed that the dysfunctions of the planning system were irreparable, even though actors at all levels of responsibility were familiar with them and despite the fact that their solution required nothing more than abandoning the phantasmagoria of a society coinciding perfectly with itself. Yet I recall that during the 1970s, most Western observers marveled at the growth of the Soviet economy and the accomplishments of Soviet technology (exemplified by the launching of *Sputnik* in 1957), to the point that they seriously considered the possibility that the Soviet Union could surpass the level of the United States. Martin Malia noted, not without irony, the confidence inspired by the reformist current at the end of the Brezhnev era (later considered by Gorbachev as a period of stagnation) and then by the arrival in power of Yuri Andropov, considered a man of modernization. Still, as Malia indicated, Andropov spoke only of a "crisis of performance" and not of the system, though he did not ignore the latter.[5] He entrusted to a sociologist the mission of investigating the condition of the country, and her results, published in the *Novosibirsk Report*, left no room for doubt. "Advancing radical criticisms in orthodox language," Malia wrote, "[Tatyana] Zaslavskaya argued that Soviet central planning had become obsolete—indeed a fetter on production—and that Soviet society, far from being the harmonious unity depicted in official propaganda, was riven by conflicts between the rulers and the ruled, and hobbled by alienation, apathy, and lack of motivation among the working class."[6]

Let me now return to the proposition with which I began: the collapse of the Soviet regime and then of the socialist bloc had not been foreseen.[7] Nevertheless, there are degrees in the unforeseeable. The forewarning signs of incurable tensions had appeared as early as 1956 and had multiplied thereafter. All attempts at reform ran into a double impossibility: maintaining the party's control over the ensemble of social life, or attacking its prerogatives without destroying it. Thus Gorbachev's route, from perestroika to glasnost and from glasnost to democratization, came to demonstrate for the last time the futility of efforts to exit the cycle in which reformers were caught. In one sense, Gorbachev reformulated Khrushchev's project, but with an incomparable audacity. Thirty years after the Twentieth Congress, it is true, the state of Soviet society and the international situation had changed appreciably. In any case, they could not be separated, since the strategy intended to construct a power capable of defying the United States by intervening throughout the world had ended in a considerable worsening of the Soviet economy. To be sure, one could rightly ask what the regime's chances for survival might have been with the help of Gorbachev's more prudent policies. It is probable that the Soviet government's prestige was weakened by the sudden abandonment of military competition with the United States, the campaign of reconciliation with the West, and the acceptance of defeat in Afghanistan. In any event, I will not try to demonstrate that the collapse of Communism had to occur at the time it did, nor will I attempt to minimize the events that precipitated that collapse. Essentially, the scenario that unfolded after 1985 showed that, if upholding the regime required its reform, and if a fully engaged reform prohibited establishing limits on it, a revolution was inevitable.

In the beginning, perestroika constituted only a new version of modernization. However, encroaching upon the interests of the apparatchiks, solidly anchored in society, was enough to arouse their violent opposition. Next came the support Gorbachev sought and obtained from liberal intellectuals and then the liberation of Andrei Sakharov (one can ask if this event has been properly appreciated, since it signified a legitimation of dissidence, even more so since the hero did not play the game of collaboration proposed to him). After that, Gorbachev encouraged the press, whose principal organs were entrusted to liberals under the name of glasnost. He decided to appeal to public opinion and the party base in order to get around the obstacles raised by the hierarchy. Gorbachev facilitated the organization of free elections (no matter the restrictions accompanying them) and announced the program that would make the Soviet Union into a socialist state founded on the rule of law. All these initiatives, in a conjuncture where conservatives mobilized and held on to their privileges, had the effect of agitating the population, stirring up nationalist demands in the republics, and launching an unmasterable movement.

As audacious as Gorbachev's policies were, his objective was not the destruction of the party. His maneuvers for treating the conservatives delicately, when he feared being seen as overwhelmed by the liberals, were a first sign. His profession of Communist faith after the failure of the putsch as well as his subsequent declarations confirmed it. That is to say, unlike Khrushchev, he took the decisive step when he decided to disassociate the state from the party, meanwhile claiming to remain at the helm of both of them. Khrushchev had concluded from his penetrating critique of bureaucracy only the necessity of reinforcing the party's control over the party—a dream. For his part, Gorbachev forged the more ambitious, but no less aberrant project of delimiting the functions of the party *in reality*, at a distance from the functions of a government deriving its legitimacy from popular suffrage. For the party was not—is it necessary for me to say it again?—an institution *inside* society, whose prerogatives one could disavow with impunity. The party *was* the prerogative. Beyond the mass of its agents, whose ineffectiveness was widely known, it had not ceased to possess legitimacy. To limit it was to destroy the symbolic pole or, as I would like to say, the imaginary pole of the social.

Knowledgeable observers believed they could conclude that the party was no longer anything, that *real* power had escaped it in order to pass into the hands of the technocrats of the Plan, managers, the army, and directors of the military-industrial complex. But, as I have written on another occasion, *this nothing partook of everything* [*ce rien tenait à tout*]. It was necessary that the party be rooted out from society so that society could be identified in its own movement and rediscover the meaning and direction of the possible. Communist power gave way like a colossus whose strength depended only on the image of the fear he had once inspired and whose muscles suddenly gave out as soon as he came out of his listlessness and groped for support around himself.[8]

We have not wondered enough about the absence of the army on the public scene when the political crisis came to a head. In other circumstances, it had decided the victory of a party faction; Khrushchev, for instance, had received the support of Georgy Zhukov.[9] This time, it remained as if petrified (the putsch was the affair of a handful of brainless soldiers). One could believe for a moment that the army was waiting for the right hour to act. In fact, even after the party's dismemberment, it did not come on the scene. Was this not the sign that it drew its legitimacy only from the party and that, once the latter was shaken and then destroyed, it proved to be disoriented? The strength of this army, which had made the world tremble, suddenly disappeared. As for the power of the KGB or of the directors of the military-industrial complex, one looked in vain for any trace of them in 1989, 1990, or 1991. Boris Yeltsin's coup d'état was carried out in a kind of institutional void. No less astonishing was the conflagration that, starting from Moscow, blew over the Communist citadels of Eastern Europe, one after the other. Poland was already half farmed out to the domination of the Kremlin leaders, and everyone knew that Hungary and Czechoslovakia remained submitted to them only for fear of the Soviet armies. On that score, the socialist bloc was fissured. But the most solid bastion, the German Democratic Republic, in spite of the strength of its army and police, was carried away in the upheaval. Countries long outside the Soviet orbit—Romania and Albania—saw the apparatuses of repression crumble. Few events have better taught the primacy of the political over relations of force.

22

Psychologism and Moralism at Fault

According to the two historians whose arguments provided me with my starting point, the end of Communism furnished the solution to problems posed by its birth and its attractiveness to a large part of the world. As I have noted, according to François Furet, a parenthesis had been closed; Communism had been relegated to the past—"the past of an illusion." According to Martin Malia, the fact that the Soviet regime "collapsed like a house of cards" proved that it had never been anything besides a house of cards. These postmortems found confirmation in the adage that the greatest desire produces the greatest harm (Raymond Aron had said, paraphrasing Pascal, "Whoever creates the angel creates the beast"). From this point of view, psychological history provides the ultimate key to the Communist adventure. This history only teaches us to survey the damages of a "great belief." Nevertheless, the fact that this belief was diffused so widely merits explanation. Thus psychological history becomes tied to the history of modern societies, for without this link, psychological history loses its inspiration. Communism thus seemed to emerge out of the very flesh of democracy, tumbling down the slope of egalitarianism until its final downfall.

One might say that desire, belief, or illusion plays such a large role in the life of the individual that, in order to have some knowledge of them, one must do more than consult the individual and rely on his professions of faith, the version he gives (possibly to himself) of the meaning of his acts, and even the interpretation he makes of his dreams. Another exigency emerges when it comes to analyzing a social formation and investigating the nature of its institutions and predominant representations.

For representations do not result from individuals' desires, beliefs, or illusions, as if, taken one at a time, individuals all reveal the same frame of mind, given similar conditions of existence or the shared attraction to those who profess a doctrine. Social representations—one might more accurately call them schemata for the apprehension of the social—have their own consistency that needs to be explained. Accomplished authors have for a long time taught us to distinguish religious belief in medieval Europe from its role when combined with political institutions; to differentiate Calvinism as a doctrine from its role when combined with economic practices; to define the role of bourgeois ideology in the transformations that resulted from the repudiation of aristocratic values; or, more generally, to consider the symbolic and the imaginary in the analysis of social facts.

This last opposition, like the others, is open to debate. Indeed, once it is admitted that political power possesses a symbolic signification, one cannot forget that it must always be visible [*ostensible*] and appeal to the imagination. That is to say, one is justified in identifying the mark of the imaginary when the One captivates most of his or its subjects to the point that they lose the meaning and direction of both their own identity and the distance that separates them from one another. Likewise, once it is admitted that the state in the modern world becomes a generative organ of the nation or, as one used to say in the nineteenth century, the teacher of the nation, one must agree that it turned into an imaginary power when it appeared as the sole source of authority, the separation of public power and civil life fading away. Generally speaking, since political power, the state, justice, equality, and freedom are not entirely real things, the question posed by their symbolic or imaginary function is not settled a priori. We can observe that social representations are ordered according to relationships that are not accidental and, at the same time, that they each bear the mark of a particular history. For example, it is one thing to know what the notion of freedom becomes in a contemporary democracy, and it is another to ask about the notion of equality. Tocqueville taught us enough about the discordance between these two notions and the variety of aspects under which each appeared for the example to seem completely convincing. But it is no less necessary to understand how dominant representations in a political system are articulated, combined, and modified together over time. Thus one sees a kind of democratic syntax asserted. Even judging from the present that it has deteriorated, the logic of this syntax still survives, as long as it has not collapsed into another language—in other words, into another regime.

There is no doubt that, with respect to democracy, the Communist regime revealed another syntax. Thus it is disconcerting that many analysts who have not hesitated to qualify it as totalitarian have always stopped at denouncing the evil spells of a doctrine—socialism—judged to be the product of a deviation from democratic ideology. Such commentators have detected in the history of Communism only the abominable adventures of an enterprise driven by egalitarianism or submission to a law of history. I have discussed this latter phenomenon. As for egalitarianism, is it true that it was the bad offspring of democratic equality and that it came to beget a new model of organization and a new style of existence? Equality, when it came to be recognized as natural, was not merely the object of a belief. It gave meaning and direction to human relationships in the space of the polity, or, independently of all affiliation to any particular polity, it instituted a nonnegotiable advance [*un irréversible*] for thought. This in spite of the fact that inequalities of all kinds remained and that, as a consequence of colonialism and racial prejudice, equality was persistently denied.

To return to Marcel Mauss's expression, equality is put in the presence of "total social facts" whose meanings are political, economical, juridical, moral, and aesthetic. Furthermore, equality penetrates the very life of the psyche, which gives in to once-forbidden thoughts. Consequently, egalitarianism—if one means the belief in real equality or, what amounts to the same thing, an imaginary of equality—appears in many ways: equality of income, the abolition of the distinction between governing and governed, and so forth. More generally, no matter the social register (school, family, sexuality), it converts the negation of a natural hierarchy into a negation of differences in positions. It is not surprising that, in a bourgeois society molded by capitalism, egalitarianism was, on the one hand, essentially conceived as the expression of a desire to dispossess the wealthy of their wealth and, on the other, resonated with socialism. Nevertheless, this egalitarianism was not cut off from a framework of democratic representations. The fiction of real egalitarianism did not cease to be combined with the idea of rights. Although they also required satisfaction and thus eluded every principle of arbitration, hence of justice, those rights bore the mark of a demand for freedoms.

Was this the case in Russia? Wildfires of egalitarianism broke out during the revolution and shortly thereafter among the peasantry, whereas egalitarian theories had previously been carried by populist currents. One would be wrong to confuse these phenomena with what Tocqueville described as a democratic inclination born from the improvement of the equality of conditions, which he discovered in America as the sign of the uniformity of society, or which he observed in France as a democracy abandoned to its untamed instincts through the fault of an elite incapable of understanding its meaning and direction or of regulating it. How could one say that the egalitarian passion, as it has been attributed to the Bolsheviks, was imported from the West? It had not been the motor of Leninist politics, even if in a first phase of the revolution the Leninists knew how to make good use of the violence rampant in the campaigns against property owners: the construction of socialism was expressly subordinated to the introduction of the norms of industrial capitalism. Even more absurd would it be to present Stalinist de-kulakization as the sign of a will toward leveling conditions. Its objective was to destroy the peasantry altogether and to make the state the owner of the totality of the means of production, thus ensuring the domination of a bureaucratic stratum over the ensemble of the population. It would exhaust the reader to revisit again the new social discrimination that, far from being the sign of the revolution skidding out of control, was essential to the regime.

23
Communism and the Constitution of the World-Space

I T IS A FACT that the Soviet regime provided a model for many countries. To different degrees, it attracted people everywhere and came to present an alternative on a planetary scale between two forms of society. The antagonism between two powers or coalitions that resulted from this alternative seemed for a moment to decide the fate of humanity. Is it necessary to conclude from the sudden decomposition of the regime that the whole world had been dreaming, its adversaries as well as its partisans? It would be more fitting to acknowledge that, during the twentieth century, a path had in reality opened. Although it was proved to be an impasse, this path revealed the intensity of shocks triggered by practices and representations paradigmatic of European societies, shocks that made the earth tremble.

The Communist enterprise is indeed illuminated by resituating it within the framework of what one today calls globalization, a process often readily attributed to Communism's defeat if only the resulting expansion of the market is considered. But the signs of this process were apparent much earlier. Certainly, the Soviet regime was something other than a last imperial adventure, driven by unprecedented means on a hitherto unthinkable scale (even though there is reason to take an interest in the fate of the idea of empire). But it is rarely observed that the formation of a *single world-space* provided the resources to conceive, beyond different cultures, political systems, and inequalities in development, a *single social state*; a total mastery of human relations under the name of the One; an abolition of divisions that, no matter their manifestations, had always implied an experience of the Other; and, lastly, a system in which the positions of dominating and dominated would be eliminated.

It was such an event I had in mind (*event* is the right word to indicate that, with Communism, something happened to humanity that cannot be dissolved in the flux of time) when I drew attention to the connection and interpenetration of schemas of institution, socialization, and representation characteristic of Western regimes, on the one hand, and, on the other, of regimes that in spite of any transformation remained semi-Asiatic. I also had this event in mind when I highlighted the birth of a new political space from the graft of two antecedent spaces onto each other. The opposition between Western and Asiatic society is no doubt crude. I introduced it not to substitute the idea of a duality of development for the idea of a unilateral history of humanity. Instead, my intention was to discern the signs of the genesis of an entirely new society in Russia at a given time. Examining the traits of a phenomenon at once localizable and having become unlocalizable after it acquired a universal meaning and affected the entire world, we are led to assess the effects of the erosion of barriers among different political systems, modes of production, and—the word is not too strong—civilizations.

There is, however, no reason to consider the advent and rise of Communism in terms of either necessity or contingency. Doing so would involve, in some respects, resorting to a theory of history. We should be led only by the investigation of the phenomenon. I have not disengaged from that phenomenon in order to grasp—from what place could I?—an ordered sequence of humanity's transformations. Nor have I lost its meaning in the search for accidents without which it would not have developed. I have asked only what it discloses. We are no longer able to differentiate between the objective and the subjective. To say that Communism developed as a consequence of the encounter and crystallization of elements from multiple sources does not imply that it depended on chemistry or geology. And to say that it signified the germination of a project that one can decipher in the intentions of a small number of individuals does not imply that those individuals were simple instruments or authors of it. The unprecedented type of party that emerged in Russia at the beginning of the twentieth century, I have already remarked, was not the product of Lenin's imagination, even if one should recognize his "genius" in having captured in a conjuncture the meaning and direction of a marriage of opposites and in having opened the way for a conception of despotism without despots, democracy without citizens, capitalism without capitalists, a proletariat without a workers' movement, and a state without a framework of laws and rights proper to it. Lenin introduced the schema of a society at once entirely articulated according to the principle of the rationality of organization and entirely incorporated according to the principle of the identification of the individual with the community.

The conjuncture to which I refer was marked by World War I. For without this event, would a revolution have removed the tsarist regime? Would the Bolsheviks have become capable of imposing the dictatorship of a party-state? These questions lead back to the hypothesis of contingency. I could limit myself to saying that the tireless reasoning of if–then dispenses with the need to understand that which *is*, and that it has no other virtue than to deliver us from the myth of necessity. Nevertheless, I would like to note first of all that Bolshevism's traits were designed a dozen years before the start of World War I. The war, though one could decide that it was the product of fortuitous causes, only precipitated (extraordinarily, it is true) a process already under way: not only an interdependence of European nations but the unification of the globe—the constitution of a world-space.

The violence of the war achieved a previously unknown degree of intensity and scale. It came to pass that a tremendous potential for the destruction of what one believed to be the accomplishments of civilization had gathered on the underside of the progress of industry and science. The idea of a mobilization of all sectors of activities, the idea of a single commandment everyone felt obliged to obey, the idea of the insignificance of the individual with respect to state power—these ideas became conceivable or at least realizable only as a consequence of the radicalization of violence, and especially its legitimation. Thus one can think that Communism (as fascism did in another situation) took from the war experience one of the sources of its project of "total domination," to use Arendt's term, a domination that extended over the broadest possible area and was rooted in the deepest depths of society. In fact, numerous authors, notably Arendt herself, pointed out the war's role in the rise of Communism, not only because it led to the breakup of the tsarist regime, but because it created a new situation, transformed relations among nations, weakened the political and social order inside each country (however different the fates of victors and vanquished), and unsettled ways of thinking.

For his part, Furet underscored in some of the most convincing pages of his book the characteristics of World War I and, notably, the phenomenon of "total mobilization" that everywhere accompanied the integration of the masses into the national community.[1] Describing revolutionary effervescence in Europe after the war, and the discredit incurred by Social Democrats and socialists for having disavowed internationalism in 1914, he observed that the victory of the Bolsheviks had been welcomed as the promise of a new era. Since events taking place in Russia far from justified the enthusiasm of part of the Left, the mistake to which some fell victim seemed due to these wartime and postwar circumstances. Furet's picture, though fair, did not clarify the politics of Western Communists over the long term, their stubborn will to bind themselves to the party of Lenin and then Stalin, as well as their ability to reproduce that party as a model. To the first mistake of initial enthusiasm one must thus add other mistakes, always fed by the illusion that the homeland of socialism could not falter. Nevertheless, according to Furet's interpretation, everything happened as if the recognized role of the war as accelerator (of globalization as well as of the movement propitious to a regime based on the total mobilization of material resources and human energies) no longer had to be considered in the history of Western societies or in the history of Germany and Italy, both carried away in the fascist experience. The idea of the opening of a passage into the heart of democratic societies (within which revolutionary and totalitarian aspirations were connected) was pushed aside. So was the idea that these aspirations were able to be fulfilled in the existence, power, and eventual capacity for expansion of the Soviet state.

We have already considered the following questions: During these decades, were French Communists blind to events taking place in Russia? Were they, dare I say, increasingly blind when signs of the unrelenting domination of the party-state multiplied under Stalin's reign? Did not a great number of them—leaders, apparatchiks, and ideologue intellectuals—perceive Soviet society *as it was*, to the point of not wanting to know or wanting to not know about the oppression and terror taking place there? Soviet society *as it was*. This means a society entirely subjugated to the norms of the party-state and opening numerous careers to new cadres; a society led by an iron hand, delivered from all kinds of parasites, having triumphed over democracy's disorders; and a society that had become a source of a great anticapitalist power while constructing an industrial empire in which the working masses obeyed the law of organization. In short, if the image of Russia forged by Communists in the West resulted from a phantasmagoria, was it not confused with the phantasmagoria of the One that governed the Soviet system? And did not that phantasmagoria of the One come to be realized in institutions and methods of action alike?

The fact is that societies in the democratic tradition all resisted the Communist current, especially in the Anglo-Saxon world. But it is also true that they all provided it opportunities. This fact is enough to make one think that they themselves concealed antagonisms conducive to the rejection of freedoms. It also makes one think that, though the conditions that made it possible were special, the establishment in one place in the world, in a large country, of a totalitarian regime viewed as revolutionary revealed these antagonisms and represented a "solution" that neither democracy nor capitalism foretold.

Furet remained satisfied with an ideological schema: the idea of Communism was born in Europe before emigrating to Russia, where, after having been introduced as a result of explosive tensions and multiple accidents (including the war), it encountered the test of reality. It then returned to its original terrain, where it kept alive the persistent desire to believe in the success of a proletarian state. In the end, nothing remains from these adventures. Yet what does this schema conceal? Communism in its Bolshevik version was presented as the product of the Marxist movement and, more generally, of revolutionary currents that had emerged during the nineteenth century, though none of these had ever been disposed toward the formation of a party designed to assume leadership of the proletariat. All revolutionary currents were branded with the utopian label. Although we cannot forget that Marx had explicitly criticized utopia, we can still acknowledge—how to deny it?—that the notion of an end to history or prehistory had a utopian character.

It is no less important to recall that these currents had in no small way contributed to the formation of workers' movements that had shaped modern democracy. In truth, utopia is not easily cut off from a social critique that refashions the spirit of the times and, to some

extent, political, economic, and legal realities. And if one speaks of utopia, one must also recognize it in the pole opposite to socialism, namely,
economic liberalism, the generator of practices that, if they had evolved
freely, would have been devastating. I would add that wanting to make
the idea of Leninism, or better yet of Stalinism, coincide with socialism wrongly omits the steadfastness of the radical Left's opposition to
Communism. The attempt to reestablish the continuity of an ideological
trajectory not only seems to do violence to the history of ideas, but also
reflects an astonishing resistance to considering Soviet Communism as
a regime in which the distinctions constitutive of all civil life, as well as
thought itself, were attacked. Out of fear of confronting a question that
weakens his confidence in Reason, the historian seems to make an effort
to keep his distance from the event, to circumscribe it in time (the past)
and the space of the world (it was a product of democratic society), and
to return it to the sphere of passions (it was a new blindness of men).
Nevertheless, as Arendt had admirably understood, in spite of its destruction, Communism leaves the trace of having crossed a threshold of
the possible.[2]

If one can agree that Communism arose from a state of the world,
there is room to fear, without giving in to catastrophism but out of simple concern for vigilance, the effects of an always narrower imbrication
of changes everywhere affecting political regimes, economic structures,
and social and religious movements of different natures. To the placidity
of liberals who see in globalization the combined development of the
market and democracy, it seems worthwhile to oppose the judgment that
Paul Valéry had formulated during the interwar years: "Henceforward
every action will be reechoed by many unforeseen interests on all sides;
it will produce a chain of immediate events—confused reverberations in
a closed space. The *effects of effects*, which were formerly imperceptible
or negligible in relation to the length of human life and to the radius of
any human power, are now felt almost instantaneously at any distance;
they return immediately to their causes, and only die away in the unpredictable."[3] Valéry, it is true, conceived of only a gathering disorder. He
did not imagine new models of domination with a universal vocation.
We have made progress in the consciousness of the unforeseeable.

NOTES

Translator's Introduction

1. Eric Hobsbawm, *The Age of Extremes: The Short Twentieth Century, 1914–1991* (New York: Penguin, 1994).

2. Mikhail Gorbachev, "Will East and West Finally Meet?" *Toronto Star*, 24 February 1992, A1.

3. André Gide, *Retour de l'URSS* (Paris: Gallimard, 1936); *Return from the USSR*, trans. Dorothy Bussy (New York: Knopf, 1937); Claude Lefort, "Retour de Pologne," *Socialisme ou Barbarie* 21 (1957), in the first edition of *Éléments d'une critique de la bureaucratie* (Geneva: Droz, 1971; Paris: Gallimard, 1979), and in *L'Invention démocratique: Les limites de la domination totalitaire* (Paris: Fayard, 1981).

4. Lefort's English translators, including the present one, have felt the need to repeat the basic facts of his biography. Lefort himself once offered a forceful meditation on how repetition haunts novelty, though his topic was not biography but the tradition of radicalism: "Le Nouveau et l'attrait de la répétition," in *Éléments d'une critique de la bureaucratie*; "Novelty and the Appeal of Repetition," trans. John B. Thompson, in *The Political Forms of Modern Society: Bureaucracy, Democracy, Totalitarianism*, ed. and intro. John B. Thompson (Cambridge, Mass.: MIT Press, 1986). For more by Lefort in English, see *Democracy and Political Theory*, trans. David Macey (Minneapolis: University of Minnesota Press, 1988), and *Writing: The Political Test*, trans. and ed. David Ames Curtis (Durham, N.C.: Duke University Press, 2000). For introductions and explorations, see Dick Howard, "Introduction to Lefort," *Telos* 22 (1974–1975): 2–30; *The Marxian Legacy*, 2nd ed. (Minneapolis: University of Minnesota Press, 1988); and *The Specter of Democracy: What Marx*

and Marxists Haven't Understood and Why (New York: Columbia University Press, 2002), esp. chap. 8; Claude Habib and Claude Mouchard, eds., *La Démocratie à l'oeuvre: Autour de Claude Lefort* (Paris: Editions Esprit, 1993); Hugues Poltier, *Claude Lefort: La découverte du politique* (Paris: Michalon, 1997), and *Passion du politique: La pensée de Claude Lefort* (Geneva: Labor et Fides, 1998); Esteban Molina, *Le Défi du politique: Totalitarisme et démocratie chez Claude Lefort* (Paris: Harmattan, 2005); and Bernard Flynn, *The Philosophy of Claude Lefort: Interpreting the Political* (Evanston, Ill.: Northwestern University Press, 2005). The last chapter of Flynn's fine book examines *Complications: Communism and the Dilemmas of Democracy* and revisits arguments made in his review essay "Totalitarianism After the Fall," *Constellations* 9, no. 3 (2002): 436–44.

5. See, for instance, Maurice Merleau-Ponty, *Le Visible et l'invisible, suivi de Notes de travail*, ed. Claude Lefort (Paris: Gallimard, 1964); *The Visible and the Invisible*, trans. Alphonso Lingis (Evanston, Ill.: Northwestern University Press, 1968), and *La Prose du monde*, ed. Claude Lefort (Paris: Gallimard, 1969); *The Prose of the World*, trans. John O'Neil (Evanston, Ill.: Northwestern University Press, 1973).

6. Claude Lefort, "La Politique et la pensée de la politique," *Les Lettres nouvelles* 32 (1963), in *Sur une colonne absente: Écrits autour de Merleau-Ponty* (Paris: Gallimard, 1978), partially translated as "Thinking Politics," trans. Taylor Carman, Mark B. N. Hansen, and Alexander Hickox, in *The Cambridge Companion to Merleau-Ponty*, ed. Taylor Carman and Mark B. N. Hansen (Cambridge: Cambridge University Press, 2004), 356–57.

7. Edgar Morin, Claude Lefort, and Jean-Marc Coudray [Cornelius Castoriadis], *Mai 1968: La Brèche: Premières réflexions sur les événements* (Paris: Fayard, 1968, 1988).

8. The term is Merleau-Ponty's. Flynn, *Philosophy of Claude Lefort*, 21.

9. Claude Lefort, *Le Travail de l'oeuvre: Machiavel* (Paris: Gallimard, 1972, 1986), 432.

10. Ronald Aronson, "Communism's Posthumous Trial," *History and Theory* 42 (2003): 245 [review of Stéphane Courtois et al., *The Black Book of Communism: Crimes, Terror, Repression*, foreword by Martin Malia, ed. Mark Kramer, trans. Jonathan Murphy (Cambridge, Mass.: Harvard University Press, 1999); François Furet, *The Passing of an Illusion: The Idea of Communism in the Twentieth Century*, trans. Deborah Furet (Chicago: University of Chicago Press, 1999); Tony Judt, *The Burden of Responsibility: Blum, Camus, Aron, and the French Twentieth Century* (Chicago: University of Chicago Press, 1998);

and Michel Dreyfus et al., eds., *Le Siècle des communismes* (Paris: Éditions de l'atelier/Éditions ouvrières, 2000))].

11. François Furet, *Le Passé d'une illusion: Essai sur l'idée communiste au XXè siècle* (Paris: Laffont, 1995); *Passing of an Illusion*; Martin Malia, *The Soviet Tragedy: A History of Socialism in Russia, 1917–1991* (New York: Free Press, 1994).

12. Aronson, "Communism's Posthumous Trial," 222–45.

13. For an appreciation, see Stephen Kotkin, "On Martin Malia (1924–2004)," *New York Review of Books*, 13 January 2005, 39.

14. "Z" [Martin Malia], "To the Stalin Mausoleum," *Daedalus* 119, no. 1 (1990), in *Without Force of Lies: Voices from the Revolution of Central Europe in 1989–90: Essays, Speeches, and Eyewitness Accounts*, ed. William M. Brinton and Alan Rinzler (San Francisco: Mercury House, 1990), 424.

15. In 1999 Martin Malia could write of the "five years of silence from the guild of Russian historians" about his book ("A Reply to Yanni Kotsonis," *Russian Review* 58, no. 4 [1999]: 676–77). See also Yanni Kotsonis, "The Ideology of Martin Malia," review of *The Soviet Tragedy*, by Martin Malia, *Russian Review* 58, no. 1 (1999): 124–30, and "Yanni Kotsonis Responds," *Russian Review* 58, no. 4 (1999): 677–78.

16. Martin Malia, "Judging Nazism and Communism," *National Interest* 69 (2002): 63–78. See also the dissection by Michael David-Fox, "On the Primacy of Ideology: Soviet Revisionists and Holocaust Deniers (In Response to Martin Malia)," *Kritika: Explorations in Russian and Eurasian History* 5, no. 1 (2004): 81–105.

17. Stéphane Courtois et al., *Le Livre noir du communisme: Crimes, terreurs et répression* (Paris: Laffont, 1997). See also Martin Malia, "The Lesser Evil?" *Times Literary Supplement*, 27 March 1998, 3.

18. See the review of the Courtois affair by Anson Rabinbach, "Communist Crimes and French Intellectuals," *Dissent* 45, no. 4 (1998): 61–66.

19. "The French Revolution is over" is the title of the first part of François Furet, *Penser la Révolution française* (Paris: Gallimard, 1978); *Interpreting the French Revolution*, trans. Elborg Forster (Cambridge: Cambridge University Press and Maison des Sciences de l'Homme, 1981).

20. Michael Scott Christofferson, *French Intellectuals Against the Left: The Antitotalitarian Moment of the 1970s* (New York: Berghahn, 2004).

21. Examining Furet, *Passing of an Illusion*, and Courtois et al., *Black Book of Communism*, together are J. Arch Getty, "The Future Did Not Work," *Atlantic Monthly*, March 2000, 113–16; Jolanta T. Pekacz, "Twentieth-Century

Communism: The Rise and Fall of an Illusion," *Canadian Journal of History* 36, no. 2 (2001): 311–16; Ronald Grigor Suny, "Obituary or Autopsy? Historians Look at Russia/USSR in the Short Twentieth Century," *Kritika: Explorations in Russian and Eurasian History* 3, no. 2 (2002): 303–19; and Aronson, "Communism's Posthumous Trial," 222–45.

22. In a personal conversation (July 2002), Malia strongly emphasized the inevitability of the utopian impulse—"People need utopia"—and its capacity to take new forms. Furet, *Passing of an Illusion*, 502–3.

23. Claude Lefort, "Esquisse d'une genèse de l'idéologie dans les sociétés modernes," *Textures* 8–9 (1974), in *Les Formes de l'histoire: Essais d'anthropologie politique* (Paris: Gallimard 1978); "Outline of the Genesis of Ideology in Modern Societies," trans. John B. Thompson, in *Political Forms of Modern Society*. For Lefort, ideology is neither, à la Furet and Malia, a set of ideas to be applied and materialized nor merely, à la Arendt, the "stringent logicality" of an idea. Remaining fixed on the symbolic field of representation misapprehends the imaginary constitution of ideology as a political form of the social (see n. 25). Lefort distinguishes among bourgeois, totalitarian, and "invisible" ideologies, the last characterizing late-modern, media-driven Western societies. Totalitarian regimes attempt to homogenize originary political and social divisions through particular institutions and discourses that distortedly profess a universal vocation. Discourse is ideological in its projection of an imaginary unity that accompanies an apparent politicization of all spheres of activity. However, the attempt to unify all social divisions cannot ever be completely accomplished, and new divisions and conflicts are engendered. Lefort's clearest departure from Hannah Arendt in chapter 16 of *Complications* is his emphasis on the party as the institution that concretizes the imaginary aspiration for a society coinciding perfectly with itself. Chapters 16 and 17 reprise elements of Lefort, "Thinking With and Against Hannah Arendt," *Social Research* 69, no. 2 (2002): 447–61. Lefort also assesses Raymond Aron's view of ideology in chapter 8 and Aleksandr Solzhenitsyn's view of ideology in chapter 19 of *Complications*. See Flynn, *Philosophy of Claude Lefort*, chap. 9.

24. On Lefort's treatment of this theme, see Miguel Abensour, "'Savage Democracy' and 'Principle of Anarchy'" (1994), trans. Max Blechman, *Philosophy and Social Criticism* 28, no. 6 (2002): 703–26. For its currency in the broader intellectual climate, see Samuel Moyn, "Savage and Modern Liberty: Marcel Gauchet and the Origins of New French Thought," *European Journal of Political Theory* 4, no. 2 (2005): 164–87, and "Of Savagery and Civil Society:

Pierre Clastres and the Transformation of French Political Thought," *Modern Intellectual History* 1, no. 1 (2004): 55–80.

25. The lineage of this inheritance is knotty. Jacques Lacan did the most in the postwar era to formulate the distinctions among what he called the Symbolic, Imaginary, and Real, but he always acknowledged his debt to Claude Lévi-Strauss. Lefort also sharpened his use of the symbolic and imaginary through engagements with sociologists and anthropologists such as Gregory Bateson, Pierre Clastres, Arthur Maurice Hocart, Abraham Kardiner, Lévi-Strauss, and Marcel Mauss, among others. Flynn cautions against seeing Lefort as borrowing from Lacan, even though the psychoanalytic provenance is implicit, in *Philosophy of Claude Lefort*, 89–94, 118–19, and passim. One might also compare Slavoj Žižek's Lacanian reading of the Soviet show trials with Lefort's discussion in chapter 17 of *Complications*. Žižek argues that proving the guilt of the accused compensated for the accuser's own guilt in having already betrayed the party's holism and the Communist *we*, in *Did Someone Say Totalitarianism? Five Interventions in the (Mis)Use of a Notion* (London: Verso, 2001), 102–40. See also the helpful article by Marc de Kesel, "Act Without Denial: Slavoj Žižek on Totalitarianism, Revolution, and Political Act," *Studies in East European Thought* 56, no. 4 (2004): 299–334. One notable difference between Lefort and Žižek seems to be that the former speaks of the imaginary but seldom of the real, of form not absence, whereas the latter's continuing pursuit of the real helps explain his reconstructed Leninism.

26. Michael Hardt and Antonio Negri also argue for the common against a postnationalist imperium of markets, media, and militaries, in *Empire* (Cambridge, Mass.: Harvard University Press, 2000), and *Multitude: War and Democracy in the Age of Empire* (New York: Penguin, 2004). But their appeal to pure immanence is at odds with Lefort's dogged insistence that political division and emptiness are constitutive of the social. See my review article on the Hardt and Negri debates, "Empire Versus Multitude: Place Your Bets," *Ethics and International Affairs* 18, no. 3 (2004–2005): 97–108.

27. Olivier Roy, *Globalized Islam: The Search for a New Ummah* (New York: Columbia University Press, 2004), and *L'Échec de l'Islam politique* (Paris: Seuil, 1992); *The Failure of Political Islam*, trans. Carol Volk (Cambridge, Mass.: Harvard University Press, 1995). Lefort makes only one reference to Islam in *Complications*: "Even after the experience of Communism and fascism, one can still find well-intentioned minds concluding that a terrorist power, such as an

Islamist one, should obviously not be refused democratic legitimacy as long as it is derived from suffrage."

28. Paul Berman, *Terror and Liberalism* (New York: Norton, 2003); Peter Beinart, "A Fighting Faith: An Argument for a New Liberalism," *New Republic*, 13 December 2004, 17, and *The Good Fight: Why Liberals—and Only Liberals—Can Win the War on Terror and Make America Great Again* (New York: HarperCollins, 2006). The discourse is mirrored by British writers John Gray, *Al Qaeda and What It Means to Be Modern* (New York: Norton, 2003), and Oliver Kamm, *Anti-Totalitarianism: The Left-Wing Case for a Neoconservative Foreign Policy* (London: Social Affairs Unit, 2005). Steering clear of updated totalitarianism in favor of an older model is Mark Lilla, "The New Age of Tyranny," *New York Review of Books*, 24 October 2002, 1–8. The self-evidence of the Islamic–totalitarian connection to neoconservatives has no shortage of examples. Besides the *National Review*, see, for example, Natan Sharansky, with Ron Dermer, *The Case for Democracy: The Power of Freedom to Overcome Tyranny and Terror* (New York: PublicAffairs, 2004).

29. Dick Howard has traced Lefort's development from antitotalitarianism to democratic theory, highlighting the force of "indetermination" in the latter, in *Specter of Democracy*, chap. 8. Samuel Moyn has pointed out the limits of "anti-" politics that oppose and do not affirm, and has emphasized Lefort's influence on a contemporary practitioner of historical-political reflection, in, for example, "Antitotalitarianism and After," introduction to Pierre Rosanvallon, *Democracy Past and Future*, ed. Samuel Moyn (New York: Columbia University Press, 2006). For an attempt to rescue aestheticized politics from totalitarian abuse, with a brief nod to Lefort, see Michael Halberstam, *Totalitarianism and the Modern Conception of Politics* (New Haven, Conn.: Yale University Press, 1999). For the difficulty of providing a systematic account of totalitarian, authoritarian, and dictatorial regimes, see Sigrid Meuschel, "Theories of Totalitarianism and Modern Dictatorships: A Tentative Approach," *Thesis Eleven* 61 (2000): 87–98. For an impassioned assessment of the post–September 11, 2001, situation and of Arendt's elimination of colonialism from her portrait of totalitarianism (its imperialist prehistory notwithstanding), see Nikhil Pal Singh, "Cold War Redux: On the 'New Totalitarianism,'" *Radical History Review* 85 (2003): 171–81. Domenico Losurdo argues that once its empirical specificity is lost, totalitarianism becomes a deductive category that lumps together dissimilar regimes and turns attention away from the West's own totalizations, in "Towards a Critique of the Category of Totalitarianism," trans. Marella Morris and John Morris, *Histori-*

cal Materialism 12, no. 2 (2004): 25–55. On totalitarianism's persistent elasticity and ambiguity as a "semantic marker" since the 1930s, see Anson Rabinbach, "Moments of Totalitarianism," *History and Theory* 45 (2006): 72–100 [review of Tzvetan Todorov, *Hope and Memory: Reflections on the Twentieth Century*, trans. David Bellos (Princeton, N.J.: Princeton University Press, 2003); Richard Overy, *The Dictators: Hitler's Germany and Stalin's Russia* (London: Allen Lane, 2004); Henry Rousso, ed., *Stalinism and Nazism: History and Memory Compared*, trans. Lucy B. Golsan, Thomas C. Hilde, and Peter S. Rogers (Lincoln: University of Nebraska Press, 2004); Ian Kershaw and Moshe Lewin, eds., *Stalinism and Nazism: Dictatorships in Comparison* (Cambridge: Cambridge University Press, 1997); and Žižek, *Did Someone Say Totalitarianism?*].

30. Pierre Rosanvallon, *Le Capitalisme utopique: Histoire de l'idée du marché* (Paris: Seuil, 1979, 1999).

Author's Introduction

Notes in brackets are my additions to the original notes. Where possible, I refer to translations of works cited; when necessary, I indicate that I have modified them.—Trans.

1. [François Furet, *Le Passé d'une illusion: Essai sur l'idée communiste au XXè siècle* (Paris: Laffont, 1995); *The Passing of an Illusion: The Idea of Communism in the Twentieth Century*, trans. Deborah Furet (Chicago: University of Chicago Press, 1999).]

2. [François Furet, *Penser la révolution française* (Paris: Gallimard, 1978); *Interpreting the French Revolution*, trans. Elborg Forster (Cambridge: Cambridge University Press and Maison des Sciences de l'Homme, 1981). See also Claude Lefort, "Penser la révolution dans la Révolution française," *Annales* 2 (1980), in *Essais sur le politique (XIXè–XXè siècles)* (Paris: Seuil, 1986); "Interpreting Revolution Within the French Revolution," in *Democracy and Political Theory*, trans. David Macey (Minneapolis: University of Minnesota Press, 1988).]

3. [Furet had been attacked from the Left for dissociating 1789 from modern revolutionary politics. Lefort seems not to have wanted his critical engagement with Furet to be taken as an endorsement of his friend's detractors.]

4. [Martin Malia, *The Soviet Tragedy: A History of Socialism in Russia, 1917–1991* (New York: Free Press, 1994); *La Tragédie soviétique: Histoire*

du socialisme en Russie, 1917–1991, trans. Jean-Pierre Bardos (Paris: Seuil, 1995).]

5. [Malia, *Soviet Tragedy*, 8; *La Tragédie soviétique*, 19.]

6. [Hannah Arendt, *The Origins of Totalitarianism* (New York: Harcourt Brace Jovanovich, 1951, 1973). See also Claude Lefort, "Hannah Arendt et la question du politique," *Cahiers du Forum pour l'indépendence et la paix* 5 (1985), in *Essais sur le politique*; "Hannah Arendt and the Question of the Political," in *Democracy and Political Theory*.]

7. [Marcel Mauss, "Essai sur le don: Forme et raison d'échange dans les sociétés archaïques" (1923–1924), in *Sociologie et anthropologie*, intro. Claude Lévi-Strauss (Paris: PUF, 1950), 274, 276; *The Gift: The Form and Reason for Exchange in Archaic Societies*, foreword by Mary Douglas, trans. W. D. Halls (New York: Norton, 1990), 78, 80 (translation modified). See also Claude Lefort, "L'Échange et la lutte des hommes," *Les Temps modernes* 64 (1951), in *Les Formes de l'histoire: Essais d'anthropologie politique* (Paris: Gallimard, 1978).]

8. [Mauss, "Essai sur le don," 276; *Gift*, 80.]

9. [Raymond Aron, *Démocratie et totalitarianisme* (Paris: Gallimard, 1965, 1970), originally published as *Sociologie des sociétés industrielles: Esquisse d'une théorie des régimes politiques* (Paris: Centre de documentation universitaire, 1958); *Democracy and Totalitarianism*, ed. and intro. Roy Pierce, trans. Valence Ionescu (Ann Arbor: University of Michigan Press, 1990).]

1. Wisdom of the Historian

1. [Martin Malia, *The Soviet Tragedy: A History of Socialism in Russia, 1917–1991* (New York: Free Press, 1994), ix; *La Tragédie soviétique: Histoire du socialisme en Russie, 1917–1991*, trans. Jean-Pierre Bardos (Paris: Seuil, 1995), 9.]

2. [Malia, *Soviet Tragedy*, 4]; *La Tragédie soviétique*, 14.

2. Critique of "Couch Liberalism"

1. Harold Rosenberg, "Couch Liberalism and the Guilty Past" (1955), in *The Tradition of the New* (New York: Horizon Press, 1959); "Le Libéralisme rampant et le passé coupable," in *La Tradition du nouveau*, trans. Anne Marchand (Paris: Éditions de Minuit, 1962).

2. [Rosenberg, "Couch Liberalism and the Guilty Past," 221]; "Le Libéralisme rampant et le passé coupable," 219.

3. [Karl Radek (1885–1939) was active in the German Communist movement following World War I. He played a brief leading role in Russia during the 1920s before falling out of favor. "Rehabilitated" in the 1930s, he was then accused of treason and infamously "confessed" at his trial in 1937. He is believed to have died in prison. Rosenberg, "Couch Liberalism and the Guilty Past," 223]; "Le Libéralisme rampant et le passé coupable," 220–21. [Radek is quoted in People's Commissariat of Justice of the USSR, *Report of Court Proceedings in the Case of the Anti-Soviet Trotskyite Centre* (Moscow: People's Commissariat of Justice of the USSR, 1937), 550.]

4. [Andrei Vyshinsky (1883–1954) was the principal Soviet prosecutor who oversaw the trials of the Stalinist purges. Rosenberg, "Couch Liberalism and the Guilty Past," 222]; "Le Libéralisme rampant et le passé coupable," 220.

5. [Rosenberg, "Couch Liberalism and the Guilty Past," 224]; "Le Libéralisme rampant et le passé coupable," 221.

6. [Rosenberg, "Couch Liberalism and the Guilty Past," 227; "Le Libéralisme rampant et le passé coupable," 225; Leslie A. Fiedler, "Hiss, Chambers, and the Age of Innocence" (1950), in *An End to Innocence: Essays on Culture and Politics* (Boston: Beacon Press, 1955), 3.]

7. [Rosenberg, "Couch Liberalism and the Guilty Past," 229, citing Fiedler, "Hiss, Chambers, and the Age of Innocence," 23–24]; "Le Libéralisme rampant et le passé coupable," 226–27.

8. [Rosenberg, "Couch Liberalism and the Guilty Past," 229]; "Le Libéralisme rampant et le passé coupable," 226–27.

9. [Rosenberg, "Couch Liberalism and the Guilty Past," 229; "Le Libéralisme rampant et le passé coupable," 227.]

10. [Rosenberg, "Couch Liberalism and the Guilty Past," 232; "Le Libéralisme rampant et le passé coupable," 230.]

11. [Rosenberg, "Couch Liberalism and the Guilty Past," 231, citing Leslie Fiedler, "McCarthy and the Intellectuals" (1954), in *End to Innocence*, 70]; "Le Libéralisme rampant et le passé coupable," 228.

12. [Rosenberg, "Couch Liberalism and the Guilty Past," 232]; "Le Libéralisme rampant et le passé coupable," 230.

13. [Rosenberg, "Couch Liberalism and the Guilty Past," 236]; "Le Libéralisme rampant et le passé coupable," 234.

14. [The Old Bolsheviks generally had been party members before 1917 and were persecuted by the Stalinist machinery during the purges of the 1930s.]

15. [Rosenberg, "Couch Liberalism and the Guilty Past," 236]; "Le Libéralisme rampant et le passé coupable," 235.

16. [Rosenberg, "Couch Liberalism and the Guilty Past," 237]; "Le Libéral-isme rampant et le passé coupable," 235.

17. [Rosenberg, "Couch Liberalism and the Guilty Past," 230]; "Le Libéral-isme rampant et le passé coupable," 228.

18. [Rosenberg, "Couch Liberalism and the Guilty Past," 238]; "Le Libéral-isme rampant et le passé coupable," 236

19. [Rosenberg, "Couch Liberalism and the Guilty Past," 238–39]; "Le Libéralisme rampant et le passé coupable," 237; ["Statement of the L.C.F.S.," *Partisan Review* 4, no. 4 (1939): 126. Rosenberg himself had signed this manifesto, as had Clement Greenberg, Dwight Macdonald, Philip Rahv, and others. The libertarian ethos of the League for Cultural Freedom and Socialism, which rebelled against the constraints of Popular Front orthodoxies, might be contrasted with that of the contemporaneous Committee for Cultural Freedom (1939), formed by Sidney Hook and a persuaded John Dewey, and that of the Americans for Intellectual Freedom (1949), the immediate forerunner to the Congress for Cultural Freedom, paragon of cold war anti-Communism.]

20. Daniel Bell, *The End of Ideology* (Glencoe, Ill.: Free Press, 1960).

21. [Harold Rosenberg, "Death in the Wilderness," in *Tradition of the New*, 258]; "Mort dans le désert," in *La Tradition du nouveau*, 256.

3. Autopsy of an Illusion

1. François Furet, *Le Passé d'une illusion: Essai sur l'idée communiste au XXè siècle* (Paris: Laffont, 1995), 14; [*The Passing of an Illusion: The Idea of Communism in the Twentieth Century*, trans. Deborah Furet (Chicago: University of Chicago Press, 1999), x (translation modified)].

2. Furet, *Le Passé d'une illusion*, 14; [*Passing of an Illusion*, x].

3. Furet, *Le Passé d'une illusion*, 11; [*Passing of an Illusion*, vii (translation modified)].

4. Claude Lefort, "Le Totalitarianisme sans Staline: L'URSS dans une nouvelle phase," *Socialisme ou Barbarie* 14 (1956), in *Éléments d'une critique de la bureaucratie* (Geneva: Droz, 1971; Paris: Gallimard, 1979); ["Totalitarianism Without Stalin," trans. Alan Sheridan, in *The Political Forms of Modern Society: Bureaucracy, Democracy, Totalitarianism*, ed. and intro. John B. Thompson (Cambridge, Mass.: MIT Press, 1986)].

5. Claude Lefort, "Le Nouveau et l'attrait de la répétition," in *Éléments d'une critique de la bureaucratie*, 360; ["Novelty and the Appeal of Repetition," trans. John B. Thompson, in *Political Forms of Modern Society*, 133].

6. Claude Lefort, "Une autre révolution," *Libre* 1 (1977), in *L'Invention démocratique: Les limites de la domination totalitaire* (Paris: Fayard, 1981), 251.

7. [For Lefort's perspective as events were unfolding, see "Réflexions sur le présent" (1989–1991), in *Écrire: À l'épreuve du politique* (Paris: Fondation Saint-Simon/Calmann-Lévy, 1992); "Reflections on the Present," in *Writing: The Political Test*, trans. and ed. David Ames Curtis (Durham, N.C.: Duke University Press, 2000).]

8. Aleksandr Solzhenitsyn, *L'Archipel du Goulag, 1918–1956: Essai d'investigation littéraire, première et deuxième parties*, 2 vols., trans. Jacqueline Lafond et al. (Paris: Seuil, 1974), 1:218; [*The Gulag Archipelago, 1918–1956: An Experiment in Literary Investigation: I–II*, trans. Thomas P. Whitney (New York: Harper & Row, 1975), 298. See also Claude Lefort, *Un homme en trop: Réflexions sur "L'Archipel du Goulag"* (Paris: Seuil, 1976)].

9. [Solzhenitsyn, *L'Archipel du Goulag*, 1:218; *Gulag Archipelago*, 298.]

10. Furet, *Le Passé d'une illusion*, 14; [*Passing of an Illusion*, ix].

11. [Furet, *Le Passé d'une illusion*, 14; *Passing of an Illusion*, ix.]

12. Furet, *Le Passé d'une illusion*, 13; [*Passing of an Illusion*, ix].

13. Furet, *Le Passé d'une illusion*, 93; [*Passing of an Illusion*, 66 (translation modified)].

14. Furet, *Le Passé d'une illusion*, 18; [*Passing of an Illusion*, 2 (translation modified)].

15. Furet, *Le Passé d'une illusion*, 19–20; [*Passing of an Illusion*, 4].

16. Furet, *Le Passé d'une illusion*, 15; [*Passing of an Illusion*, xi].

4. Marx's False Paternity

1. François Furet, *Le Passé d'une illusion: Essai sur l'idée communiste au XXè siècle* (Paris: Laffont, 1995), 15; [*The Passing of an Illusion: The Idea of Communism in the Twentieth Century*, trans. Deborah Furet (Chicago: University of Chicago Press, 1999), xi].

2. Furet, *Le Passé d'une illusion*, 14–15; [*Passing of an Illusion*, x].

3. [Boris Souvarine (1895–1984) was a worker and journalist who, after World War I, was active in the Third International and helped lead the French Communist Party. His early criticisms of Stalin and his refusal to side with Trotsky set him on the path that eventually culminated in a decidedly anti-Communist socialism. He later edited the journal *Le Contrat social*.] Boris Souvarine, *La Critique sociale, 1931–1934* (Paris: Éditions de la Différence, 1983), 9.

4. Souvarine, *La Critique sociale*, 8.

5. The Idea of Revolution and the Revolutionary Phenomenon

1. François Furet, *Le Passé d'une illusion: Essai sur l'idée communiste au XXè siècle* (Paris: Laffont, 1995), 96; [*The Passing of an Illusion: The Idea of Communism in the Twentieth Century*, trans. Deborah Furet (Chicago: University of Chicago Press, 1999), 68].

2. Furet, *Le Passé d'une illusion*, 96; [*Passing of an Illusion*, 68].

3. [Giuseppe Ferrari, *Machiavel: Juge des révolutions de notre temps*, preface by Georges Navet (1849; Paris: Payot et Rivages, 2003). For a discussion of this work, see Claude Lefort, "La Révolution comme principe et comme individu," in *Différences, valeurs, hiérarchie: Mélanges offerts à Louis Dumont* (Paris: École des Hautes Études en Sciences Sociales, 1984), and *Essais sur le politique (XIXè–XXè siècles)* (Paris: Seuil, 1986); "The Revolution as Principle and as Individual," in *Democracy and Political Theory*, trans. David Macey (Minneapolis: University of Minnesota Press, 1988). On Machiavelli, see, notably, Claude Lefort, *Le Travail de l'oeuvre: Machiavel* (Paris: Gallimard, 1972, 1986); the essays collected in *Les Formes de l'histoire: Essais d'anthropologie politique* (Paris: Gallimard, 1978); and "Machiavel et la *verità effetuale*," in *Écrire: À l'épreuve du politique* (Paris: Fondation Saint-Simon/Calmann-Lévy, 1992); "Machiavelli and the *Verità Effetuale*," in *Writing: The Political Test*, trans. and ed. David Ames Curtis (Durham, N.C.: Duke University Press, 2000).]

4. [For Lefort on Tocqueville, see "Reversibilité: Liberté politique et liberté de l'individu," *Passé-Présent* 1 (1982), in *Essais sur le politique*; "Reversibility: Political Freedom and the Freedom of the Individual," in *Democracy and Political Theory*; "De l'égalité à la liberté: Fragments d'interprétation de *De la démocratie en Amérique*," *Libre* 3 (1978), in *Essais sur le politique*; "From Equality to Freedom: Fragments of an Interpretation of *Democracy in America*," in *Democracy and Political Theory*; and "Tocqueville: Démocratie et art d'écrire" (1989–1992), in *Écrire*; "Tocqueville: Democracy and the Art of Writing," in *Writing*.]

5. [Gordon S. Wood, *The Creation of the American Republic, 1776–1787* (Chapel Hill: University of North Carolina Press, 1969)]; *La Création de la république américaine*, trans. François Delastre, preface by Claude Lefort (Paris: Belin, 1991); Bernard Bailyn, *The Ideological Origins of the American Revolution* (Cambridge, Mass.: Harvard University Press, 1967).

6. Lefort, "Préface," in Wood, *La Création de la république américaine*, 8.

7. Furet, *Le Passé d'une illusion*, 46; [*Passing of an Illusion*, 31–32].

8. Furet, *Le Passé d'une illusion*, 47; [*Passing of an Illusion*, 32].

9. Furet, *Le Passé d'une illusion*, 48; [*Passing of an Illusion*, 33].

10. Furet, *Le Passé d'une illusion*, 46; [*Passing of an Illusion*, 31–32 (translation modified)].

11. Marc Ferro, *La Révolution de 1917*, vol. 1, *La Chute du tsarisme et les origines d'Octobre* (Paris: Aubier, 1967; Albin Michel, 1992); [*The Russian Revolution of February 1917*, trans. J. L. Richards (Englewood Cliffs, N.J.: Prentice-Hall, 1972); *La Révolution de 1917*, vol. 2, *Octobre, naissance d'une société* (Paris: Aubier, 1976); *October 1917: A Social History of the Russian Revolution*, trans. Norman Stone (London: Routledge & Kegan Paul, 1980)]; and *Des soviets au communisme bureaucratique: Les mécanismes d'une subversion* (Paris: Gallimard, 1964).

12. [The *cahiers de doléances* were lists of grievances collected on the local level, a practice existing for several centuries as a means to gauge popular sensibilities. The *cahiers* presented to the États Généraux in 1789 are understood to have helped launch the French Revolution.]

13. Boris Souvarine, *Staline: Aperçu historique du bolchévisme* (Paris: Plon, 1935), 138–39; [*Stalin: A Critical Survey of Bolshevism*, trans. C. L. R. James (New York: Alliance, 1939), 145 (translation modified)].

14. Ferro, *Des soviets au communisme bureaucratique*, 157.

15. [The Soviet Union had a number of different secret police formations that succeeded one another: the Cheka (1917–1922); Gosudarstvennoe Politicheskoe Upravlenie, or GPU (1922–1934); Narodnyi Komissariat Vnutrennikh Del, or NKVD (1934–1954); and Komitet Gosudarstvennoi Bezopasnosti, or KGB (1954–1991).]

16. Souvarine, *Staline*, 243; [*Stalin*, 259 (translation modified)].

17. Souvarine, *Staline*, 50; [*Stalin*, 48–49; Vladimir Ilyich Lenin, *What Is to Be Done?* (1902), in *Collected Works*, 45 vols. (Moscow: Foreign Languages Publishing House, 1960–1970), 5:383–84; Lenin, cited in Karl Kautsky, "Die Revision des Programms der Sozialdemokratie in Oesterreich," *Die Neue Zeit* 20, no. 1 (1901–1902): 79–80].

18. Leon Trotsky, quoted in Souvarine, *Staline*, 66; [*Stalin*, 64–65. See also, in part, Leon Trotsky, *Our Political Tasks* (1904; London: New Park, 1979), 77, 124].

19. Furet, *Le Passé d'une illusion*, 179–80; [*Passing of an Illusion*, 148. My emphasis.]

20. Leon Trotsky, *Staline*, trans. Jean van Heijenoort (Paris: Grasset, 1948), xiii; [*Stalin: An Appraisal of the Man and His Influence*, ed. and trans. Charles Malamuth (New York: Harper, 1941), xv].

6. The Jacobin Phantom

1. [Georgy Plekhanov (1856–1918) was a revolutionary leader and founder of the Russian social democracy movement. Early on, he sided with the Mensheviks against the Bolsheviks. Returning to Russia from exile during the revolution, he left disenchanted and died shortly thereafter.]

2. [Thermidor refers to the overthrow on July 27, 1794, or 9 Thermidor in the revolutionary calendar, of Robespierre and the Terror.] I called attention to Trotsky's various appreciations of a Soviet Thermidor in "La Contradiction de Trotski et le problème révolutionnaire," *Les Temps modernes* 39 (1949), reprinted as "La Contradiction de Trotsky," in *Éléments d'une critique de la bureaucratie* (Geneva: Droz, 1971; Paris: Gallimard, 1979); ["The Contradiction of Trotsky," trans. Alan Sheridan, in *The Political Forms of Modern Society: Bureaucracy, Democracy, Totalitarianism*, ed. and intro. John B. Thompson (Cambridge, Mass.: MIT Press, 1986)].

3. [Claude Lefort, "La Terreur révolutionnaire," *Passé-Présent* 2 (1983), in *Essais sur le politique (XIXè–XXè siècles)* (Paris: Seuil, 1986); "The Revolutionary Terror," in *Democracy and Political Theory*, trans. David Macey (Minneapolis: University of Minnesota Press, 1988).]

4. [Claude Lefort, "Edgar Quinet: La Révolution manquée," *Passé-Présent* 2 (1983), in *Essais sur le politique*; "Edgar Quinet: The Revolution That Failed," in *Democracy and Political Theory*. See also Lefort's presentation of Jules Michelet, *La Cité des vivants et des morts: préfaces et introductions* (Paris: Belin, 2002).]

5. François Furet, *Penser la Révolution française* (Paris: Gallimard, 1978), 81; [*Interpreting the French Revolution*, trans. Elborg Forster (Cambridge: Cambridge University Press and Maison des Sciences de l'Homme, 1981), 56].

6. [Louis de Saint-Just, "Rapport sur les factions de l'étranger" (March 13, 1794), in *Oeuvres de Saint-Just*, intro. Jean Gratien (Paris: Éditions de la Cité Universelle, 1946), 213.]

7. Dominique Colas, *Le Léninisme* (Paris: PUF, 1982), 146. [Colas cites Vladimir Ilyich Lenin, "Contribution à l'histoire de la dictature" (1920), in *Oeuvres*, 45 vols. (Paris: Éditions sociales, 1961), 31:366; "A Contribution to the History of the Question of the Dictatorship: A Note," in *Collected Works*,

45 vols. (Moscow: Foreign Languages Publishing House, 1960–1970), 31:353, and "La Révolution prolétarienne et la renégat Kautsky" (1918), in *Oeuvres*, 28:224; "The Proletarian Revolution and the Renegade Kautsky," in *Collected Works*, 28:236.]

8. V. I. Lenin, "Les Taches immédiates du pouvoir des soviets" (April 28, 1918), in *Oeuvres choisies*, 2 vols. (Moscow: Éditions en langues étrangères, 1947), 2:396–97; ["The Immediate Tasks of the Soviet Government," in *Selected Works in Two Volumes*, 2 vols. in 4 (Moscow: Foreign Languages Publishing House, 1951), 2(1):480–81].

9. [Lenin, "Les Taches immédiates du pouvoir des soviets," 398; "Immediate Tasks of the Soviet Government," 481–82.]

10. Lenin, "Les Taches immédiates du pouvoir des soviets," 387; ["Immediate Tasks of the Soviet Government," 470 (translation modified)].

11. Lenin, "Les Taches immédiates du pouvoir des soviets," 394; ["Immediate Tasks of the Soviet Government," 478–79 (translation modified)].

12. Colas, *Le Léninisme*, 189ff.

13. [In March 1921, sailors at the naval base at Kronstadt rebelled against Bolshevik rule. The rebellion was forcibly put down. See Lefort, "La Contradiction de Trotsky et le problème révolutionnaire"; "Contradiction of Trotsky," 47–48.]

7. A Liberal Matrix for the Dictatorship of the Proletariat?

1. François Furet, *Le Passé d'une illusion: Essai sur l'idée communiste au XXè siècle* (Paris: Laffont, 1995), 39; [*The Passing of an Illusion: The Idea of Communism in the Twentieth Century*, trans. Deborah Furet (Chicago: University of Chicago Press, 1999), 24].

2. Claude Lefort, "L'Image du corps et le totalitarisme" (1974), *Confrontation* 2 (1979), in *L'Invention démocratique: Les limites de la domination totalitaire* (Paris: Fayard, 1981), 170; ["The Image of the Body and Totalitarianism," trans. Alan Sheridan, in *The Political Forms of Modern Society: Bureaucracy, Democracy, Totalitarianism*, ed. and intro. John B. Thompson (Cambridge, Mass.: MIT Press, 1986), 301–2].

3. [Furet, *Le Passé d'une illusion*, 39; *Passing of an Illusion*, 24.]

4. [Furet, *Le Passé d'une illusion*, 40; *Passing of an Illusion*, 25.]

5. Furet, *Le Passé d'une illusion*, 40; [*Passing of an Illusion*, 25].

6. [Furet, *Le Passé d'une illusion*, 41; *Passing of an Illusion*, 26.]

7. [Furet, *Le Passé d'une illusion*, 41; *Passing of an Illusion*, 26.]

8. Furet, *Le Passé d'une illusion*, 173–74; [*Passing of an Illusion*, 142].

9. Leon Trotsky, *Staline*, trans. Jean van Heijenoort (Paris: Grasset, 1948), 584; [*Stalin: An Appraisal of the Man and His Influence*, ed. and trans. Charles Malamuth (New York: Harper, 1941), 421].

10. [For Lefort on Leo Strauss, see *Le Travail de l'oeuvre: Machiavel* (Paris: Gallimard, 1972, 1986), 259–305, and "Trois notes sur Leo Strauss," in *Écrire: À l'épreuve du politique* (Paris: Fondation Saint-Simon/Calmann-Lévy, 1992); "Three Notes on Leo Strauss," in *Writing: The Political Test*, trans. and ed. David Ames Curtis (Durham, N.C.: Duke University Press, 2000).]

11. [Leo Strauss, *Liberalism Ancient and Modern* (New York: Basic, 1968)]; *Le Libéralisme antique et moderne*, trans. Olivier Berrichon Seyden (Paris: PUF, 1990), and "The Crisis of Our Time" and "The Crisis of Political Philosophy," in *The Predicament of Modern Politics*, ed. Harold J. Spaeth (Detroit: University of Detroit Press, 1964). [The two essays were revised and combined in Strauss, "Political Philosophy and the Crisis of Our Time," in *The Post-Behavioral Era: Perspectives on Political Science*, ed. George J. Graham and George W. Carey (New York: McKay, 1972).]

12. [Strauss, *Liberalism Ancient and Modern*, v; *Le Libéralisme ancien et moderne*, 7–8.]

13. [Strauss, *Liberalism Ancient and Modern*, vii]; *Le Libéralisme ancien et moderne*, 10.

14. [Claude Lefort, "Droits de l'homme et politique," *Libre* 7 (1980), in *L'Invention démocratique*; "Politics and Human Rights," trans. Alan Sheridan, in *Political Forms of Modern Society*.]

15. Alexis de Tocqueville, *De la démocratie en Amérique*, in *Oeuvres complètes*, 18 vols., ed. Jacob Peter Mayer (Paris: Gallimard, 1951), 1(1):34; [*Democracy in America*, trans. Arthur Goldhammer (New York: Library of America, 2004), 39. Lefort cites Tocqueville as saying "un corps politique de société" instead of "un corps de société politique"].

16. Tocqueville, *De la démocratie en Amérique*, 1(1):34; [*Democracy in America*, 40].

17. Tocqueville, *De la démocratie en Amérique*, 1(1):38; [*Democracy in America*, 44–45].

18. Tocqueville, *De la démocratie en Amérique*, 1(2):16, 17; [*Democracy in America*, 489, 490].

19. Alexis de Tocqueville, *L'Ancien Régime et la Révolution*, in *Oeuvres complètes*, 2(2):199; [*The Old Regime and the Revolution*, 2 vols., ed. and intro.

François Furet and Françoise Mélonio, trans. Alan S. Kahan (Chicago: University of Chicago Press, 2001), 2:163].

20. Furet, *Le Passé d'une illusion*, 174; [*Passing of an Illusion*, 142 (translation modified)].

21. Furet, *Le Passé d'une illusion*, 41; [*Passing of an Illusion*, 26].

8. *Democracy and Totalitarianism*

1. [Raymond Aron, *Démocratie et totalitarianisme* (Paris: Gallimard, 1965, 1970), originally published as *Sociologie des sociétés industrielles: Esquisse d'une théorie des régimes politiques* (Paris: Centre de documentation universitaire, 1958); *Democracy and Totalitarianism*, ed. and intro. Roy Pierce, trans. Valence Ionescu (Ann Arbor: University of Michigan Press, 1990). Lefort previously discussed this text on the occasion of the Soviet Union's and Communism's unraveling: "Réflexions sur le présent" (1989–1991), in *Écrire: À l'épreuve du politique* (Paris: Fondation Saint-Simon/Calmann-Lévy, 1992); "Reflections on the Present," in *Writing: The Political Test*, trans. and ed. David Ames Curtis (Durham, N.C.: Duke University Press, 2000), 266–69.]

2. [The two previous Soviet constitutions were written in 1918 and 1924.]

3. Aron, *Démocratie et totalitarianisme*, 247. [The translation omits this line (165).]

4. [During the revolution, Nikolai Bukharin (1888–1938) had argued, against Lenin and Trotsky, that Russia stay in World War I as a prelude to world revolution. Editor of *Pravda*, member of the Politburo, and head of the Comintern, Bukharin fell in and out of favor with Stalin until he was finally tried and executed in 1938. Longtime Bolshevik Grigory Zinoviev (1883–1936) returned from exile in 1917 on the same train as Lenin. Also playing leading roles in the Politburo and Comintern, Zinoviev became, after Lenin's death, part of the ruling troika with Stalin and Lev Kamenev (1883–1936). When the troika succeeded in driving out Trotsky, Stalin in turn attacked Zinoviev and Kamenev. Their trials and executions in 1936 opened the Great Purges.]

5. Aron, *Démocratie et totalitarianisme*, 261; [*Democracy and Totalitarianism*, 174–75 (translation modified)].

6. [Especially in the Khrushchev and Brezhnev eras, "collective leadership" was invoked as a precaution against the kind of dictatorial concentration of power that Stalin had exercised.]

7. [Aron, *Démocratie et totalitarianisme*, 248; *Democracy and Totalitarianism*, 165–66 (translation modified).]

8. [Aron, *Démocratie et totalitarianisme*, 247; *Democracy and Totalitarianism*, 165 (translation modified).]

9. [Aron, *Démocratie et totalitarianisme*, 247; *Democracy and Totalitarianism*, 165.]

10. Aron, *Démocratie et totalitarianisme*, 249; [*Democracy and Totalitarianism*, 166 (translation modified)].

11. Dominique Colas, *Textes constitutionnels soviétiques* (Paris: PUF, 1987), 9.

12. ["Constitution (Fundamental Law) of the Russian Socialist Federated Soviet Republic" (1918), pt. 2, chap. 5, art. 9, in Aryeh L. Unger, *Constitutional Development in the USSR: A Guide to the Soviet Constitutions* (New York: Pica, 1982), 27–28.]

13. Colas, *Textes constitutionnels soviétiques*, 12–13.

14. ["The USSR Constitution of 1936," chap. 10, art. 126, in Unger, *Constitutional Development in the USSR*, 156.]

15. Aron, *Démocratie et totalitarisme*, 249; [*Democracy and Totalitarianism*, 166 (translation modified)].

16. Aron, *Démocratie et totalitarisme*, 249; [*Democracy and Totalitarianism*, 166 (translation modified)].

17. Aron, *Démocratie et totalitarisme*, 251; [*Democracy and Totalitarianism*, 168].

18. [Aron, *Démocratie et totalitarisme*, 256; *Democracy and Totalitarianism*, 171.]

19. Aron, *Démocratie et totalitarisme*, 256; [*Democracy and Totalitarianism*, 171 (translation modified)].

20. [Lefort's discussion of ideology here bears comparison with that in "Esquisse d'une genèse de l'idéologie dans les sociétés modernes," *Textures* 8–9 (1974), in *Les Formes de l'histoire: Essais d'anthropologie politique* (Paris: Gallimard, 1978); "Outline of the Genesis of Ideology in Modern Societies," trans. John B. Thompson, in *The Political Forms of Modern Society: Bureaucracy, Democracy, Totalitarianism*, ed. and intro. John B. Thompson (Cambridge, Mass.: MIT Press, 1986).]

21. [Aron, *Démocratie et totalitarisme*, 274; *Democracy and Totalitarianism*, 184.]

22. Aron, *Démocratie et totalitarisme*, 274; [*Democracy and Totalitarianism*, 184 (translation modified)].

23. [Aron, *Démocratie et totalitarisme*, 274; *Democracy and Totalitarianism*, 185.]

24. [Aron, *Démocratie et totalitarisme*, 274; *Democracy and Totalitarianism*, 185.]

25. [Sergey Kirov (1886–1934) rose to prominence after the revolution and was rewarded by Stalin in 1926 by being placed in charge of the Leningrad party. Kirov's popularity ended up turning Stalin against him. His murder in December 1934 was used by Stalin as a pretext for launching the trials of Zinoviev, Kamenev, and others.]

26. [Yury Piatakov (1890–1937) had sided with Bukharin during the revolution over the question of Russian participation in World War I. A pivotal figure in Ukraine, his oppositional efforts within the party led to his expulsion from it in 1927, though he returned to prominence in the early 1930s. After standing trial in 1936 alongside Karl Radek and others, he was executed the following year.]

27. [Despite being troubled by Bolshevik organizing principles even before World War I, Aleksey Rykov (1881–1938) played key leadership roles from the Petrograd Soviet forward. He served as chairman of the Council of People's Commissars (1924–1929) and joined in the machinations against Trotsky, though Stalin removed him from power soon thereafter. In 1938 he was tried and executed alongside Genrikh Yagoda (1891–1938) and others. Yagoda was a senior official in the Checka. In 1934 Stalin placed him in charge of the secret police, from where he oversaw the opening of the Great Purges, which quickly consumed him.]

28. [Mikhail Tukhachevsky (1893–1937) was a key military commander during the revolutionary wars, chief of staff for the Red Army from 1925 to 1928, and marshal of the Soviet Union in 1935. He was arrested in 1937 on charges of espionage and Trotskyist conspiracy and was executed alongside other military commanders.]

29. [Martin Malia, *The Soviet Tragedy: A History of Socialism in Russia, 1917–1991* (New York: Free Press, 1994), 268]; *La Tragédie soviétique: Histoire du socialisme en Russie, 1917–1991*, trans. Jean-Pierre Bardos (Paris: Seuil, 1995), 326.

30. [Malia, *Soviet Tragedy*, 269]; *La Tragédie soviétique*, 327.

9. The Myth of the Soviet Union in the West

1. [De-kulakization refers to the programmatic offensive against Soviet peasants in the 1930s following the institution of agricultural collectivization.

Kulak had meant a wealthy farmer, but the term eventually applied to almost any peasant who stood in the way of Stalinist policies.]

2. François Furet, *Le Passé d'une illusion: Essai sur l'idée communiste au XXè siècle* (Paris: Laffont, 1995), 175; [*The Passing of an Illusion: The Idea of Communism in the Twentieth Century*, trans. Deborah Furet (Chicago: University of Chicago Press, 1999), 143].

3. Furet, *Le Passé d'une illusion*, 177; [*Passing of an Illusion*, 145].

4. [Furet, *Le Passé d'une illusion*, 177; *Passing of an Illusion*, 146.]

5. [Furet, *Le Passé d'une illusion*, 177; *Passing of an Illusion*, 146.]

6. Furet, *Le Passé d'une illusion*, 295–300; [*Passing of an Illusion*, 251–56].

7. Furet, *Le Passé d'une illusion*, 14; [*Passing of an Illusion*, ix].

8. Furet, *Le Passé d'une illusion*, 15; [*Passing of an Illusion*, x].

9. [Claude Lefort, "La Méthode des intellectuels progressiste," *Socialisme ou Barbarie* 23 (1958), in *Éléments d'une critique de la bureaucratie* (Geneva: Droz, 1971; Paris: Gallimard, 1979).]

10. [Julius Martov (1873–1923) was a left-wing Menshevik leader who argued, against his comrades and with the Bolsheviks, for Russian withdrawal from World War I. He then led the Mensheviks' opposition to the Bolsheviks until the former were abolished. He was forced into exile the year he died.]

11. Marc Ferro, *L'Occident devant la Révolution soviétique: L'histoire et ses mythes* (Brussels: Éditions Complexe, 1991).

12. [Boris Souvarine, *Staline: Aperçu historique du bolchévisme* (Paris: Plon, 1935); *Stalin: A Critical Survey of Bolshevism*, trans. C. L. R. James (New York: Alliance, 1939)]; Yvon [Robert Guihéneuf], "Ce qu'est devenue la Révolution russe," *Les Brochures de la révolution prolétarienne* 2 (n.d.); [*Ce qu'est devenue la Révolution russe*, preface by Pierre Pascal (Paris: Librairie du travail, 1936); Ante Ciliga, *Au pays du grand mensonge*, trans. A. Gourevitch (Paris: Gallimard, 1938); *The Russian Enigma*, trans. Fernand G. Renier and Anne Cliff (London: Labour, 1940; Westport, Conn.: Hyperion Press, 1973). See also Claude Lefort, "Le Témoignage d'Antón Ciliga," *Les Temps modernes* 60 (1950), in *Éléments d'une critique de la bureaucratie*].

13. [André Gide, *Retour de l'URSS* (Paris: Gallimard, 1936); *Return from the USSR* (New York: Knopf, 1937).]

14. [The Section française de l'internationale ouvrière was founded in 1905. In 1920, elements favorable to the Russian Revolution broke away to form the French Communist Party. Rapprochement between the two parties in the mid-1930s culminated in the Popular Front of 1936.]

15. [Jan Valtin (Richard Julius Herman Krebs) (1904–1951) was a German Communist best known for his lengthy memoir about his exploits as an international secret agent, his survival of the Nazi camps, and his eventual emigration to the United States to escape postwar Stalinism. See his *Out of the Night* (New York: Alliance, 1941; Oakland, Calif.: AK Press, 2004)]; *Sans patrie, ni frontières* (Paris: Wapler, 1941; Paris: Lattès, 1975).

16. Furet, *Le Passé d'une illusion*, 411; [*Passing of an Illusion*, 356].

17. [Furet, *Le Passé d'une illusion*, 412; *Passing of an Illusion*, 358 (translation modified).]

18. [László Rajk (1909–1949) served as interior minister and foreign secretary of Hungary after World War II. Arrested for his opposition to Stalinism, his trial, "confession," and execution became a symbol of Hungarian nationalism, especially in 1956. Rudolf Slánsky (1901–1952) was general secretary of the Czechoslovakian Communist Party immediately after the war. He was also arrested for his opposition to Stalinism, and his trial, which resulted in his execution, is furthermore remembered for its anti-Semitism.]

19. [See also Claude Lefort, "L'Insurrection hongroise," *Socialisme ou Barbarie* 20 (1956–1957), and "Retour de Pologne," *Socialisme ou Barbarie* 21 (1957), in the first edition of *Éléments d'une critique de la bureaucratie* and in *L'Invention démocratique: Les limites de la domination totalitaire* (Paris: Fayard, 1981).]

10. The French Communist Party After World War II

1. Edgar Morin, *Autocritique* (Paris: Julliard, 1959).

2. [Victor Kravchenko, *I Chose Freedom: The Personal and Political Life of a Soviet Official* (New York: Scribner, 1946)]; *J'ai choisi la liberté: La vie publique et privée d'un haut-fonctionnaire soviétique*, trans. Jean de Kerdéland (Paris: Éditions Self, 1947), preface by Pierre Daix (Paris: Olivier Orban-Nouvelle Éditions Baudinière, 1980); Guillaume Malaurie, with Emmanuel Terré, *L'Affaire Kravchenko* (Paris: Laffont, 1982).

3. [Margarete Buber-Neumann (1901–1989) was the daughter-in-law of the philosopher Martin Buber. On her time in Siberia and Ravensbrück, see her *Als Gefangene bei Stalin und Hitler* (Zurich: Europa Verlag, 1949; Munich: Verlag der Zwölf, 1949); *Under Two Dictators*, trans. Edward Fitzgerald (New York: Dodd Mead, 1949). On her well-known encounter with Milená Jesenská, see her *Kafkas Freundin Milena* (Munich: Müller, 1963); *Mistress to*

Kafka: The Life and Death of Milena, intro. Arthur Koestler (London: Seck-er & Warburg, 1966), republished as *Milena*, trans. Ralph Mannheim (New York: Seaver, 1988), reprinted as *Milena: The Tragic Story of Kafka's Great Love* (New York: Arcade, 1997).]

4. Ante Ciliga, *Au pays du grand mensonge*, trans. A. Gourevitch (Paris: Gallimard, 1938); [*The Russian Enigma*, trans. Fernand G. Renier and Anne Cliff (London: Labour, 1940; Westport, Conn.: Hyperion, 1973)].

5. [David Rousset, *L'Univers concentrationnaire* (Paris: Pavois, 1946); *The Other Kingdom*, trans. Ramon Guthrie (New York: Reynal & Hitchcock, 1947; New York: Fertig, 1982), and *A World Apart*, trans. Yvonne Moyse and Rog-er Senhouse (London: Secker & Warburg, 1951); International Commission Against Concentration Camp Practices, *Les Conditions de la liberté en URSS: Le rôle de la décision administrative dans la procédure soviétique* (Paris: Pa-vois, 1951); *Police-State Methods in the Soviet Union*, ed. Jerzy G. Gliksman, trans. Charles R. Joy (Boston: Beacon Press, 1953).]

6. Jean-Paul Sartre and Maurice Merleau-Ponty, "Les Jours de notre vie," *Les Temps modernes* 51 (1950): 1155.

7. [The young Lefort was embroiled in a high-profile debate with Sartre at that time: Jean-Paul Sartre, "Les Communistes et la paix," *Les Temps modernes* 81 (1952), and *Les Temps modernes* 84–85 (1952); Claude Lefort, "Le Marxisme et Sartre," and Sartre, "Réponse à Lefort," *Les Temps modernes* 89 (1953); Lefort, "De la réponse à la question," *Les Temps modernes* 104 (1954). Sartre's two pieces were reprinted in *Situations VI: Problèmes du marxisme 1* (Paris: Gal-limard, 1964), and *Situations VII: Problèmes du marxisme 2* (Paris: Gallimard, 1965); *The Communists and the Peace, with a Reply to Claude Lefort*, trans. Martha H. Fletcher, John R. Kleinschmidt, and Philip R. Berk (New York: Bra-ziller, 1968). Lefort's two interventions were reprinted in *Éléments d'une cri-tique de la bureaucratie* (Geneva: Droz, 1971; Paris: Gallimard, 1979).]

8. [Romain Rolland (1866–1944), Nobel Prize laureate, visited the Soviet Union in 1935.]

9. [Maurice Merleau-Ponty, *Les Aventures de la dialectique* (Paris: Galli-mard, 1955); *Adventures of the Dialectic*, trans. Joseph Bien (Evanston, Ill.: Northwestern University Press, 1973).]

10. [Georges Cogniot (1901–1978) was a Communist legislator and editor of the French Communist Party paper, *L'Humanité*. Roger Garaudy (b. 1913) was a major party philosopher in postwar France, advocating Catholic–Com-munist dialogue during the 1960s and 1970s. In the early 1980s, he turned toward Islam, and in 1998 he was convicted of Holocaust denial by a French

court. Jean Kanapa (1921–1978), former student of Sartre, served as editor of *La Nouvelle critique* and slowly climbed the party hierarchy. In 1972 he was placed in charge of the party's section on foreign relations. Jean-Toussaint Desanti (1914–2002) joined the party during World War II and left subsequent to the 1956 events in Hungary. He was a philosophy professor at the Sorbonne, specializing in phenomenology and epistemology. Henri Lefebvre (1901–1991) was one of the most prolific and significant thinkers in the Marxist humanist tradition. He joined the party in 1928 and was expelled in 1958 for his anti-Stalinism. Maurice Caveing (b. 1923) is a philosopher of mathematics. Also participating was Victor Leduc (1911–1993), who edited the review *Action* after World War II and took up increasingly critical positions against the party, especially after 1956. He joined the Socialist Party in 1970, became national secretary, and advocated worker self-management (*autogestion*).] Roger Garaudy et al., *Mésaventure de l'antimarxisme: Les malheurs de M. Merleau-Ponty, avec une lettre de Georg Lukàcs* (Paris: Éditions sociales, 1956).]

11. [Hannah Arendt, *The Origins of Totalitarianism* (New York: Harcourt Brace, 1951, 1973), 362]; *Le Système totalitaire* [part III of *The Origins of Totalitarianism*], trans. Jean-Loup Bourget, Robert Davreau, and Patrick Lévy (Paris: Seuil, 1972), 89.

12. [Arendt, *Origins of Totalitarianism*, 362; *Le Système totalitaire*, p. 89.]

13. Arcadi Vaksberg, *Vchinski: Le procureur de Staline: Les grands procès de Moscou*, trans. Dimitri Sesemann (Paris: Albin Michel, 1991).

14. [Sartre and Merleau-Ponty, "Les jours de notre vie," 1160.]

15. [Sartre and Merleau-Ponty, "Les jours de notre vie," 1160.]

16. [Sartre and Merleau-Ponty, "Les jours de notre vie," 1161. My emphasis.]

17. [Sartre and Merleau-Ponty, "Les jours de notre vie," 1162.]

18. [Sartre and Merleau-Ponty, "Les jours de notre vie," 1161.]

19. [Claude Lefort, "Le Nom d'Un," in Étienne de La Boétie, *Le Discours de la servitude volontaire*, ed. Miguel Abensour, intro. Miguel Abensour and Marcel Gauchet, commentary by Pierre Clastres et al. (Paris: Payot, 1976, 1993).]

11. Utopia and Tragedy

1. [Martin Malia, *The Soviet Tragedy: A History of Socialism in Russia, 1917–1991* (New York: Free Press, 1994), 15]; *La Tragédie soviétique: Histoire*

du socialisme en Russie, 1917–1991, trans. Jean-Pierre Bardos (Paris: Seuil, 1995), 28.

2. [Mikhail Heller and Aleksandr Nekrich, *Utopia in Power: The History of the Soviet Union from 1917 to the Present*, trans. Phyllis B. Carlos (New York: Summit Books, 1986); Malia, *Soviet Tragedy*, 15]; *La Tragédie soviétique*, 27.

3. [Malia, *Soviet Tragedy*, 15]; *La Tragédie soviétique*, 27.

4. [Malia, *Soviet Tragedy*, 16]; *La Tragédie soviétique*, 28.

5. [Malia, *Soviet Tragedy*, 16]; *La Tragédie soviétique*, 28.

6. [Malia, *Soviet Tragedy*, 496]; *La Tragédie soviétique*, 563.

7. [Malia, *Soviet Tragedy*, 498]; *La Tragédie soviétique*, 566.

8. [Malia, *Soviet Tragedy*, 14]; *La Tragédie soviétique*, 26–27.

9. [Carl J. Friedrich and Zbigniew K. Brzezinski, *Totalitarian Dictatorship and Autocracy* (Cambridge, Mass.: Harvard University Press, 1956, 1965). Friedrich and Brzezinski's depiction of totalitarianism became orthodox in American foreign policy circles, stymying the widespread acceptance of alternative analyses of Soviet society, such as Hannah Arendt's. Their recipe of ideology, party, terror, and central state monopoly, applying equally to Soviet Communism and fascism, was later targeted by revisionist and pluralist Sovietologists.]

10. [Malia, *Soviet Tragedy*, 8]; *La Tragédie soviétique*, 19.

11. [Malia, *Soviet Tragedy*, 8]; *La Tragédie soviétique*, 19.

12. The Political and the Social

1. [Raymond Aron, *Démocratie et totalitarianisme* (Paris: Gallimard, 1965, 1970), originally published as *Sociologie des sociétés industrielles: Esquisse d'une théorie des régimes politiques* (Paris: Centre de documentation universitaire, 1958), 287; *Democracy and Totalitarianism*, ed. and intro. Roy Pierce, trans. Valence Ionescu (Ann Arbor: University of Michigan Press, 1990), 193.]

2. [On the cycle of lectures, see Raymond Aron, *Mémoires: 50 ans de réflexion politique* (Paris: Julliard, 1983); *Memoirs: Fifty Years of Political Reflection*, foreword by Henry A. Kissinger, trans. George Holoch (New York: Holmes and Meier, 1990), 235–36, 266–81.]

3. Aron, *Démocratie et totalitariansme*, 27; [*Democracy and Totalitarianism*, 7].

4. Aron, *Démocratie et totalitariansme*, 25; [*Democracy and Totalitarianism*, 6].

5. Aron, *Démocratie et totalitariansme*, 28–29; [*Democracy and Totalitarianism*, 8].

6. Aron, *Démocratie et totalitariansme*, 33; [*Democracy and Totalitarianism*, 11–12. Lefort misquotes Aron as saying that "even if we *do agree* with the Greek philosophers who held that human life is essentially politics"].

7. Aron, *Démocratie et totalitariansme*, 328; [*Democracy and Totalitarianism*, 222].

8. Aron, *Démocratie et totalitariansme*, 328; [*Democracy and Totalitarianism*, 222].

9. Aron, *Démocratie et totalitariansme*, 30; [*Democracy and Totalitarianism*, 9 (translation modified)].

10. Aron, *Démocratie et totalitariansme*, 334; [*Democracy and Totalitarianism*, 226 (translation modified)].

11. Aron, *Démocratie et totalitariansme*, 334; [*Democracy and Totalitarianism*, 227].

12. Aron, *Démocratie et totalitariansme*, 344; [*Democracy and Totalitarianism*, 235 (translation modified)].

13. Aron, *Démocratie et totalitariansme*, 345; [*Democracy and Totalitarianism*, 235–36].

14. [Claude Lefort, "Le Totalitarianisme sans Staline: L'URSS dans une nouvelle phase," *Socialisme ou Barbarie* 14 (1956), in *Éléments d'une critique de la bureaucratie* (Geneva: Droz, 1971; Paris: Gallimard, 1979); "Totalitarianism Without Stalin," trans. Alan Sheridan, in *The Political Forms of Modern Society: Bureaucracy, Democracy, Totalitarianism*, ed. and intro. John B. Thompson (Cambridge, Mass.: MIT Press, 1986), 73–74.]

15. Aron, *Démocratie et totalitariansme*, 345; [*Democracy and Totalitarianism*, 236 (translation modified). My emphasis.]

16. Leon Trotsky, *La Révolution trahie*, trans. Victor Serge (Paris: Grasset, 1936), 269; [*The Revolution Betrayed: What Is the Soviet Union and Where Is It Going?* trans. Max Eastman (Garden City, N.Y.: Doubleday, 1937; New York: Pathfinder, 1972), 238].

17. Trotsky, *La Révolution trahie*, 281; [*Revolution Betrayed*, 249].

18. Marc Ferro, *Des soviets au communisme bureaucratique: Les mécanismes d'une subversion* (Paris: Gallimard, 1964), 119ff.

19. [Martin Malia, *The Soviet Tragedy: A History of Socialism in Russia, 1917–1991* (New York: Free Press, 1994), 178, 194]; *La Tragédie soviétique: Histoire du socialisme en Russie, 1917–1991*, trans. Jean-Pierre Bardos (Paris: Seuil, 1995), 231, 249.]

20. [Malia, *Soviet Tragedy*, 201]; *La Tragédie soviétique*, 255–56.

21. [Malia, *Soviet Tragedy*, 201; *La Tragédie soviétique*, 256.]

22. Ante Ciliga, *Au pays du grand mensonge*, trans. A. Gourevitch (Paris: Gallimard, 1938); [*The Russian Enigma*, trans. Fernand G. Renier and Anne Cliff (London: Labour, 1940; Westport, Conn.: Hyperion, 1973)]. See also Claude Lefort, "Le Témoignage d'Antón Ciliga," *Les Temps modernes* 60 (1950), in *Éléments d'une critique de la bureaucratie* (Geneva: Droz, 1971; Paris: Gallimard, 1979).

23. Ciliga, *Au pays du grand mensonge*, 89; [*Russian Enigma*, 101].

24. Ciliga, *Au pays du grand mensonge*, 68; [*Russian Enigma*, 74].

25. Ciliga, *Au pays du grand mensonge*, 69; [*Russian Enigma*, 76].

26. [Sergo Ordzhonikidze (1886–1937) was a member of the Politburo and close associate of Stalin until the latter learned of his attempts to protect individuals under investigation (including Victor Kravchenko). Ordzhonikidze was found dead the night before he was to have delivered a speech in which he allegedly intended to denounce Stalin.]

27. [Malia, *Soviet Tragedy*, 209]; *La Tragédie soviétique*, 264.

28. [Malia, *Soviet Tragedy*, 206]; *La Tragédie soviétique*, 261.

29. Trotsky, *La Révolution trahie*, 161, 165; [*Revolution Betrayed*, 139, 142].

30. Pierre Chaulieu [Cornelius Castoriadis], "Les Rapports de production en Russie," *Socialisme ou Barbarie* 2 (1949), in *La Société bureaucratique*, vol. 1, *Les Rapports de production en Russie* (Paris: Union générale d'éditions, 1973); ["The Relations of Production in Russia," in *Political and Social Writings*, vol. 1, *From the Critique of Bureaucracy to the Positive Content of Socialism*, trans. David Ames Curtis (Minneapolis: University of Minnesota Press, 1988)].

13. An Intentional Movement

1. [Martin Malia, *The Soviet Tragedy: A History of Socialism in Russia, 1917–1991* (New York: Free Press, 1994), 54]; *La Tragédie soviétique: Histoire du socialisme en Russie, 1917–1991*, trans. Jean-Pierre Bardos (Paris: Seuil, 1995), 81.

2. [Malia, *Soviet Tragedy*, 52; *La Tragédie soviétique*, 79, 85.]

3. [Malia, *Soviet Tragedy*, 60]; *La Tragédie soviétique*, 88.

4. [Malia, *Soviet Tragedy*, 60–61; *La Tragédie soviétique*, 88.]

5. [Karl A. Wittfogel, *Oriental Despotism: A Comparative Study of Total Power* (New Haven, Conn.: Yale University Press, 1957; New York: Vintage, 1981)]; *Le Despotisme oriental: Étude comparative du pouvoir total*, preface by

Pierre Vidal-Naquet, trans. Anne Marchand (Paris: Éditions de Minuit, 1964). Vidal-Naquet's preface was substantial and strongly critical.

6. [Malia, *Soviet Tragedy*, 58]; *La Tragédie soviétique*, 86.

7. [Malia, *Soviet Tragedy*, 59]; *La Tragédie soviétique*, 87.

8. [Malia, *Soviet Tragedy*, 60; *La Tragédie soviétique*, 87.]

9. [Wittfogel, *Oriental Despotism*, 391ff.]; *Le Despotisme oriental*, 510ff.

10. [David Ryazanov (1870–1938) helped found the Marx and Engels Institute and oversaw the early stages of the publication of their complete works. In 1931 he was tried as part of the Menshevik center and eventually was shot to death in a prison camp. Eugene Varga (1879–1964) was a Hungarian-born economist who worked in the Soviet Union. Sympathetic to Trotsky, he and his revisionism ran afoul of Stalin, especially after World War II. Wittfogel, *Oriental Despotism*, 401–2]; *Le Despotisme oriental*, 521.

11. [Leon Trotsky, *Histoire de la Révolution russe*, trans. Maurice Parijanine, 2 vols. (Paris: Seuil, 1950), 1:15–26, 419–26; *The History of the Russian Revolution*, trans. Max Eastman (New York: Simon and Schuster, 1932; Ann Arbor: University of Michigan Press, 1957), 3–15, 463–70.]

12. [Trotsky, *Histoire de la Révolution russe*, 25; *History of the Russian Revolution*, 14.]

13. [Trotsky, *Histoire de la Révolution russe*, 21; *History of the Russian Revolution*, 9.]

14. Miklós Molnar, *Marx, Engels et la politique internationale* (Paris: Gallimard, 1975). This book is a superlative study of the Marxist theory of the Asiatic mode of production and its links to the conception of international politics.

15. Molnar, *Marx, Engels et la politique internationale*, 189–90, 225–26.

16. Molnar, *Marx, Engels et la politique internationale*, 112. [Molnar cites Karl Marx, "Speech at the Polish Meeting in London" (January 22, 1867), in Karl Marx and Friedrich Engels, *Collected Works*, 50 vols. (New York: International, 1975–2005), 20:201.]

17. [In 1878 Vera Zasulich (1849–1919) attempted to assassinate the governor general of St. Petersburg. She became an early Russian follower of Marx, whose works she translated. An associate of Georgy Plekhanov, she sided with the Mensheviks in 1905 and was unreceptive to the Bolsheviks during the revolution of 1917. Karl Marx and Friedrich Engels, "Preface to the Russian Edition of 1882," in *The Communist Manifesto*, intro. Gareth Stedman Jones (London: Penguin, 2002), 196.]

18. Molnar, *Marx, Engels et la politique internationale*, 184.

19. V. I. Lenin, cited in Boris Souvarine, *Staline: Aperçu historique du bol-*

chévisme (Paris: Plon, 1935), 48; [*Stalin: A Critical Survey of Bolshevism*, trans. C. L. R. James (New York: Alliance, 1939), 46].

20. Karl Kautsky, *Le Bolchevisme dans l'impasse*, trans. Bracke [Alexandre M. Desrousseaux] (Paris: PUF, 1931, 1980), 11–12; [*Bolshevism at a Deadlock*, trans. Bertha Pritchard (New York: Rand School, 1931), 14].

21. Edgar Quinet, *La Révolution* (1865; Paris: Belin, 1987), 70. [For Claude Lefort on this nineteenth-century pioneer of liberal historiography of the French Revolution, see "Edgar Quinet: La Révolution manquée," *Passé-Présent* 2 (1983), in *Essais sur le politique (XIXè–XXè siècles)* (Paris: Seuil, 1986); "Edgar Quinet: The Revolution That Failed," in *Democracy and Political Theory*, trans. David Macey (Minneapolis: University of Minnesota Press, 1988). See also Claude Lefort, "Philosophe?" *Poésie* 37 (1985), in *Écrire: À l'épreuve du politique* (Paris: Fondation Saint-Simon/Calmann-Lévy, 1992); "Philosopher?" in *Writing: The Political Test*, trans. and ed. David Ames Curtis (Durham, N.C.: Duke University Press, 2000), and "La Révolution comme religion nouvelle" (1988), in *The French Revolution and the Creation of Political Culture, 1789–1848*, ed. François Furet and Mona Ozouf (Oxford: Pergamon, 1989), and in *Écrire*; "The Revolution as New Religion," in *Writing*.]

22. Marc Ferro, *Des soviets au communisme bureaucratique: Les mécanismes d'une subversion* (Paris: Gallimard, 1964), 182–83.

23. [Souvarine, *Staline*, 29; *Stalin*, 24. My emphasis.]

24. [Sergey Nechayev (1847–1882) was a revolutionary leader at St. Petersburg University in the late 1860s. He briefly went underground before being caught; he died in prison. Some give partial attribution to Mikhail Bakunin for Nechayev's *Rules That Should Inspire a Revolutionist* (1869), sometimes also misleadingly entitled *Revolutionary Catechism*. Souvarine, *Staline*, 29–30; *Stalin*, 25. My emphasis.]

25. [Petr Tkachev (1844–1886) was a journalist and political agitator whose émigré paper, *The Tocsin*, served as a hub for Russian Jacobinism. He collaborated with Nechayev. Souvarine, *Staline*, 30; *Stalin*, 26 (translation modified).]

26. [Souvarine, *Staline*, 30; *Stalin*, 26.]

27. [Souvarine, *Staline*, 31–32; *Stalin*, 27–28.]

14. The Party Above All

1. Georgy Plekhanov, quoted in Boris Souvarine, *Staline: Aperçu historique du bolchévisme* (Paris: Plon, 1935), 57; [*Stalin: A Critical Survey of Bolshevism*, trans. C. L. R. James (New York: Alliance, 1939), 54].

15. Disincorporation and Reincorporation of Power

1. [Raymond Aron, *Démocratie et totalitarianisme* (Paris: Gallimard, 1965, 1970), originally published as *Sociologie des sociétés industrielles: Esquisse d'une théorie des régimes politiques* (Paris: Centre de documentation universitaire, 1958), 267; *Democracy and Totalitarianism*, ed. and intro. Roy Pierce, trans. Valence Ionescu (Ann Arbor: University of Michigan Press, 1990), 179 (translation modified).]

2. Ernst Kantorowicz, *The King's Two Bodies: A Study in Medieval Political Theory* (Princeton, N.J.: Princeton University Press, 1957); *Les Deux corps du roi: Essai sur la théologie politique au Moyen Âge*, trans. Jean-Philippe Genet and Nicole Genet (Paris: Gallimard, 1989).

3. [Claude Lefort discusses the disincorporation of power in "L'Image du corps et le totalitarisme" (1974), *Confrontation* 2 (1979), in *L'Invention démocratique: Les limites de la domination totalitaire* (Paris: Fayard, 1981); "The Image of the Body and Totalitarianism," trans. Alan Sheridan, in *The Political Forms of Modern Society: Bureaucracy, Democracy, Totalitarianism*, ed. and intro. John B. Thompson (Cambridge, Mass.: MIT Press, 1986).]

4. [See, for instance, Claude Lefort, "La Logique totalitaire," *Kontinent Skandinavia* 3–4 (1980), in *L'Invention démocratique*; "The Logic of Totalitarianism," trans. Alan Sheridan, in *Political Forms of Modern Society*; "Démocratie et avènement d'un 'lieu vide,'" *Psychanalystes: Bulletin du Collège de Psychanalystes* 2 (1982); and "Permanence du théologico-politique?" *Le Temps de la Réflexion* 2 (1981), in *Essais sur le politique (XIXè–XXè siècles)* (Paris: Seuil, 1986); "The Permanence of the Theologico-Political?" in *Democracy and Political Theory*, trans. David Macey (Minneapolis: University of Minnesota Press, 1988).]

16. Hannah Arendt on the Law of Movement and Ideology

1. [Hannah Arendt, *The Origins of Totalitarianism* (New York: Harcourt Brace, 1951, 1973), 460–61; *Le Système totalitaire* (part III of *The Origins of Totalitarianism*), trans. Jean-Loup Bourget, Robert Davreau, and Patrick Lévy (Paris: Seuil, 1972), 204.]

2. [Arendt, *Origins of Totalitarianism*, 461; *Le Système totalitaire*, 205.]

3. I will not pause to consider how Raymond Aron criticized Arendt's use of the concept of essence in his famous essay "L'Essence du totalitarianisme,"

Critique 80 (1964); ["The Essence of Totalitarianism According to Hannah Arendt," trans. Daniel J. Mahoney, *Partisan Review* 60, no. 3 (1993): 366–76].

4. [Arendt, *Origins of Totalitarianism*, 461; *Le Système totalitaire*, 205.]

5. [Arendt, *Origins of Totalitarianism*, 462; *Le Système totalitaire*, 206.]

6. [Arendt, *Origins of Totalitarianism*, 462–63; *Le Système totalitaire*, 207.]

7. [Arendt, *Origins of Totalitarianism*, 463–64; *Le Système totalitaire*, 208–9.]

8. [Arendt, *Origins of Totalitarianism*, 464; *Le Système totalitaire*, 209.]

9. [Arendt, *Origins of Totalitarianism*, 465–66]; *Le Système totalitaire*, 211–13.

10. [Arendt, *Origins of Totalitarianism*, 468]; *Le Système totalitaire*, 215.

11. [Arendt, *Origins of Totalitarianism*, 468; *Le Système totalitaire*, 215.]

12. [Arendt, *Origins of Totalitarianism*, 469; *Le Système totalitaire*, 217.]

13. [Arendt, *Origins of Totalitarianism*, 469; *Le Système totalitaire*, 217.]

14. [Arendt, *Origins of Totalitarianism*, 469]; *Le Système totalitaire*, 217.

15. [Arendt, *Origins of Totalitarianism*, 471]; *Le Système totalitaire*, 220–21.

16. [Arendt, *Origins of Totalitarianism*, 461; *Le Système totalitaire*, 205.]

17. [Arendt, *Origins of Totalitarianism*, 466]; *Le Système totalitaire*, 212.

18. [Arendt, *Origins of Totalitarianism*, 468; *Le Système totalitaire*, 215.]

19. These two essays were included in Hannah Arendt, *Between Past and Future: Eight Exercises in Political Thought* (New York: Viking, 1961; London: Penguin, 1977); *La Crise de la culture: Huit exercises de pensée politique*, trans. Patrick Lévy et al. (Paris: Gallimard, 1972).

20. [Arendt, *Between Past and Future*, 87]; *La Crise de la culture*, 117.

21. [Arendt, *Between Past and Future*, 88; *La Crise de la culture*, 117.]

22. [Arendt wrote, "We can take almost any hypothesis and *act* upon it, with a sequence of results in reality which not only make sense but *work*" (*Between Past and Future*, 87; *La Crise de la culture*, 117).]

23. [Arendt, *Between Past and Future*, 87; *La Crise de la culture*, 117.]

24. [Arendt, *Origins of Totalitarianism*, 465]; *Le Système totalitaire*, 211.

25. [Arendt, *Origins of Totalitarianism*, 465; *Le Système totalitaire*, 211.]

17. The Perversion of the Law

1. [Hannah Arendt, *The Origins of Totalitarianism* (New York: Harcourt Brace, 1951, 1973), 462]; *Le Système totalitaire* [part III of *The Origins of To-*

talitarianism], trans. Jean-Loup Bourget, Robert Davreau, and Patrick Lévy (Paris: Seuil, 1972), 207.

2. [Claude Lefort, "L'Image du corps et le totalitarisme" (1974), *Confrontation* 2 (1979), in *L'Invention démocratique: Les limites de la domination totalitaire* (Paris: Fayard, 1981); "The Image of the Body and Totalitarianism," trans. Alan Sheridan, in *The Political Forms of Modern Society: Bureaucracy, Democracy, Totalitarianism*, ed. and intro. John B. Thompson (Cambridge, Mass.: MIT Press, 1986).]

3. [The statement is a clear reference to Stéphane Courtois et al., *Le Livre noir du communisme: Crimes, terreurs et répression* (Paris: Laffont, 1997); *The Black Book of Communism: Crimes, Terror, Repression*, foreword by Martin Malia, ed. Mark Kramer, trans. Jonathan Murphy (Cambridge, Mass.: Harvard University Press, 1999).]

4. Aleksandr Solzhenitsyn, *L'Archipel du Goulag, 1918–1956: Essai d'investigation littéraire, première et deuxième parties*, 2 vols., trans. Jacqueline Lafond et al. (Paris: Seuil, 1974); [*The Gulag Archipelago, 1918–1956: An Experiment in Literary Investigation: I–II*, trans. Thomas P. Whitney (New York: Harper & Row, 1975)].

5. Solzhenitsyn, *L'Archipel du Goulag*, 1:112; [*Gulag Archipelago*, 145].

18. The Fabrication of the Social

1. Aleksandr Solzhenitsyn, *L'Archipel du Goulag, 1918–1956: Essai d'investigation littéraire, première et deuxième parties*, 2 vols., trans. Jacqueline Lafond et al. (Paris: Seuil, 1974), 1:299; [*The Gulag Archipelago, 1918–1956: An Experiment in Literary Investigation: I–II*, trans. Thomas P. Whitney (New York: Harper & Row, 1975), 419].

2. Solzhenitsyn, *L'Archipel du Goulag*, 1:112; [*Gulag Archipelago*, 146].

19. Voluntary Servitude

1. Étienne de La Boétie, *Le Discours de la servitude volontaire*, ed. Miguel Abensour, intro. Miguel Abensour and Marcel Gauchet, commentary by Pierre Clastres et al. (Paris: Payot, 1976, 1993), 114–15; [*The Politics of Obedience: The Discourse on Voluntary Servitude*, intro. Murray N. Rothbard, trans. Harry Kurz (Montreal: Black Rose, 1997), 52].

2. [La Boétie, *Le Discours de la servitude volontaire*, 115; *Politics of Obedience*, 52.]

3. La Boétie, *Le Discours de la servitude volontaire*, 150; [*Politics of Obedience*, 77 (translation modified)].

4. [La Boétie, *Le Discours de la servitude volontaire*, 152; *Politics of Obedience*, 78.]

5. [Claude Lefort discusses this phrase in *Un homme en trop: Réflexions sur "L'Archipel du Goulag"* (Paris: Seuil, 1976), chap. 2.]

6. [Merle Fainsod, *Smolensk Under Soviet Rule* (Cambridge, Mass.: Harvard University Press, 1958), 12]; *Smolensk à l'heure de Staline*, trans. Gisèle Bernier (Paris: Fayard, 1967), 28.

7. Aleksandr Solzhenitsyn, *L'Archipel du Goulag, 1918–1956: Essai d'investigation littéraire, première et deuxième parties*, 2 vols., trans. Jacqueline Lafond et al. (Paris: Seuil, 1974), 1:131; [*The Gulag Archipelago, 1918–1956: An Experiment in Literary Investigation: I–II*, trans. Thomas P. Whitney (New York: Harper & Row, 1975), 174].

8. [Hannah Arendt, *The Origins of Totalitarianism* (New York: Harcourt Brace, 1951, 1973), 462]; *Le Système totalitaire* [part III of *The Origins of Totalitarianism*], trans. Jean-Loup Bourget, Robert Davreau, and Patrick Lévy (Paris: Seuil, 1972), 207.

9. [Arendt, *Origins of Totalitarianism*, 472–73]; *Le Système totalitaire*, 221, 223–24.

20. Impossible Reform

1. "Vingtième Congrès du Parti communiste de l'Union soviétique," *Cahiers du communisme* (1956). The citations are borrowed from my essay "Le Totalitarianisme sans Staline: L'URSS dans une nouvelle phase," *Socialisme ou Barbarie* 14 (1956), in *Éléments d'une critique de la bureaucratie* (Geneva: Droz, 1971; Paris: Gallimard, 1979), 171 and passim. [This citation was not included in the partially translated version: "Totalitarianism Without Stalin," trans. Alan Sheridan, in *The Political Forms of Modern Society: Bureaucracy, Democracy, Totalitarianism*, ed. and intro. John B. Thompson (Cambridge, Mass.: MIT Press, 1986); see "Report of the Central Committee of the Communist Party of the Soviet Union to the Twentieth Party Congress, delivered by N. S. Khrushchov [*sic*], First Secretary, CC, CPSU," *New Times*, 16 February 1956, 62.]

2. [Nikolai Bulganin (1895–1975), former mayor of Moscow and head of the state bank, was defense minister under Stalin and then premier under Khrushchev before the latter took the title for himself in 1958. Mikhail Suslov

(1902–1982) was named to the Central Committee in 1941 and was active in the campaign against Tito. He later supported Brezhnev against Khrushchev. Anastas Mikoyan (1895–1978) joined the Central Committee in 1923 and served as first deputy premier in the 1950s and early 1960s before becoming chairman of the Presidium of the Supreme Soviet in 1964/1965.]

3. ["Report of the Central Committee of the Communist Party of the Soviet Union to the Twentieth Party Congress," 58 (translation modified).]

4. ["Report of the Central Committee of the Communist Party of the Soviet Union to the Twentieth Party Congress," 55.]

5. ["Report of the Central Committee of the Communist Party of the Soviet Union to the Twentieth Party Congress," 56.]

6. ["Report of the Central Committee of the Communist Party of the Soviet Union to the Twentieth Party Congress," 69.]

7. [Claude Lefort discusses Solzhenitsyn's term *egocrat* in *Un homme en trop: Réflexions sur "L'Archipel du Goulag"* (Paris: Seuil, 1976), chap. 3, as well as in "L'Image du corps et le totalitarisme" (1974), *Confrontation* 2 (1979), in *L'Invention démocratique: Les limites de la domination totalitaire* (Paris: Fayard, 1981); "The Image of the Body and Totalitarianism," trans. Alan Sheridan, in *Political Forms of Modern Society*.]

21. Planning and Social Division

1. Gérard Duchêne, "L'Officiel et le parallèle dans l'économie soviétique," *Libre* 7 (1980): 151–88.

2. Duchêne, "L'Officiel et le parallèle dans l'économie soviétique," 180.

3. Duchêne, "L'Officiel et le parallèle dans l'économie soviétique," 181.

4. Duchêne, "L'Officiel et le parallèle dans l'économie soviétique," 181. My emphasis.

5. [Martin Malia, *The Soviet Tragedy: A History of Socialism in Russia, 1917–1991* (New York: Free Press, 1994), 408; *La Tragédie soviétique: Histoire du socialisme en Russie, 1917–1991*, trans. Jean-Pierre Bardos (Paris: Seuil, 1995), 472.]

6. [Malia, *Soviet Tragedy*, 408]; *La Tragédie soviétique*, 472.

7. [One might profitably contrast what follows to Claude Lefort's perspective in "Réflexions sur le présent" (1989–1991), in *Écrire: À l'épreuve du politique* (Paris: Fondation Saint-Simon/Calmann-Lévy, 1992); "Reflections on the Present," in *Writing: The Political Test*, trans. and ed. David Ames Curtis (Durham, N.C.: Duke University Press, 2000).]

8. [The image is taken directly from Étienne de La Boétie, *The Politics of Obedience: The Discourse on Voluntary Servitude*, intro. Murray N. Rothbard, trans. Harry Kurz (Montreal: Black Rose, 1997), 53.]

9. [Georgy Zhukov (1896–1974) was a military hero of World War II and, as defense minister in 1956, ordered Soviet troops into Hungary.]

23. Communism and the Constitution of the World-Space

1. François Furet, *Le Passé d'une illusion: Essai sur l'idee communiste au XXè siècle* (Paris: Laffont, 1995), 71; [*The Passing of an Illusion: The Idea of Communism in the Twentieth Century*, trans. Deborah Furet (Chicago: University of Chicago Press, 1999), 55. Furet cites Ernst Jünger, "Die Total Mobilmachung," in *Krieg und Krieger* (Berlin: Junker und Dünnhaupt, 1930); "Total Mobilization," trans. Joel Goeb and Richard Wolin, in *The Heidegger Controversy: A Critical Reader*, ed. Richard Wolin (Cambridge, Mass.: MIT Press, 1993)].

2. [Claude Lefort, "Reculer les frontières du possible," *Esprit*, January 1981; "Pushing Back the Limits of the Possible," trans. John B. Thompson, in *The Political Forms of Modern Society: Bureaucracy, Democracy, Totalitarianism*, ed. and intro. John B. Thompson (Cambridge, Mass.: MIT Press, 1986).]

3. [Paul Valéry, "Avant-propos," in *Regards sur le monde actuel et autres essais* (1931), in *Oeuvres*, 2 vols., ed. Jean Hytier (Paris: Gallimard, 1960), 2:924; "Foreword," in *History and Politics*, trans. Denise Folliot and Jackson Mathews, preface by François Valéry, intro. Salvador de Madariaga, in *The Collected Works of Paul Valéry*, 15 vols., ed. Jackson Mathews (New York: Pantheon, 1962), 10:16.]

INDEX